The Big History Question

THE
BIG
HISTORY
QUESTION

SNAPSHOTS OF
AUSTRALIAN
HISTORY

Frank G. Clarke

Kangaroo Press

THE BIG HISTORY QUESTION

First published in Australia in 1998 by Kangaroo Press
an imprint of Simon & Schuster Australia
20 Barcoo Street, East Roseville NSW 2069

A Viacom Company
Sydney New York London Toronto Tokyo Singapore

National Library of Australia
Cataloguing-in-Publication data

Clarke, F. G. 1943–

The big history question: snapshots of australian history

Bibliography.
Includes index.

ISBN 0 86417 954 5

1. Australia – History I. Title

994

Set in Bembo 10.5/13.8
Printed in Australia by Griffin Press, Adelaide

10 9 8 7 6 5 4 3 2 1

Contents

Conversion Table

1 inch = 2.5 cm

1 foot = 30.5 cm

1 yard = 0.9 m

1 mile = 1.6 km

1 acre = 0.4 hectare

1 gallon = 4.5 litres

1 ounce = 28 grams

1 pound (weight) = 0.45 kilogram

1 pound (money) = $2.00

Preface

My interest in Australian history began as a very young child. In my first year at school, in 1948, we learned about the great Australian outlaw and bushranger Ned Kelly. Our teacher—an Irish nun—must have been a brilliant story-teller, for she kept a class of young children rapt and attentive as she wove, into her account of Ned Kelly, the old tale of the wrongs of Ireland at the hands of the English. She depicted Ned as a son of Ireland foully done to death in colonial Australia by the agents of English injustice. That dramatic and sad story became my first narrative of Australian history—and I have never forgotten it. I did not know it then, but I was hooked for life. Thereafter, we small boys played bushrangers and troopers rather than cowboys and Indians, and we all aspired to become 'as game as Ned Kelly', when we grew up.

The taste for the romance and adventure of Australian history has never left me, although as a professional historian, I have had to learn to discriminate between myth and reality in a way that my first teacher never did. As I developed, I encountered the books of the famous Australian popular authors—such as the great Ion Idriess, Douglas Lockwood, Bill Wannan, and Hector Holthouse. These writers introduced me to the richness of my country's past, despite its somewhat chequered appearance, and taught me that, while much of it was uplifting and inspirational, there were dark pages that also had to be turned if one was to access the complete narrative. But, above all else, they were master story-tellers who possessed the gift of making whatever they wrote about come to life.

When I began teaching Australian history at Macquarie University in 1973, I found that the students really engaged with the subject when the broad general sweep of history, and impersonal historical forces and processes, could be illustrated with stories and examples from the lives of real people. Whenever I met former students in the following years, it became very clear that what they remembered best from the broad narrative of Australian history were these stories.

Early in 1997, I began to participate in regular broadcasts on Australian history themes with the Australian Broadcasting Corporation (ABC). Over the weeks and months, this developed into a weekly session on Wednesday evenings as part of Angela Catterns' regular national evening program. I would pose a question on some aspect of Australian history, and the listeners—who came from as far afield as Darwin in the Northern Territory and Launceston in Tasmania—

would ring in with their answers. It was a lot of fun. We received calls from outback desert camps, from truckies on the road on mobile phones, from a farmer in northern New South Wales harvesting in the cool of the night and calling in from the cabin of his harvester, and from people sitting at home and listening to the evening show with their families.

It soon became abundantly clear that there was a great deal of knowledge and interest in Australian history among the ABC's listeners. It was a rare night when I could pose a question that no-one could answer, and it was very obvious that our fascination with Australian history and its stories was shared by a great many of our fellow Australians. After the program, we would receive numerous letters and telephone calls from listeners—with suggestions for future questions, as well as commentary and additional information on previous questions. *The Big History Question*—as Angela dubbed this part of her program—seemed to have caught the interest of a receptive and well-informed audience who would often suggest that the program's material be made available in a book.

What follows is a selection of forty-three topics from the ones which I prepared to go to air. They have been chosen as a representative sample, and include material from all Australian colonies and states, and from both the nineteenth and twentieth centuries.

It only remains for me to conclude by repeating the message printed on the covers of the study guides used by the students whom I teach at Macquarie University:

Warning: Scientific Tests Show that Australian History can be Addictive!

Frank G. Clarke
Macquarie University
June 1998

1
Daisy Bates

Daisy Bates was known to Aborigines as 'Kabbarli'. Why did she falsify her personal history? Why is she recognised as the founding mother of modern anthropology in Australia? And is Edwardian dress really suitable for camping with Aborigines?

The name of this extraordinary woman will forever be associated with Australian Aborigines. She unintentionally became a pioneer of modern anthropological techniques because of her decision to live within Aboriginal communities for prolonged periods. At the time she made this decision (in about 1912), it was a radical—almost a revolutionary—step for a lone white woman. In her preparedness to defy contemporary conventions of acceptable behaviour for a married woman, Daisy Bates seems almost modern. However, as we shall see, this propensity to live her own life (whatever other people might think) showed up well before her involvement with Aboriginal society, and well before she had even contemplated—if she ever did—her ultimate destiny of becoming the founding mother of modern anthropology in Australia.

She was born Daisy Mary O'Dwyer in the County of Tipperary, Ireland, in October 1859, and received an education suitable for a female from the more genteel levels of nineteenth-century British society. Her mother died when Daisy was only five, and her father when she was still in her teens. Her upbringing was then undertaken by Sir Francis and Lady Outram in London, where she developed a familiarity with English literature and a clear writing style—which was to stand her in good stead in her later career as self-taught anthropologist, professional journalist and Aboriginal welfare worker. At this early stage of her life, Daisy also demonstrated another attribute that was destined to flower in her later years—she became fluent in both French and German, and thereby developed a facility for learning languages. In later years, she was to master over 180 separate Aboriginal dialects.

Despite her own claims to have arrived the following year, Daisy landed in Australia in 1883 in search of a drier climate to help combat a threatened onset of tuberculosis. She was 24 years of age. She found work as a governess on a cattle station near Charters Towers in North Queensland where she met and became enamoured of a British migrant working as a stockman on the station. His name was Edwin Murrant which he was later to change to Henry Harboard

Morant—the legendary 'Breaker Morant' who wrote ballads for the *Bulletin*, and who was later executed by the British during the Boer War for killing prisoners. Daisy and Edwin Murrant were married in Charters Towers on 13 March 1884. A month after the wedding, Murrant was charged with the theft of a saddle and some pigs, and, although he was discharged a week later, the couple separated and apparently never met again. Daisy kept this marriage a close secret and never referred to it in any of her papers.

For the rest of 1884 Daisy worked as a governess to the Bates family on a property near Nowra to the south of Sydney. There she met John Bates, the eldest son of the family. He proposed to her, and they were married in Nowra in February 1885. Clearly, she never mentioned her first marriage only eleven months earlier, and we have to accept that Daisy committed bigamy in marrying the hapless drover, John Bates, who became and remained her innocent dupe for the rest of his life. This was not such a risk for her to take, for there was no centralised system of recording births, deaths, and marriages at that time in Australia, and, unless she was so unfortunate as to encounter in one colony somebody who knew of her marriage in a small country town in a different colony, her reputation was safe. Indeed, even today such centralised record-keeping does not exist, and registers of marriages are still kept quite separate from one another in each state.

Daisy Bates soon discovered that her second marriage was no more successful than her first, despite producing a son in a little over a year. She found her new husband reluctant to give up his life as a wandering drover, and, following the birth of their son, the two spent very little time together. It has also been suggested that John's intense dislike for Aborigines did little to increase harmony between them, and that Daisy's increasing interest in Aborigines annoyed her husband. Whatever the truth of this, there is no doubt that Daisy's independence of spirit would not leave her shackled in a domestic role for very long. In 1894, she abandoned her seven-year-old son to the care of the Bates family and returned to Britain alone. Once more, inconvenient social conventions were ignored when they threatened to cramp the style of Daisy Bates.

In England, Daisy worked as a professional journalist for the next five years, until *The Times* of London sent her back to Australia in 1899 to investigate claims that the settlers of the north-west of Western Australia were treating the Aborigines with great cruelty, that Aborigines were treated no better than slaves on the cattle stations of Western Australia, and that in poor seasons the Aborigines were actually starving.

In Western Australia, she renewed contact with her husband, and travelled extensively with him through much of the north-west inland in the region of Port Headland, Roebourne, and Carnarvon. Her report for *The Times* amounted to a vindication of the pastoralists she encountered, despite contrary evidence provided

Daisy Bates with Aborigines in the Musgrave Ranges, South Australia, c.1920s.
(State Records of South Australia)

to her by the Roman Catholic Bishop of Western Australia, Matthew Gibney. She even maintained that Aborigines preferred to be chained at the neck, because it left their hands free! This period also marks the final break with her husband and son, and she went to live in Perth, where she made her living in journalism.

In May 1904, Daisy gained employment with the State Government of Western Australia which paid her to compile vocabulary lists and a grammar of Aboriginal languages throughout the state. Daisy was now in her forty-fifth year, and, for the rest of her active life, her involvement would be with Aboriginal people and their culture. From this time, until she finally retired in 1935, the name of Daisy Bates was inescapably connected with the detailed study of Australia's indigenous population.

She also revolutionised the methodology of such study. It had always been—and remained so for many decades to come—the usual practice for ethnographers and anthropologists to make comparatively short field-trips, which were designed primarily to find evidence to support or to refute their theories regarding native peoples. To this end, most scholars in the field would travel into rural areas of outback Australia and interview Aboriginal survivors and tribal remnants who lived and worked on the cattle stations. But, in 1918, Daisy established a permanent camp with the Aborigines at Ooldea on the newly opened trans-Australia railway line in South Australia. There she lived for the next seventeen years, and immersed herself in the daily life of her subjects, until she had become so acclimatised that she was able, in her own words, to 'think black'.

The Aborigines trusted her with a great deal of secret and sacred knowledge that had hitherto been guarded from the whites. They also gave her the Aboriginal name of *Kabbarli* (grandmother). By living with the Aborigines in this way, and by observing the rhythms and patterns of still-functioning tribal societies, Daisy Bates's observations provided a most accurate and valuable picture of the complexities of traditional Aboriginal societies. Her work is particularly useful for what it has to tell us about the role of *women* in the secular and religious life of Aboriginal society. Male anthropologists in the early years of the twentieth century tended to concentrate on Aboriginal *men* and their affairs, and tended to imagine that women had no initiations and rituals of their own.

Nevertheless, Daisy Bates was a person of her time, and, looking at her work now, we can see in her books that she was an evolutionary Darwinist and a prominent exponent of the belief that Aborigines were a dying race, and that they needed to receive welfare until they disappeared. This may seem decidedly old-fashioned today, but there is no doubting the well-spring of genuine compassion that motivated her—and her withdrawal to the hard and lonely life at Ooldea provides evidence of her strength of mind and stubbornness of purpose. Moreover, her attitudes also reflect something of the hypocrisy and double standards of that time. For example, in later life, she became the upholder of propriety in sexual matters, and often passed adverse judgment on the morals of the Aborigines. She stuck resolutely to a style of Edwardian dress that was quite inappropriate for life in an Aboriginal encampment. This even extended to her always avoiding skin contact with Aborigines—even when she was nursing them—by wearing gloves. Her prejudices were strong, irrational, and occasionally hurtful. For example, she worshipped the British royal family and its representatives in Australia—Federal Governors-General and State Governors. She despised the Labor Party, trade unions, Germans, and the children of Aboriginal and settler sexual unions—whom she described as 'half-breeds'.

By 1935, Daisy was starting to slow down. At 75 years of age, the rigours of camp life had begun to exact their toll on an ageing body. She left Ooldea and retired to Pyap on the Murray River, and later on she lived at Wynbring Siding. She resided in a tent at both locations and spent her time writing her popular book on Aboriginal people and their culture—*The Passing of the Aborigines* (1938). After 1942 Daisy finally gave up her tent, and lived the last years of her life in an old-people's home in Adelaide. She died in 1951, at the age of 91.

With all of the fascinating and contradictory aspects of her character, Daisy Bates rates as one of the most unconventional and original women in twentieth-century Australia. Although her views on Aboriginal people are no longer acceptable, her contributions to the development of modern anthropology must surely entitle her to the distinction of being recognised as the founding mother of that discipline in Australia.

2

Jack Howe—the Ringer or Gun-Shearer

Jack Howe's name lives on as an item of apparel still worn in the rural sector. What is this fashion garment? Why was Jack so famous? What well-known Australian song immortalises Jack and his ilk? And what is a 'bare-bellied yoe' anyway?

Jack Howe was born in Queensland some time in 1861. His father did not register the birth properly, so a more precise date is not possible. John Robert Howe, to give him his full name, was the son of a circus acrobat—whose major claim to fame was an ability to jump from a springboard in a flying somersault and to clear fourteen horses—and a young Irish widow named Louisa Chadburne. The couple married, and eventually produced five children—of whom Jack Howe was the eldest.

Perhaps as a result of an inherited athleticism, young Jack developed into something of a prodigy as a youth and young adult. He grew into a giant of a man weighing more than 250 pounds (about 105 kg) with an enormous barrel chest, and the thigh muscles and arm muscles of a prize-fighter or a professional strongman. His hands were described as being the size of small tennis racquets. But this extraordinary physical development did not result in clumsiness or a lack of co-ordination; rather it produced a high level of achievement in athletic activities, and even in dancing. Even while he worked as a professional shearer, Howe continued to win foot-races, long-jumping and high-jumping contests, and dancing competitions for the Irish Jig and the Sailor's Hornpipe.

The combination of physical strength and manual dexterity made Jack Howe a formidable shearer. As a teenager, he had already earned a reputation as a fast and clean shearer with the traditional blades or hand-shears, and he claimed a record at the time—of 196 sheep in a 5–6-hour period. It was the combination of speed and clean cutting that drew attention to his shearing. There were many fast shearers in New South Wales, but they had something of a reputation for ragged cutting, for not taking all the wool off the sheep, and for nicking the animals and damaging them. Some stock owners preferred slower, more thorough, shearing even though, among the shearers themselves, the premium was on speed and endurance.

Jack Howe began to attain real fame in the 1890s after he had made his base at Blackall in Queensland. At Alice Downs in October 1892, he shore 321 lambs with blades in a single day. Later in that same year, and using machines for the first time, Howe shore 237 sheep in one day at Barcaldine Downs. The first record was commemorated with a gold medal presented by a business company in Cootamundra, and the second saw Howe presented with a personally inscribed shearing-machine presented by Wolseley—the company that manufactured them. All this attention made Jack Howe something of a role model in the industry, and his fame was spread far and wide across rural Australia and New Zealand by the itinerant shearers. A measure of his influence and his legendary status can be seen in the sleeveless flannel shirt, later replaced by the blue singlet, that became, for many years, the unofficial uniform of the shearer—and was always called a 'Jackie Howe'. His record for hand-shearing was never beaten, and was not surpassed by a machine for a further 58 years. His record for machine-shearing lasted until 1950.

'Ringer' is a term that came to be applied to a champion shearer, to the one who scored the highest tally of sheep shorn at a particular shed over a stipulated period. Another expression for the best shearer was 'gun-shearer'. Whenever a gun-shearer like Jack Howe was at work, he attracted visitors from miles around—many of them with notebooks to keep a tally of the scores, and to provide evidence should the tales of their hero's exploits ever be doubted. Considerable gambling also accompanied the shearing contests which became a favourite form of outback entertainment.

The pastoralist would drive the sheep for shearing into a yard, and some of these would be drafted into a holding pen from which each shearer would select his animals until the pen had been emptied, when it was refilled from the mob in the yard. Canny hands always looked for the young animals with soft wool on the back and little or none on the belly. These were the easiest to shear, and, since the shearers were paid on the number of sheep shorn, the more of this type they could select, the higher their tally and their pay. These one- and two-year-old animals were known as 'bare-bellied yoes' (or 'bare-bellied joes'), whereas the older and more difficult sheep were called 'cobblers'. Because their fleeces were full of burrs and other snags which hindered a shearer's stroke and slowed him down, cobblers were usually left to the last—hence the pun in the name ('a cobbler's last'). Each animal selected by a shearer was picked up and flipped onto its back, and then manhandled from the holding pen to the shearer's station—where it was held fast by hand and knees for shearing. The sheep were often large and heavy, and a day's shearing—in conditions of heat and dust that verged on the intolerable—was no place for the weak.

The enormous tallies achieved by Jack Howe often attracted the envy, as well as the admiration, of his fellow shearers, and in some sheds men would try to distract him—to break his rhythm and concentration. Sometimes they would

Team of shearers with hand-shears. This is the type of team in which Jack Howe earned his reputation.

jump on his back, occasionally they would tickle him, often they would play practical jokes on him—and it was even known for them to throw his sheep back in the pen in a vain attempt to slow him down. However Jack's size and athletic ability protected him from too much rough-housing, and the genuine admiration which most shearers felt for this legendary character ensured a comparatively peaceful working environment.

Howe's popularity was further enhanced by his early and continued commitment to the Shearers Union, in which he was active from 1887 onwards, and in which he held minor office as a delegate on the union's central committee for two years. In later life, he became president of the Blackall Workers' Political Organisation in 1909.

No matter how fit a man might be, shearing exacts a heavy physical toll on its practitioners. The constant bending and hauling of heavy sheep on a daily basis usually leads to severe back problems that are complicated by rheumatism brought on by the damp. By 1900, even Jack Howe had had enough. He had married ten years earlier, and his health, together with the need to care for his wife and increasing family—ten children in all—caused him to abandon the scene of his triumphs and exchange the shearing shed for the life of a publican. Jack Howe remained a hotel-keeper for the next eighteen years, until, in 1918, he decided to retire, and purchased two farms. When he left Blackall the following year, he received an enormous public farewell, but he did not live long to enjoy his retirement, and died in July 1920.

In the Australian outback, shearing was probably the most physically demanding, most specialised, and most skilled occupation on the sheep stations. To city folk, the nomadic shearers typified the wide open spaces, the freedom, and the dangerous loneliness of the inland. Shearers were usually represented as larger-than-life; as hard workers, hard drinkers, and free spenders whose money— earned so arduously on the stations—often disappeared in a wild spree at the first pub they encountered down the track.

Shearing attracted 'characters', yet the towering reputation enjoyed by Jack Howe among his peers is a clear indication that the legend is based on truth, and that he trod the shearing boards of nineteenth-century outback Queensland like a giant among pygmies, and epitomised the peerless gun-shearer so deeply embedded in the bush mythology of nineteenth-century Australia.

The song *Click Go The Shears* is surpassed only by *Waltzing Matilda* as Australia's best-known folk song. It celebrates the era of the blade-shearer and the rivalry which a gun-shearer like Jack Howe always had to face from men who were natural competitors, even when a formal competition was not in progress. The first and last verses of the song illustrate something of the life of the shearers, and the chorus demonstrates the way in which the gun-shearer established the standard for all the other shearers to emulate or try to better.

CLICK GO THE SHEARS

Out on the board the old shearer stands,
Grasping his shears in his thin bony hands.
Fixed is his gaze on a bare-bellied yoe,
Glory, if he gets her, won't he make the Ringer go!

Chorus:
Click go the shears, boys, click, click, click.
Wide is his blow and his hands move quick.
The Ringer looks around and is beaten by a blow,
And curses the old snagger with the bare-bellied yoe.

There we leave him standing, shouting for all hands,
While all around him the other shearers stand.
His eyes are on the keg which now is lowering fast.
He works hard, he drinks hard, and goes to hell at last!

3
The Battle of Brisbane

What was the Battle of Brisbane all about? How were the explosive ingredients of sex and money involved? Did Australians enjoy being saved by the Yanks? And why was the Battle of Brisbane 'hushed up' by the Australian Government?

When Singapore fell to the Japanese in February 1942, 15 000 Australian soldiers went into captivity. The Australian Government, under the leadership of Prime Minister John Curtin, was left to face the nightmare possibility that had disturbed the sleep of Australian colonists since Europeans first arrived on these shores— the nightmare of having to stand alone to face an Asian invasion. The British Navy, under whose protective mantle Australia had sheltered since 1788, was pre-occupied with preserving British freedom in the European theatre of war, and could not be relied upon for the defence of Australia. And so it was, in these dire straits, that in December 1941 John Curtin signalled a desperate change in strategy when he called unequivocally for help from the United States of America:

> Without any inhibitions of any kind, I make it quite clear that Australia looks to America, free of any pangs as to our traditional links with the United Kingdom ... and we shall exert all our energies towards the shaping of a plan with the United States ... Which will give our country some confidence of being able to hold out until the tide of battle swings against the enemy.[1]

The Americans were delighted to have Australia as a base from which to mount and launch the counter-attack against the Japanese, and soon General Douglas MacArthur, the Supreme Commander of all Allied forces in the south-west Pacific area, landed in Australia and set up his headquarters. The first American troops arrived in Brisbane in March 1942. The Japanese Air Force was launching bombing raids against Darwin and Broome—and invasion seemed imminent. In these circumstances, the American soldiers were welcomed as saviours with enthusiasm and gratitude by most Australians. It was not until historians investigated the Japanese archives after the war, that it was discovered that the Japanese Government had rejected as impractical any plan to invade and occupy Australia.

Meanwhile, Australia's battle-hardened troops returned from fighting Rommel's army in the Middle East. At Kokoda and Milne Bay in New Guinea,

Wartime propaganda photographs attempted to portray the Australian–American relationship as close and friendly. (Australian History Museum, Macquarie University)

"Wot'll you do, Cabby, when the Yanks go?"
"Wot'll YOU do, sister?"

As usual, the cartoonists got much closer to the truth of the relationship.
(Taken from Patsy Adam-Smith, *Australian Women at War*, Melbourne, 1984)

together with conscript militia, the Australians inflicted the first defeats on land suffered by the Japanese in World War II. However, when General MacArthur made an announcement of these victories, he spoke only of 'Allied troops', and this enraged the Australians who felt that the few American soldiers involved at Milne Bay had shown cowardice in the face of the enemy. Relationships between the men of the two armies began to decline.

There were other reasons contributing to the growing hostility. These reasons were racial, sexual, and economic. Australia, at this time, still operated a 'White Australia' policy, yet there were significant numbers of Negro soldiers in the American forces. The customs and cultures of the two peoples seemed very different, and behaviour which Americans saw as just joking about in fun, was regarded by Australians as tasteless and boastful. For example, in one episode commented upon by a contemporary Australian officer (Major-General Iven Mackay), a drunken American soldier entered a bar and called out: 'Here I am Aussies! Come to save you from the Japanese'. The result was a minor riot.

In a letter sent in October 1942 to the American President Franklin D. Roosevelt, the American Ambassador to Australia commented on Australians in the following terms:

> They are a fine, outstanding people, who can be led but not driven. They are individually jealous of the general standard of equality oft-asserted against social classification.[2]

The Ambassador went on to state that Australians generally felt gratitude to the United States for saving them from Japan, and he carefully ignored the reports of the countless fist-fights and brawls in city pubs, cinemas and restaurants.

The main explanation for the increasing tension, however, was fundamentally economic, although with sexual overtones. The American soldiers were paid substantially more than their Australian counterparts. At the lowest level, American privates earned twice as much as did Australian privates, and the differential grew larger with the officers. Moreover, the American soldiers, via their military PX stores, had access to a range of goods not available to the general community, or, if they were available, it was only at a vastly greater price than the subsidised PX stock. Cigarettes cost Australian soldiers four times what the Americans could buy them for. It is also a fact of life that those with more money to spend get more attention from those with something to sell—and taxi drivers, publicans, and good-time girls flocked around the Americans like bees around a honey-pot. The economic advantage enjoyed by the Americans spilled over into sexual relationships, and there is no doubt that Australian girls were attracted to the free-spending, polite, and easy-going Yanks. Jealousies flared when Australian soldiers found that Australian women often seemed to prefer the company of visiting servicemen in preference to that of their fellow countrymen.

By 26 November 1942, American Thanksgiving, Brisbane had become a smouldering powder-keg with well over 100 000 soldiers of both armies in close proximity. The violence was triggered by an altercation between an American private—who had been selling cigarettes bought at the PX to Australian soldiers—and three Australian privates who were out looking for trouble. An American military policeman intervened, and the Australians turned on him, kicking and punching him to the ground. His fellow military police saw that he was in trouble and came to his assistance, and the Battle of Brisbane was on.

Violence escalated quickly. Despite its being defended by the civilian police as well as the military police, a crowd of about 3000 Australians attacked the main Brisbane PX store, and looted it. The American military police carried shotguns, and a number of shots were fired. One Australian private was killed, and another seven were wounded, but rumours of a much higher death-rate swept through the Australian Army—together with a story that the Americans had used 'Tommy guns' and had killed a girl standing innocently in the foyer of a picture theatre. A further eight Australians were treated for baton injuries. Wholesale brawling between the men of the two armies then erupted, and street fighting lasted for the next two days. There were no American deaths. In all, eleven Americans required hospitalisation for their injuries, and a further ten were treated for less serious complaints.

The newspapers were subject to wartime censorship, and reported the events as a small-scale military riot between a handful of Australian troops and the American military police. But American military records tell a similar story to that recounted by Australian witnesses and participants—of an Australian capital city in the hands of rioting mobs and out of control for a full two days. Indeed, it was not until Australian officers brought in troops from outside the Brisbane area, that peace was restored on the third day.

Ironically, the censorship that was designed to cool down a dangerous and volatile situation actually made things worse, because it allowed the rumours to fester unchecked by accurate and truthful information. For the rest of the war, and for decades thereafter, wild stories about the Battle of Brisbane circulated throughout Australia, with a much exaggerated death-toll and casualty list. The bitterness between the armies remained a constant feature for the remainder of the war, and was probably not eradicated until the two armies stood side by side once more in Korea and Vietnam.

4

William Buckley—Australia's Wild White Man

Who was William Buckley? Why is he regarded as the first champion of reconciliation with the Aboriginal people? And how does a white man manage to be thought of as the ghost of an Aboriginal warrior?

William Buckley looms as a larger-than-life figure in the early accounts of the settlement of Victoria, and his account of his life reads like a work of extraordinary fiction rather than as a true narrative of events. Yet no-one can fault his memoir as he dictated it to a Hobart journalist in the final years of his life, and we are left with a sense of wonder at Buckley's courage and tenacity as he carved out a life for himself as a fully accepted member of Victoria's Aboriginal society. For thirty-two years, he never saw another white man nor ever heard a word of English spoken.

Born in 1780, in the small Cheshire village of Marton, William Buckley enjoyed the healthy rural existence of the English peasant. His physical development reflected this wholesome and invigorating lifestyle, as he grew into a robust and vigorous youth, strongly built and just-on two metres in height. His father possessed only a small portion of leased land, and, in order to give the young Buckley a better start in life, his parents sent him to live with his grandparents in Macclesfield, a nearby town about eight kilometres away. There he learnt to read but not to write, and, by the age of fifteen, his grandfather apprenticed him to a local bricklayer with the intention that he would learn the trade and be able to make his living as a builder of houses.

For the next four years William struggled to force an 'unsettled nature' (his own later description of himself) into conformity with society's expectations of him. He did not succeed, although his tough training certainly increased his strength and endurance. By 1799, England was at war with revolutionary France, and army recruitment was stepped up dramatically. To a young man with a thirst for travel and adventure, the lure of the war proved irresistible. His size and strength made the army very interested in him, and, in 1799, he joined up. William's regiment became part of an expeditionary force sent to fight the French in Holland. This campaign was a dreadful military catastrophe, and William was wounded badly in the right hand. He was lucky to be one of the soldiers evacuated when the retreat was ordered in October 1799.

The dreary routine of daily army life proved to be just as galling to a spirited young man of action as had the tedium of life as an apprentice bricklayer, and William Buckley spent considerable time carousing in pubs with his friends. One day he was accosted by a young woman he had not seen before and asked to take a bolt of cloth to a woman who lived in the barracks so that she could make it into clothes. William obliged, but the cloth was stolen, and he found himself facing a charge of receiving stolen goods. He was found guilty at his trial, and received a sentence of transportation.

Now his situation had really deteriorated. As a convicted military felon, he was put to work in a prison gang—building new fortifications on the Thames River at Woolwich near London. The work proved demanding and exhausting, and he was subject at all times to the threat of the lash for even the most minor infractions of discipline. For William Buckley, this proved to be almost insupportable, and he came to hate all authority, swearing that if he ever regained his freedom, he would die before he would ever submit to such physical and mental torments again.

In 1803, William found himself included in an expedition to found a new convict colony in the Port Phillip District of New South Wales under the command of Captain David Collins. Since Collins had been part of the first fleet that had brought the British to Australia in 1788, it was felt by the authorities in London that his experience would be of great benefit to the fledgling settlement. And a convict with Buckley's physique and range of skills would be of great utility in any new colonising venture.

When the two ships of the expedition arrived in Port Phillip Bay in the month of October, Collins landed his party in the vicinity of present-day Sorrento on the Mornington Peninsula. The site was not well chosen, being especially short of water, and Collins soon decided to transfer the little band across Bass Strait to Van Diemen's Land, and to abandon any attempt to establish a settlement in the vicinity of Port Phillip Bay. It was not normal practice at this time for convict commandants to share their private thoughts and plans with the prisoners under their control, so William Buckley had no inkling that such changes were afoot, when, with two companions, he escaped the rigours of convict life and took to the bush.

The escapers had no real plan other than to try to walk to Sydney where they could pass themselves off as shipwrecked mariners. If life in the wild proved to be too arduous, they could always return to the settlement. They would certainly incur punishment, but Collins was known to be a fair man, and at least they would be fed. The trouble was that, soon after the escape, Collins abandoned the site. Just before the expedition sailed away, William's two companions decided to surrender, for they had found the hardships of foraging for sustenance in a harsh and hostile country to be beyond their capacities. Only William, determined to

William Buckley as he first appeared to the colonists of the Port Phillip
Bay District in 1836.

be free at any price, remained at large when, in May 1804, the last ship sailed out
of Port Phillip Bay. He was not to see another white man for the next thirty-one
years.

For a considerable time he eked out an existence on shell-fish which he was
able to scavenge from the rocks along the seashore, and on wild berries which he

gathered as he wandered. He built a small hut for himself, and struggled to come to terms with the loneliness and the knowledge that he had become a real-life Robinson Crusoe.

Eventually, he was found by local Aborigines who shared a meal with him and appeared friendly, although William felt great fear about what his discovery might portend for the future. At length, he realised that he had exhausted the food supplies in his immediate vicinity, and also that he was becoming progressively weaker. There would be only one outcome if he remained where he was. So with some trepidation, William Buckley set out to follow a native trail wherever it took him. By this time, he had become very weak, and could walk for only a short distance before stopping to rest. His legs were in very bad shape, and he was grateful when he discovered the grave of a dead Aborigine with a broken spear at its head. William took the broken spear as a walking-stick to help support his weight, and continued his slow, shuffling progress along the track.

Suddenly, he was surrounded by Aborigines, but they recognised the spear as belonging to a former member of their tribe, and assumed that William was the returned ghost of their friend who had picked up his spear out of habit. In Aboriginal religion, beings returning from the spirit world had much in common with a newborn baby. They had to learn all over again their language, their culture, and their relationships with all the members of their extended tribe. This marked the beginning of William's gradual induction into the tribal structure of Aboriginal society, and these people became his new family whom he grew to love dearly over the next three decades. During this time he took a wife and she produced a daughter of whom he felt very proud, although he saw her on only rare occasions.

He proved an apt pupil, and quickly mastered the language of his tribe. He accompanied them on their seasonal wanderings as they moved from place to place in response to the rhythms of the land and the different foodstuffs it produced. He met the adjoining tribes whenever the Aborigines got together to share trade and ceremonial activities. His own tribe forbade him to become involved in the incessant warfare and payback violence that he found to be such an important part of traditional Aboriginal existence, and he was often forced to sit and watch episodes of formalised (although usually managed) ferocity which distressed him enormously. All in all, William Buckley spent the next thirty years living the life of a traditional Aborigine before that timeless relationship to the land came to be disrupted by the arrival of permanent white colonists. His detailed account of the traditional Aboriginal way of life is still the best we have—because it is written from the inside by a sensitive and sympathetic observer.

In 1836, the settlement of the Port Phillip District finally took place, when pastoralists from Van Diemen's Land arrived with their flocks of sheep and attempted to arrange treaties with the Aborigines for the sale of their lands. To the surprise of the settlers, they were approached by a huge man clad in animal skins who walked slowly out of the bush into their midst and sat with great dignity with the blacks who were visiting their camp. At first, William was unable to converse in English. It had been over thirty years since he had spoken his own native tongue, but as the settlers used the name of different things, his memory returned, and he was able to begin a slow and halting conversation. The newcomers were amazed to find that he was a white man, and that he possessed an intimate knowledge of the Aboriginal culture and language.

This situation caused him considerable distress, because the final inevitable outcome was clearly going to be complete dispossession of the Aborigines. He was not trusted by the whites, who believed him to be far too sympathetic towards the blacks; and the Aborigines made him aware of the pain they felt in seeing him wearing white man's clothes and living increasingly within white society. As the spiral of violence climbed ever higher, William Buckley found himself trapped between two cultures and forced inevitably to choose one over the other. He chose to rejoin his own people, and—to remove himself from such a harrowing confrontation—he requested that he be sent to Van Diemen's Land. His Aboriginal family wept at his departure, and he never returned to them.

In Van Diemen's Land, William married and tried to live a normal life. He found this impossible, as his fame had made him well known, and his enormous size made it impossible for him to merge into the anonymity he so desperately craved. He refused ever to disparage Aboriginal culture or to discuss his experiences with the blacks in a climate of opinion that reflected the ignorance and hostility of white colonial society, and consequently he earned an inaccurate and unjust reputation as a dull or slow-witted individual. He dictated his memoirs late in life in an attempt to provide for his wife and adopted daughter, and died in Hobart in 1856.

5

The Hungry Mile

What was the 'Hungry Mile'? Why are dock-workers so committed to solidarity? Are Government schemes to 'reform' the waterfront a modern idea? And why was 'Pig-Iron Bob' called 'Pig-Iron Bob'?

The stretch of Sydney's Sussex Street leading to the docks was known colloquially to the wharf labourers as the 'hungry mile'. This title reflected the anger and resentment of the dockside workers over the primitive conditions of employment in operation in the years between the two world wars, and the genuine privation they and their families endured as a result.

Men seeking employment gathered early each morning at the gates of the wharves—and waited to be allocated work. The employers had the whip-hand in this situation, and gave or withheld work on a whim. Because of the entrenched hostility between the employers and the Waterside Workers Federation—dating back to the great maritime strikes of the 1890s—it was suspected that this pick-up procedure at the dock gates was often used to even up a few old scores, and to deny work to well-known union activists. An employers' blacklist existed, and men on that list were often denied work—except at times when there was some urgency to clear up a backlog on the wharves. The State Government passed legislation giving preference to returned servicemen after World War I, and this permitted the employers to play-off each group against the other, and effectively to divide the workforce and weaken the union. On occasion there would be serious riots on the waterfront as too many men fought for too few jobs. The riots would drive the non-union workers away for a few days, but then hunger would drive them back to the gate looking for work. It was a very combustible situation. At times men would scuffle and fight for the piece of paper known as a 'starting docket' which entitled them to a day's work on the wharves.

This degrading method of distributing work, known as the Bull System, was loathed by the wharfies who described it as a slave market. Following the morning pick-up, hundreds of unsuccessful applicants would drift up the hungry mile in a dispirited mob clutching the few pence they had left in their pockets, and wondering how they were going to feed their families that night. As Australia plunged into the Great Depression of the 1930s the desperation grew more urgent, and the numbers of men searching for work at the pick-up gate each morning skyrocketed. Waterside workers were given first preference, and those

During the recession of the 1920s and the depression of the 1930s, men queued for work on the docks, and those who were unsuccessful walked the hungry mile up Sussex Street in Sydney, and queued for the dole. This photograph shows a disempowered workforce. (Australian History Museum, Macquarie University)

who were outsiders got what was left over (if any). The Bull System was not replaced until 1943, when the wartime emergency made the continuation of such an inefficient scheme no longer viable, and the nation's manpower resources had to be distributed more effectively. Political bias in offering employment was forced to give way in the face of an overpowering reality, and the employers' blacklist of the earlier days—whereby the stevedoring companies would warn one another about union activists—disappeared. But, prior to this, every port city had its own local equivalent of Sydney's hungry mile.

Such improvements in conditions did not happen easily, and employers opposed the union 'tooth-and-nail'. In New South Wales there were riots and fighting in 1925 when the Federal Government attempted to break the unions by deporting the Irish-born Tom Walsh—president of the Seamen's Union; and the Scandinavian-born Jacob Johnson—one of the leaders in the waterfront unrest of the early 1920s. In Western Australia, the years after World War I were marked by bitter confrontation on the Fremantle wharves, and the State

Government organised an armed force of police and strike-breakers to break the power of the union. All around Australia, the employers orchestrated a concerted campaign to retain control of the waterfront and to keep the workforce subservient and dependent on the Bull System. In the 1930s, in Melbourne, a wharf labourer was shot by the police in a riot on the waterfront, and a number of other members of the union were gaoled for eleven years.

The industrial unrest on Australia's waterfront has sometimes given rise to anger in the wider community, but there have been a number of occasions when Australia has had good cause to be grateful for the radicalism and preparedness of the wharfies to challenge the hegemony of conservative governments. Perhaps the best known of these incidents occurred in 1937 and 1938, when the wharf labourers refused to load ships carrying scrap iron to Japan. The wharfies argued that this pig-iron would be used to augment the Japanese munitions and armaments industries, and that Australian soldiers would soon find themselves facing bullets and shells made from Australia's own scrap iron. The conservative government in Canberra, spurred on by its ambitious Attorney-General, Robert Gordon Menzies, attempted to bring the union to heel with the Crimes Act, and to force the men to continue loading the pig-iron for Japan. Menzies failed in this endeavour, and history has shown that the union was right and the government was wrong on this issue. One by-product of the confrontation was the hated nick-name of 'Pig-Iron Bob' that was conferred on Menzies by the wharf labourers at this time, and which he carried for the rest of his political career.

However, a federal Labor government, and the exigencies of World War II, saw the final dismantling (in 1943) of this iniquitous system of work allocation to political favourites and industrial neuters. This brought an end to the pain and anguish suffered by working men as they trudged to-and-fro on Sydney's hungry mile. The memory of the unfairness and the wrongs experienced in these years has become part of the mythology of today's wharf labourers, and helps to explain their reputation for intransigence and radicalism.

THE HUNGRY MILE

They tramp there in their legions on the morning dark and cold.
To beg the right to slave for bread from Sydney's lords of gold;
They toil and sweat in slavery, 'twould make the devil smile,
To see the Sydney wharfies tramping down the hungry mile.
On ships from all the seas they toil, that others of their kind,
May never know the pinch of want, nor feel the misery blind
That makes the lives of men a hell in those conditions vile;
That are the hopeless lot of those who tramp the hungry mile.

The slaves of men who know no thought of anything but gain,
Who wring their brutal profits from the blood and sweat and pain
Of all the disinherited that slave and starve the while,
Upon the ships beside the wharves along the hungry mile.
But every stroke of that grim lash that sears the souls of men
With interest due from years gone by, shall be paid back again
To those who drive these wretched slaves to build the golden pile,
And blood shall blot the memory out—of Sydney's hungry mile.
The day will come, aye, come it must, when these same slaves shall rise,
And through the revolution's smoke, ascending to the skies,
The master's face shall show the fear he hides behind his smile,
Of these his slaves, who on that day shall storm the hungry mile.
And when the world grows wiser and all men at last are free,
When none shall feel the hunger nor tramp in misery
To beg the right to slave for bread, the children then may smile,
At those strange tales they tell of what was once the hungry mile.

A. ANTONY

6

The Rabbit Plague

What possible reasons could the colonists have had for introducing the greatest environmental pest in Australian history? Why did the rabbit prosper so well? And what have calici and myxo got to do with it all?

The European rabbit is an introduced species in Australia, and has been responsible for the extensive destruction of native flora and the erosion and degradation of huge areas of Australia's most productive farmland. The rabbit population exploded in the nineteenth century, and the rabbits defied all the attempts of colonial governments to eradicate them. The irony is that the distraught settlers were directly responsible for the damage they inflicted on themselves—by having gone to considerable pains to successfully import the vermin and establish them in viable numbers to produce a self-supporting population. For close on 150 years, Australian farmers and pastoralists have had cause to curse the well-meaning ignorance that lay behind this most damaging of all animal importations.

In rural England, rabbits were a traditional part of the countryside. They provided an important addition to the diet of the peasant and labouring classes, for they could be caught without the need for expensive equipment, and were in sufficient numbers to retain relatively stable populations despite widespread human hunting. Many poorer folk in rural districts kept hutch-bred rabbits for food, and these had developed a heavier bone and flesh structure through centuries of selective breeding. The furs were also valued for their warmth and attractiveness, and children were fond of the rabbit as a domestic pet. The English thus believed that rabbits served a variety of useful purposes in return for very little outlay of effort on their part.

Consequently, rabbits arrived in Australia with the first fleet in 1788, and there is no doubt that further importations occurred during the first 60–70 years of European settlement. In Van Diemen's Land, an early colonist, Dr William Crowther, introduced rabbits in 1826, and they also accompanied the first settlers to the new Colony of Western Australia in 1829. We know that rabbits were introduced into the district around Port Phillip when it was permanently colonised after 1836, because one of the pioneer pastoralists named Alfred Joyce commented on their infesting his property by 1843. Sealers and whalers deliberately released rabbits onto the islands of Bass Strait and off the coast of South Australia, in an attempt to establish colonies of these most useful food animals.

One of the most striking things that emerges from all these introductions is that the rabbits did not initially appear to be the pest that they were to become later in the nineteenth century. The reason seems to lie in the farming practices adopted by the early pastoralists. When Europeans first drove their flocks of sheep into a new district, they inflicted mayhem on the existing ecological balance. Not only did the sheep destroy the native grasses, but they also competed with a variety of native herbivore species—such as kangaroos, wallabies, and wombats. In addition, the sheep were subjected to attack from Aborigines and from a variety of native animal predators—including dingoes, native cats, eagles, hawks, and crows. The reaction of the pastoralists was to shoot and bait-out as many of the competing herbivores and predators as they could—including the Aborigines. Over the decades, one effect of this was that it opened up an ecological niche by removing all the native predators that had hitherto inhibited the growth of rabbit populations. It was another unforeseen consequence of the application of European agrarian practices to the Australian landscape.

It would be wrong, however, to assume that the rabbit plague was merely the product of chance. The name of Thomas Austin is habitually connected with the pestilent increase in their numbers in the second half of the nineteenth century. Austin has been unjustly saddled with the responsibility for the plague when, in fact, it lies with the wider settler society. In the 1850s and 1860s, throughout Australia, groups known as 'acclimatisation societies' were established in an effort to correct what colonists regarded as the shortcomings of nature in their new country. British attitudes to landscape were embedded in a culture which found wilderness disturbing and unsettling, and which placed a higher premium on landscapes moulded to conform to aesthetic precepts more appropriate to the closely settled countryside of rural England than to the sparsely populated immensity of the inland. As part of this attempt to render the strangeness of Australia into something more familiar and acceptable, the acclimatisation societies introduced dozens of exotic plants and animals. The European bee, the horse, the trout, the fox, the donkey, the blackberry, the starling, the thrush, the blackbird—and the rabbit—are just a few of the new species that made a vigorous adaptation to Australian conditions as a result of the deliberate intervention of these societies. The environmental damage which they and the many other foreign species have since wrought in Australia beggars the imagination.

Thomas Austin, therefore, should not be singled-out for special obloquy. He was only one among many colonists involved in this process, when in 1859, he imported wild English rabbits which he crossbred with hutch-bred domestic rabbits and released on his property, *Barwon Park*, near Geelong in Victoria. Austin had constructed special burrows for his rabbits, and they acclimatised with great rapidity in the now predator-free environment. By 1865, he reported that he and his guests had shot an estimated 20 000 rabbits in sport that year, and that there were still at least 10 000 rabbits on the property. Two years later, when the young Duke of Edinburgh toured Australia, Thomas Austin invited him to a rabbit-shoot on the evening of his first day in Victoria. The Duke was delighted, and, in the cool of the evening, with the assistance of two bearers to load his guns, he potted over 400 rabbits in the space of three hours.

Catalogue of desperate measures to deal with a desperate situation. Nineteenth-century attempts to defeat the rabbit plague proved quite ineffectual.

The descendants of Austin's rabbits spread across the whole of eastern and central Australia within a generation, so that, as early as 1868, the squatters in Victoria's Western District had been forced to employ full-time trappers. In 1869, one property owner estimated that he had spent nearly ten thousand pounds to clear his property alone of more than two million rabbits. With no efficient predators to hinder their spread, the rabbits forced the abandonment of sheep runs, caused a drastic reduction in the annual wool-clip, and completely devastated entire districts, leaving them denuded of grass, and with the trees stripped of their bark as high as the rabbits could reach.

By the 1880s, the tide had reached Queensland, as rabbits in countless millions moved further and further north. Their burrowing undermined sandhills, and their voracious eating left no plants to hold the earth together. The result was that sand drifted into river beds and choked the waterholes; it covered the trees which lined the creeks, and made the land uninhabitable by European farmers. In Western Australia, even the vast and waterless Nullarbor Plain proved to be inadequate protection against the onslaught. By the 1890s, overlanders travelling to the desert goldrush of Kalgoorlie and Coolgardie had deliberately carried rabbits with them which they released in the goldfields districts. The Government of Western Australia met the problem by building a rabbit-proof fence over 2000-kilometres long, in a vain attempt to quarantine the rabbits to the goldfields and the northern region, but the rabbits moved faster than the fence could be erected, and people carelessly left the gates open, so the fence became an expensive and useless 'white elephant'. Only in the far north of the country did the climate and the predator population restrict the establishment of huge rabbit populations.

Within fifty years of Thomas Austin's innovation, rabbits had colonised every major pastoral and farming district in Australia, had effectively halved the value of the annual wool-clip, and had stripped large areas of the country bare of all herbage, thereby accelerating its destruction through erosion and sand drift. Despite many attempts by individual farmers to shoot, trap, and otherwise hunt rabbits into extinction, the numbers did not even begin to decline until the introduction of the contagious disease myxomatosis almost 100 years later in the 1950s. Then a dramatic culling took place, but it was not complete, and, in the following years, the tenacious rabbit had developed a partial immunity to myxomatosis, and the numbers began to expand once more. In 1997, a new weapon—known as the calicivirus—was introduced, and once again rabbit populations are in decline. There can be no complacency, however, as the rabbit's ability to develop immunity to the first disease (myxomatosis) demonstrates the resilience of this hardy and thoroughly well-acclimatised pest.

7

Black Mary—the First Female Aboriginal Bushranger

'Black Mary' was the first female Aboriginal bushranger. Who was she? Why did she call herself 'Thunderbolt's Lady'? What was remarkable about her life on the run? And what happened to her in the end?

Mary Ann Ward was born in 1834, the first child of a mixed-race relationship between the transported convict James Bugg (sometimes known as Briggs), and his Aboriginal partner, Charlotte. When Aborigines attacked the out-station on which James Bugg worked as a convict overseer in June 1835, his life was saved by Charlotte who fired a gun and frightened off the intruders, although James received a severe beating in the raid.

Another child, a son John, was born to the couple in 1836, and the arrival of these two children brought the little family to the attention of the Australian Agricultural Company which was James' employer. It was company policy to discourage cohabitation between the races, and to disallow marriage across the racial divide. The existence of the two infants complicated matters, but since both parents desired the best for them, the company arranged for Mary Ann and John to be sent to the Orphan School in Sydney and to be educated so as to equip them for life amidst the white settlers, in preference to the life of tribal Aborigines. James and Charlotte were separated by the company, but later got together again and produced a further four children. The four were christened on the same day as James and Charlotte were married in 1848. James and Charlotte lived for the rest of their lives on their own small property.

In the meantime, Mary Ann and John were taken from their parents to be civilised in Sydney, and Mary Ann received the sort of basic education given to girls of the lowest class of the white population, which enabled her to read, and equipped her for a life as a domestic servant. She then returned to the Gloucester area of New South Wales to be with her parents and siblings; and there, at 14 years of age, she married an ex-constable named Edmund Baker. Soon after, Mary Ann gave birth to her first child, and she and her husband found employment on a station in the Mudgee district. It is here that she made the acquaintance of the drover, horsebreaker, and bushman, Fred Ward.

In 1856, Fred Ward was convicted of receiving stolen horses and was sent to the convict depot on Cockatoo Island in Sydney Harbour. He was released four years later on a ticket-of-leave to the station on which Mary Ann was working, and found, when he arrived, that her husband had died in his absence. They became lovers, were married by a local Methodist minister, and moved in search of work to the Dungog area. Fred Ward was required, under the terms of his probation, to present himself to the authorities at Mudgee. He stole a horse to make one of these regular appearances, and was caught and reconvicted. Ward was sent once more to the notorious Cockatoo Island, and, two weeks afterwards, Mary Ann gave birth to their first child—a daughter whom she named Marina Emily Ward. Mary Ann was 26 years of age, and now the mother of two small children.

Legend has it that Cockatoo Island was escape-proof until Mary Ann swam out to the island in the night with food and a file with which Fred Ward filed through his irons and disappeared into the sea. The story goes that Mary Ann guided the escape from the harbour shore by holding up a lantern in the darkness towards which Ward and a companion swam. The couple became fugitives from then on, with a price on their heads, so it is clear that the authorities believed that Mary Ann had been deeply involved in the escape. After this point, Fred Ward was never recaptured.

Fred Ward and Mary Ann fled north on stolen horses, robbing huts and settlers for a gun and supplies. Ward embraced the life of a bushranger and soon became known as 'Captain Thunderbolt'. They lived rough in the mountains for the next four years, with their children, and Thunderbolt is recorded as robbing huts, hotels, and the mails. Mary Ann gave birth to her next child in 1864, and we can only speculate on the restrictions on movement that she must have experienced as a heavily pregnant woman, and then as a nursing mother—with two other small children for whom to care. Despite the dangers and the pressure of living on the run during this period, the couple never became brutal, and it is worth recording that, although Thunderbolt and Mary Ann were hunted like wild animals, they never killed any of their victims or pursuers. The daring style and 'Robin-Hood' character of their operations attracted a grudging admiration from the authorities who progressively increased the reward on Thunderbolt, until by 1865 it had reached two hundred pounds.

Mary Ann worked as Thunderbolt's accomplice in his ventures. She dressed as a man, rode astride, and conducted herself in such a way that she was usually mistaken for a young boy. She spoke the 'flash' language of the colonial lower classes and was defiant towards the incompetent police who finally captured her. She was described as being skilled at all forms of station work—including the cutting-out and butchering of an animal chosen for the table. She possessed all the bush skills of her mother's people, and could evade pursuit and live off the

THE REIGN OF TERROR.
A FIGURE SPECIALLY DEDICATED TO THE ADMIRERS OF ROBBERY AND MURDER.

This archetypal figure of a bushranger from the mid-nineteenth century represents the fear engendered in ordinary colonists by the activities of outlaws like Thunderbolt and Mary Ann. (*Sydney Punch* 1864)

land most effectively. What finally brought her into the hands of the authorities was her children. In 1865 a heavily pregnant Mary Ann was captured when the police raided their camp on the Narran River where they had been for the last eight months. Thunderbolt escaped, but Mary Ann was taken, and left at the nearby Wilbie Station while the chase for Thunderbolt and his other companions continued. The strength of the relationship between these two outlaws can be seen in Thunderbolt's reaction. He retraced his steps, raided the station, and stole Mary Ann away.

In March of the following year, the police once again caught up with the fugitives, and surprised them in the process of butchering a bullock for food. Thunderbolt escaped once again on the back of a superb thoroughbred, but Mary Ann could not evade capture as she had to protect her new baby and her other two infants. The police took Mary Ann and her children into custody, and she rode in her usual style with the baby and the toddler slung in saddlebags on either side of her horse, and with her eldest son riding another. She escaped, but was recaptured and taken to Stroud where her older two children were taken from her. She was brought before a magistrate with her babe-in-arms. There she faced the charge of being 'an idle and disorderly person and a companion of reputed thieves, having no visible means of support or fixed place of residence'. Mary Ann was sentenced to six-months imprisonment at the East Maitland gaol.

The case became a political 'bone-of-contention' in the New South Wales Parliament where some members complained bitterly at the application of the vagrancy laws to a person of Aboriginal background. What sort of justice was it that sought to apply laws (from which Aborigines were specifically exempted) to Mary Ann Ward—who was referred to in the House as 'Thunderbolt's Gin'? It was clear that Mary Ann's Aboriginality had itself become an issue. Opposition politicians argued that to take an Aboriginal person from the bush was identical to taking a European person from their home, and it would have been a great injustice for the authorities to enter a person's home, remove them by force, and then charge them with being a vagrant. Similarly, Mary Ann had been dragged from her natural abode, the bush, and accused of vagrancy solely because of her connection with Thunderbolt. The Attorney-General recommended that Mary Ann be released, and she rejoined Thunderbolt after leaving her children in the care of family or friends.

In 1867, she had a further brush with the law involving a length of allegedly stolen calico which was in her possession, and for which she was unable to account. Once again, Mary Ann's race became an issue, and she got off when her supporters argued in court that, as an Aboriginal person, she might have been unaware that, by failing to prove that she had come by the drapery legitimately, she could be convicted of a crime.

For the next eight months, Thunderbolt was reported to be accompanied on his robberies by an unknown young male accomplice, so it seems more than likely that, without her children, Mary Ann had resumed her activities as his partner-in-crime, in her former guise of a young man.

There are two stories of the end of Mary Ann.

One story holds that she died of pneumonia in the bush in 1867. She was taken by her husband, in a dying state, to a settler's house near Muswellbrook, and died the following night. The post-mortem showed that the cause of death was inflammation of the lungs brought on by exposure. It may well have been tuberculosis, as, when Thunderbolt was finally shot dead in 1870, he was found to be in the final stages of tuberculosis himself.

The second story is that Mary Ann returned to her children following the death of Thunderbolt, remarried on a further two occasions, and produced another thirteen children in these later relationships. According to the death certificate for this woman—who died aged 70 in 1905—her name was Mary Ann, daughter of James Briggs and Charlotte, surname unknown. She was said to be of Maori extraction, and to have been born in the Bay of Islands in New Zealand. However, on one of her children's birth registrations, she listed her birthplace as Gloucester, and Burgess as her maiden name. The similarities are certainly very close, and the story of a Maori background may have been a ploy to explain her darker complexion in an acceptable way to an increasingly intolerant and racially prejudiced society.

We will never know for sure which of these stories is the truth, but we do know, without the shadow of a doubt, that 'Black Mary', or 'Thunderbolt's Lady' (as she described herself), was Australia's first Aboriginal woman bushranger. Other bushrangers had occasional Aboriginal females as companions, but none of these relationships were long-lasting, nor did they produce the bevy of children that resulted from the devotion between these two remarkable people. The descendants of Thunderbolt and Mary Ann continue to live in Kempsey, and in Redfern in Sydney. In 1996, the life and times of their famous forebears became the subject of a popular stage play by the young playwright Julie Janson.

8

The New Italy Settlement

What was the New Italy settlement? What did the French have to do with it? Who was the 'con-man' who hatched the whole idea? And what eventually happened to the Italians who were 'conned'?

The story of New Italy begins with a French nobleman—Charles Marie Bonaventure du Breil, Marquis de Rays (1832–93). Like many members of the French aristocracy, de Rays found himself deprived by the French Revolution of the privileges enjoyed by his noble ancestors, and, even after the restoration of the Bourbons in 1816, the prestige and fortune of such people never recovered. When de Rays was born in 1832, the future for men of his class was one of living a quiet life on the family estates, or seeking adventure and fortune in distant lands. As an adult, the young Marquis de Rays travelled extensively, visiting North America, Africa, and Indo-China, and began to develop an interest in colonisation theories, and the wealth that could be extracted from colonising ventures by those who controlled and organised them.

In 1877 he decided to promote his own scheme of colonisation. It was poorly thought out, and amounted to a complicated confidence trick on would-be settlers and investors. He had not even selected a location for his model colony at this time, and began by proposing that it be established in the north-west of Australia. The British authorities testily informed de Rays that a French colony in Australia was out of the question, and suggested that the eager promoter look elsewhere. He then turned his attention to the French empire, and applied for land on New Caledonia to be allocated to his colony. The French Government was as unresponsive as the British had been. Finally, the Marquis announced that the colony, to be known as 'La Nouvelle France' would be set up on the islands north of Australia, namely East New Guinea, New Britain, and New Ireland.

During this period of increasingly frantic searching for a site for his new venture, de Rays had been assiduously promoting his colony throughout western Europe. The confidence-trickster took out advertisements in the French press, in which he extolled the plan as an opportunity for investors to make a fortune without having to leave the comfort of their own homes. He opened agencies in towns across Europe to attract investors, and, once the site had finally been chosen, he set out also to find a workforce to develop the colony for the absentee landlords. It was at this stage that de Rays' propaganda impacted upon a group of

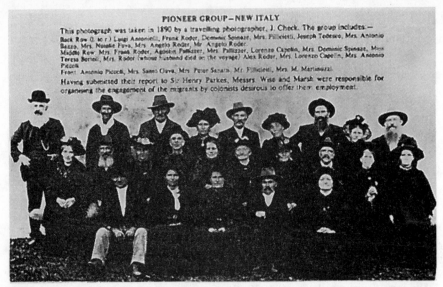

Pioneer Group, New Italy. (Taken from Anne-Gabrielle Thompson, *Turmoil -Tragedy - to Triumph: The Story of New Italy,* (Stanthorpe, 1980).

impoverished peasants from the Venetian rural hinterland.

The advertisements and the publicity painted a picture of a fertile Garden of Eden—a tropical paradise where the climate was temperate; a land cooled by Pacific Ocean breezes; a paradise of prodigious fertility; a land where epidemics and contagious diseases were unknown. De Rays promised that every family of agriculturalists wishing to settle in the colony would be assigned twenty acres of land with a four-room house already on it. Those who paid 1800 francs in gold before they left Europe would:

- become the immediate owners of land and house;
- be transported free to the new colony; and
- receive (once arrived at their destination) six-months' supplies to maintain themselves until they could plant and harvest their first crop.

Those who did not possess the means to pre-purchase their land and house were expected to:

- make a nominal down-payment of 1000 francs for a whole family; and
- work at the direction of the colony's administration for five years, following which they, too, would qualify for ownership of the package of house and land.

To landless Italian peasants who lived on the margins of starvation, the prospects held out to them by this propaganda seemed positively glittering. The promises made by the Marquis de Rays represented a ray of hope for them and, more importantly, for their children.

The French Government opposed de Rays' scheme, and refused to issue passports to the hundreds of deluded Venetians who had become caught up in the scam. De Rays arranged for them to travel to Barcelona in Spain where he had purchased a ship named the *India* to carry his migrants to 'La Nouvelle France'. In July 1880, more than 300 emigrant Italians embarked on a perilous voyage to one of the most misrepresented colonies in the chequered history of European expansion overseas.

When they arrived, they found, to their surprise, that the fertile Garden of Eden which they had been led to expect—with its cleared land and little four-roomed cottages—did not exist. They were the victims of an unscrupulous confidence-man. The land was not particularly fertile, and the climate was disease-ridden. The migrants began to die. When the monsoon season began in the second half of December, the trickle of deaths grew ominously and food began to run out. By February 1881, the survivors had had enough of this false paradise, and they deserted en masse to the nearby French penal colony of New Caledonia. There, the Italians were fed and offered temporary lodgings, but they had become alienated from, and suspicious of, the French—and refused resolutely to leave their ship. They had determined to reach Australia at all costs.

The British Consul on New Caledonia forwarded the migrants' request to New South Wales, where it came before the Colonial Secretary, Sir Henry Parkes, and the Governor, Lord Loftus. Parkes compassionately gave permission for the Italians to be brought to Sydney and treated as shipwrecked mariners. The French administration on New Caledonia advanced the funds, and a ship belonging to the Australian Steamship Navigation Company—which regularly plied between Noumea and New South Wales—was made available to transport to Sydney the 217 Italians who wished to resettle in Australia. The remaining fifteen survivors elected to remain in New Caledonia.

On 7 April 1881, the hapless victims of de Rays' rash venture sailed into Sydney Harbour, where they received a warm and sympathetic welcome from the general public and from the small resident Italian community. The colonial government, however, was unwilling to facilitate a separate ethnic community settling down all together in one locality. This was an era of unashamed assimilationism, and the government believed that the Italians should be distributed throughout colonial society, thereby being forced to learn the English language and colonial habits. Although such a course would inevitably split up friends and families as they went their separate ways, it would be for the ultimate benefit of the immigrants in the long run. After all, the Italians could always keep in touch with one another via the post office and the telegraph.

To the close-knit Italians who had shared the trials and tribulations of the previous year, this prospect of being split up proved deeply disturbing, and it was with extreme reluctance that they dispersed through the community and took up whatever work they could obtain. They never gave up the hope of coming together again, and, in 1882, some Italians began to apply for selections of land in the Grafton region, where the land was reasonably fertile, and where they could find employment in the local timber industry. Over the following years, others joined them, and the nucleus of the New Italy settlement grew out of the reassembling families of de Rays' innocent greenhorns.

They worked together, clearing their selections, building their houses, digging large cool cellars, and growing an increasing variety of vegetables and other cash crops. They manufactured their own wine, developed a silk industry with its associated orchards of mulberry trees, shore their own sheep, and designed and built their own knitting and spinning machines. The drive for self-sufficiency, together with the habits of thrift and careful use of resources that they had brought with them from Italy, made them resourceful and successful colonists. The migrants quickly gained the reputation of being hard-working and reliable workers in the timber-felling industry, and of being industrious labourers on nearby farms. Slowly the community established itself and created a permanent presence. By 1884, a school had been established with a full-time teacher, although it was government policy that Italian be forbidden in the classroom, and all instruction had to be conducted in the English language. By 1898, there were 232 inhabitants in the New Italy settlement, but this marked the high-water mark of the enterprise.

The problem was two-fold. To start with, the community of Italians was not large enough to become self-sustaining in its own right; and, secondly, the assimilation policy enforced through the education system had its inevitable effects as the children moved out into the wider colonial and national society. As the twentieth century moved into its first and second decades, the population of New Italy flattened out—and then declined. Younger families moved away to buy their own farms in Queensland, and the old-timers began to die out. The settlement remained inhabited until 1955, but its decline had become irreversible.

Today, the area has been reclaimed by the bush, and practically all traces of this Italian colony have disappeared. There is a museum and a memorial commemorating the lives of these hardy pioneers, and a modern multicultural Australia honours the bravery and the courage of these immigrants who absolutely refused to become the passive victims of a French criminal—or of a harsh fate.

9

Frank Jardine—the Twice-Buried Pastoralist

Who was Frank Jardine? What was remarkable about the expedition he led from Rockhampton to Cape York? Why did Aboriginal mothers use his name to discipline their naughty children? And why would a man be buried twice?

Frank Jardine was born at Orange in New South Wales on 28 August 1841 and educated at Sydney Grammar School. He was the eldest son of John Jardine, a pastoralist and magistrate who was originally from Scotland. In 1863, a new northern settlement named *Somerset*, on the tip of the Cape York Peninsula, was established in order to provide a refuge for shipwrecked mariners in the dangerous waters of the Torres Strait, and to ensure protection and a port-of-call for the growing maritime trade centred on the Torres Strait and the north Pacific region. John Jardine received the appointment of Government Resident at the new settlement, and, accompanied by a party of twenty-five Royal Navy marines and a medical officer, he occupied the site of Somerset. It was anticipated in Brisbane that the little base would become the nucleus of a much larger trading venture, and speculators purchased town allotments in Somerset, sight unseen, in anticipation of turning a handsome profit.

John Jardine believed in the plans for northern development. He travelled to Somerset by sea, but arranged for his two eldest sons, Frank and Alex, to travel overland from Rockhampton with stock, and to set up a cattle station in the vicinity of Somerset. This was a distance of approximately 2400 kilometres, through incredibly harsh and completely unknown country that had never before been traversed by Europeans. Furthermore, it involved passing through the territories of several Aboriginal tribes that were known to be fiercely protective of their countries. It was also to include travelling at the height of the northern wet season—quite a task to entrust to the leadership of a young twenty-two-year-old man and his twenty-year-old brother.

Nothing daunted, the little expedition—of six Europeans, four Aborigines, 42 horses and 250 head of cattle—left Rockhampton on 14 May 1864 and embarked upon a ten-month trek that was to become a legend of endurance and adventure, and went a long way towards establishing the larger-than-life persona of Frank Jardine. They carried supplies sufficient for four months, and were well armed with breech-loading rifles and two revolvers for each white

Frank Jardine

man. For almost the entire length of the journey, the Jardine party found itself continuously harassed by various tribes of Aborigines who contested the passage of the expedition through their respective countries. It would be true to say that Frank Jardine shot his way through to Somerset. His personal tally of dead Aborigines, which he recorded by cutting notches on the stock of his carbine, lay at 47 by the time the party reached its goal ten months later. These notches commemorated only confirmed kills, and did not include Aborigines who died later in the bush or were shot and unaccounted for, as part of the never-ending running battle to which this murderous expedition amounted.

Early in November, as they camped in a dry creek bed, the campfire got away and set fire to the tinder-dry grass, setting off a major conflagration. The upshot of this carelessness amounted to the loss of nearly all their supplies—of food, tents and camping equipment, and clothing and footwear—and forced Frank Jardine, as the leader of the expedition, to rely entirely on his bush skills to feed and guide the group through impossible country for the remaining three months. In the meantime, the incessant attacks of the Aborigines, who hung on the flanks of the party and forced it into fierce rearguard actions on a daily basis, steadily depleted the herd and the horses, to the point where there were only three effective horses remaining for managing the cattle, and the rest of the members of the expedition were reduced to walking. They had lost their clothes and wore only brief coverings of canvas. For footwear they relied on sandals they manufactured from paperbark. They lived on whatever game they could shoot, and on the eggs of the wild brush-turkeys which they found. Under the driving will of Frank Jardine, the remaining cattle were not abandoned when they became bogged in mud, or stranded on the banks of rivers swollen in the floods of the wet season, but were manhandled and pulled through all the difficulties as the expedition stubbornly continued north. The journey became a saga of survival under the most difficult of circumstances. After one encounter alone with the Aborigines in December, on the banks of the Mitchell River, they counted the bodies of thirty dead warriors.

On 2 March 1865, Frank Jardine and his party finally reached Somerset. They looked like wild men with their emu-skin caps, sunburnt bodies, canvas loincloths, and paperbark sandals. Indeed, the only thing that distinguished Frank and Alex Jardine from the Aborigines who accompanied them, was the carbines they carried slung across their backs, and the revolvers tucked into cartridge belts around their waists. They had twelve horses and fifty head of cattle left, but all members of the expedition had survived intact. All in all, it was an amazing example of bushmanship and epic perseverance from one of such tender years; but it must also be acknowledged that Frank Jardine's was a reputation built squarely on the corpses of several hundred Aborigines who had opposed the passage of the expedition. In human terms, the cost had been extraordinarily high.

Frank Jardine went on to establish the cattle station his father had envisaged on the north shore of Newcastle Bay in the vicinity of Somerset, and, as part of that process, many more Aborigines died. Jardine became the terror of the Aboriginal people in the Cape York area because of the ferocity with which he responded to attacks on his station or his stock, and he demonstrated on many occasions that he held the lives of Aboriginal people very cheaply. His personal tally of dead Aborigines is estimated in the hundreds. For their part, the Aborigines loathed and feared him, and it is reported that Aboriginal mothers would threaten their misbehaving children with a visit from the bogey-man Frank Jardine.

In European society, on the other hand, Frank Jardine won respect and admiration. In 1886, the Royal Geographical Society elected both Frank and Alex as Fellows of the Society, and awarded them both the Murchison Grant for their services to exploration. Frank married a Polynesian girl at Somerset in 1873. She was the niece of the King of Samoa. They produced two sons and two daughters. When the settlement of Somerset was closed by the government in 1879, and all those early land speculators had lost their money, Frank Jardine stayed on and founded several additional stations. The most distant of these was *Bertiehaugh* on the Ducie River, which he established in 1887, and defended against the Aborigines by constructing a fort which he equipped with a brass swivel-gun, and fifty rifles and muskets.

Frank Jardine lived on in the Cape York district for the rest of his life. He became involved in the pearling industry, and in a number of private campaigns against native pirates from the region. He died of leprosy at Somerset on 19 March 1919, and was laid to rest in a grave near the beach. The story is that the local Aborigines were so frightened of this man in life that they feared his ghost would continue to terrorise them after his death. In order to make it harder for the ghost to find its way back, the body was dug up and reburied head downwards. The truth of this old story is unknown, and perhaps it is only one final and ambiguous episode in the legend of Frank Jardine. His exploits and explorations are officially recognised in the naming of the Jardine River and the Jardine River National Park, which is one of the chief wilderness areas in Queensland.

10
Darwin and the Electric Telegraph

Why was the Northern Territory originally called *Arnhem Land*? Where does the name 'Northern Territory' come from? What name did the authorities unsuccessfully try to impose on the town of Darwin? And why was the electric telegraph so important to Australia in general—and to Darwin in particular?

Australia's Northern Territory was originally named Arnhem Land by the Dutch—after their ship the *Arnhem* which explored the northern coastline of the continent in 1623. In 1803, the explorer Matthew Flinders visited the area as part of his expedition to chart the coasts of the whole continent. The harbour on which Darwin is built was sighted by John Lort Stokes in 1839. He named it Port Darwin in honour of his friend and former shipmate from the voyage of the *Beagle*, the scientist Charles Darwin.

Attempts were made from the early 1820s onwards to establish a northern settlement. The spur for this aspiration was the desire of colonists and British merchants to participate in the thriving trade of the South-East Asian area. A number of small convict trading colonies were attempted at Port Essington, north of the present site of Darwin, but they were all abandoned because of health problems and the implacable hostility of the local Aborigines.

In 1863, the territory passed from the control of New South Wales to South Australia, and it is from this time that the name 'Northern Territory' began to be applied—as this new area of South Australian authority was north of that colony and its capital city of Adelaide. The Surveyor-General of South Australia, George Goyder (1826–98), planned a new settlement, and, in 1869, he led an expedition to the area and established a small outpost with a population comprising 135 men and a few women. Goyder planned an ambitious future for the nascent colony, and anticipated a future population of around 30 000 people who would reside in the administrative centre—a town he named Palmerston in honour of the British statesman and Prime Minister. Traders and residents ignored the name, and continued to use the name 'Port Darwin', and the official name (of 'Palmerston') fell into disuse. By 1911, when responsibility for the territory passed to the Commonwealth Government, the authorities recognised local usage, and 'Darwin' became the city's official name.

In 1872, Darwin became a key link in the overland telegraph line which

Palmerston (Darwin) Telegraph Station, 1871.

connected Australia to the wider world—and finally shattered the sense of isolation felt by colonists of European extraction on the other side of the world from their countries of origin. The telegraph revolutionised communications within Australia, and helped to break down regional loyalties which might otherwise have militated against the movement towards a federation of the six independent Australian colonies. Telegraphic communications made the different colonial communities more aware of one another and of the common problems they all faced. The capital cities of Adelaide, Melbourne and Sydney were connected by wire in 1858; Victoria and Tasmania in 1859; and, by 1870, Darwin was connected with Adelaide by a telegraph line that followed the route laid down by the explorer John McDouall Stuart in his epic journey from Adelaide to Darwin a decade earlier. The service was extended to Perth in 1877, and the building of the line across 1500 kilometres of the Nullarbor Plain—probably the most arid land in the country—ensured rapid communications for the first time throughout the entire continent.

The effects of the telegraphic revolution became even more radical in 1872, when Darwin became the link connecting Australia with Great Britain, via a world-wide international cable telecommunications system that stretched from London to the four corners of the British empire through huge undersea cables that stretched between Europe and India, India and Java, and then to Australia. For the first time, news could reach Australia in less than twenty-four hours from

Europe, and urgent communications could be sent in a matter of a few hours only.

A measure of the profound impact which this Darwin-based development had on eradicating the isolation that had always been a part of Australian psychology since the first settlement can be gained when we consider that, during the early decades of the nineteenth century, it had taken a minimum of ten months to receive communications sent from England to New South Wales. As ship-building improved, sailing times began to diminish, but in 1850 it was still a period of at least four months. With the building of the great clipper-ships during the 1850s—expressly designed for fast sailing over large distances—the time-lag dropped to about three months. In 1869, when the opening of the Suez Canal shortened the sailing time even further, a trip between England and Australia still took approximately seven weeks. To have this cut to a mere few hours overcame, at one stroke, the isolation felt by the inhabitants of this European outpost on the far side of the globe.

Henry Parkes, who had just become Premier of New South Wales when the first international transmission began, expressed the sense of wonder evoked in colonists by the new technology, when he described the technology as: 'a magical business, uniting us hand-in-hand, as it were, to the parent land'.[3]

There were practical, as well as psychological, advantages for Australians. For the first time, the purveyors of rural produce could keep tabs on the financial markets of England. Primary producers could follow the fluctuations in the prices on offer for their exports, and could send instructions to their English agents to sell or withhold their products in response to the way they interpreted English market fluctuations. Political news flowed through the telegraph and strengthened the crimson thread of kinship most Australian colonists still felt for Britain. It was the telegraph that enabled the colony of New South Wales to send an expeditionary force to the Sudan in 1885, in time to join British forces in their attack on the Mahdi and his followers, as punishment for the death of General Gordon at Khartoum.

The high costs of telegraphs, however, restricted the volume of international traffic, although, within Australia, the colonial newspapers began to print daily telegraphic intelligence about the other colonies, including the weather, the movement of ships, the prices of goods, and sporting news—especially the results of horse-racing and cricket. In later years, the telegraph played a major role in the co-ordinated pursuit of bushrangers, especially the famous Kelly Gang. By 1865, the inhabitants of the colonies of New South Wales and Victoria were sending more than half a million messages a year to one another, and nearly every primary producer who had dealings outside his own local area came to rely on the service in one way or another. Henceforth, the farmer or grazier

THE DANGERS OF LINE REPAIRING IN NORTHERN QUEENSLAND.

The dangers of line repairing in Northern Queensland according to *Sydney Punch,* 1870.

could buy or sell land, stock, or produce, in the best possible market by remote control.

Other more immediate benefits flowed through to Darwin as a result of its role as the nexus point for domestic and international telegraphic communications. Telegraph workers discovered gold at Pine Creek in 1871, and, by the early 1880s, thousands of people had flooded into the region. A railway was built to link Darwin with Pine Creek, and it was constructed largely by Chinese coolies. The growing population of permanent settlers made the Northern Territory attractive to overlanders who drove their herds there, and established a thriving cattle industry, and Darwin became the port through which their supplies were shipped. The work of laying and maintaining the overland telegraph line led to the settlement of the town known as Alice Springs in central Australia, when workers chanced upon abundant fresh-water springs in that most unlikely and inhospitable region. Eventually, the Government of South Australia determined to link Port Augusta and Darwin by railway, but abandoned the project after the line reached Oodnadatta in 1891—on the grounds that it was too expensive. The Commonwealth extended the line as far as Alice Springs after it took over the territory in 1911, but the rest of the line between Alice Springs and Darwin still remains to be constructed.

It is hard to overemphasise the effect on Australia and Australians of the electric telegraph. In an age when people had grown up accepting, as a part of nature, that information could travel only as fast as ships could sail or steam, or only as fast as men could ride, pigeons could fly, or operators could signal to each other with smoke or flags from nearby hill-tops—the communications revolution seemed to be nothing short of a miracle. That it also helped in the establishment of Darwin and a permanent northern settlement, became, later on, a matter of national importance for trade and strategic reasons.

11

Lachlan Macquarie—Slave Owner

How could the famous 'liberal' Governor own slaves, and yet keep a clear conscience? Who was George Jarvis? And what sort of life could be lived by a black slave in status-conscious colonial society?

Governor Lachlan Macquarie (1761–1824) has gone down in Australian history as the 'convicts' friend', and is generally regarded as one of the most liberal governors the convict colony of New South Wales ever had. His reputation for liberalism flows from his belief that the former criminals resident in Australia were entitled to regain their previous status in civil society after they had served their time—if their behaviour showed evidence of reformation. Other officials in the colonies took a contrary view, and maintained that a conviction for a transportable offence ought to stay with the felon for the rest of his or her life, and that freed convicts should never be allowed to regain their former positions of rank or respectability—whatever their conduct.

Macquarie's reputation for liberal views, however, seems narrowly based on his humane attitudes towards the convicts under his care, and his paternalistic concern for Aboriginal welfare. We tend to forget that slavery was not abolished throughout the British Empire until 1834, and that supposedly enlightened men could quite legally purchase slaves and keep them as private property—so long as the slave did not set foot on English soil. Immediately a slave set foot on the soil of England, under a ruling handed down by the Lord Chief Justice late in the eighteenth century, that individual automatically became free.

Therefore, when Lachlan Macquarie—an impoverished scion of a proud Scottish family—took up a military career, he was more than happy to be posted for service in India, for it was in the Far East that ambitious men could find the opportunities to make their fortunes. In India, Macquarie married his first wife, Jane Jarvis, and in 1795 the young couple were living in Calicut—having recently moved there from Bombay to save money and enjoy an easier and more economical regimental lifestyle. Ranking British officers at this time did not expect to be able to live on their military salaries, and men from poor but respectable backgrounds (such as Macquarie) were forced to make savings wherever they could. It was part of this search for a genteel way of life that probably led Macquarie into becoming a slave owner. His private journal for 24 January 1795 carries the following matter-of-fact entry:

Lachlan and Elizabeth Macquarie. (Archives Office of Tasmania)

Lieut. Gray returned from Cochin, and brought me two very fine, well-looking healthy Black Boys; both seemingly of the same age, and I should suppose from their size and appearance that they must be between six and seven year old. The stoutest of them Mrs Macquarie has called Hector after my Brother: and the smallest I have called George after her Brother.

Lieut. Gray has executed his commission much to our satisfaction, for which I conceive myself much obliged to him—The Two Slave Boys cost One Hundred and Seventy Rupees.

We had the Boys immediately well washed, their Hair cut and combed, and well clothed.[4]

The tender years of the two children renders the above entry particularly horrifying, and it makes little difference that the slaves were apparently treated kindly. It is also worth noting that a horse cost ten times more than a child in India at this time. The larger boy, Hector, disappears fairly early from the story. It seems that he was kidnapped by slave dealers a short time later, and Macquarie never saw him again. However, the smaller child, George, stayed with Lachlan Macquarie for the rest of his life, and accompanied the Governor and his second wife to the convict colony of New South Wales in 1810. By this time, George Jarvis (as he was known) would have been about twenty-one years old, and had become the personal body-servant of Lachlan Macquarie. For the remainder of the Governor's life, George, the Indian-born slave, would be at his side, even attending him at his death bed in 1824.

Nor was George destined to live a life of loneliness as a black slave in a white society. In Sydney, the Macquaries needed many servants to maintain the vice-regal lifestyle. One of these was a convict chambermaid, named Mary Jelly, who arrived in New South Wales late in Macquarie's term of office in January 1820. At Government House, Mary made the acquaintance of George Jarvis, and the two were married at St Philip's Church, Sydney, on 22 March 1820. Their first child, a daughter, was born on 19 December 1820, but died within a week on Christmas Day. On 1 September 1821, Mary Jarvis was granted an absolute pardon by the Governor, and this allowed her to accompany her husband to England when Macquarie and his family returned to London aboard the *Surrey*, in February 1822. When Macquarie and his entourage embarked in Sydney, Mary was five-months pregnant. She gave birth to George's daughter on 5 May.

In Britain, George and Mary Jarvis accompanied Lachlan and Elizabeth Macquarie on their return to the estate which Macquarie had purchased in Scotland, on the Isle of Mull, as a result of the prize-money he had accumulated during his service in India. He had named the property *Jarvisfield* in honour of his first wife—whose death from tuberculosis in the tropics had caused him much grief. George travelled with Macquarie to London in 1824 when the former governor was engaged in defending his reputation against the biased and unfair attacks of Commissioner J.T. Bigge on Macquarie's administration in New South Wales. George was present on 1 July 1824 when Macquarie died in London, and received his freedom as a bequest in Macquarie's last will and testament. The Jarvis family stayed on as retainers to Elizabeth Macquarie, and Mary attended the death bed of Elizabeth on 11 March 1835—and took a major role, with the relatives of the deceased, in organising the funeral preparations. We have no record of when George or Mary died.

It is one of the paradoxes of Australian history that this man—the most liberal, humane, and paternalistic of all the governors of the convict period—should have owned another human being as a species of private property. It goes to show that, while today we may admire Macquarie as a forward-looking and enlightened administrator, his attitudes emphatically were those of a man of his times, and he possessed all the strengths and weaknesses of a military man in the era when slavery was both legal and still morally acceptable. Lachlan Macquarie—slave owner—apparently saw nothing incompatible in having a genuine concern for the rights and welfare of the British convicts entrusted to his care, and, at the same time, in being the master of other human beings who had no legal rights whatsoever, and were nothing more than a form of portable equity or valuable livestock.

12

Sir George Arthur and the Black Books

George Arthur's name will forever be connected with the infamous penal settlement of Port Arthur. But does he deserve such a memorial? Why did the British Colonial Office regard the administrative talents of Sir George Arthur so highly? And what were the 'Black Books' anyway?

No Governor in the history of Van Diemen's Land looms larger than the notorious George Arthur, possibly because his name is forever connected with Port Arthur—the colony of secondary punishment that was deliberately designed to deter convicts from committing additional crimes in the colony, by making the punishment for such colonial infractions both savage and incessant. This is unfortunate in many ways, because it tends to dominate Arthur's reputation, and to obscure the reasons that led this Governor to be one of the most respected colonial administrators—in the eyes of his employers at the Colonial Office in London—ever sent to Australia. At the same time, he was also one of the most hated and feared men in the colony over which he presided, and his invention of the so-called Black Books has much to do with these two contradictory opinions.

George Arthur was born in 1784 in Plymouth, England, and joined the army as a young man aged twenty. This was the period of the Napoleonic wars, and the youthful officer soon found himself on active service against the French. Arthur served in Italy, Sicily, Egypt, and the Low Countries. In 1814 he was appointed as Lieutenant-Governor of Honduras, where his sympathetic treatment of the slaves won the commendation of the British Government—which was coming increasingly under the influence of humanitarian abolitionists led by William Wilberforce. In the Colonial Office, abolitionist influence was strong, especially in the person of the permanent Under-Secretary, the influential James Stephen, and Arthur's character was much admired. In 1822, he left Honduras, and shortly thereafter was appointed to the position of Lieutenant-Governor of Van Diemen's Land—a position he occupied from 1824 until 1836.

When Arthur arrived in Van Diemen's Land, he found the colony to be in some disarray after the disastrous commands of Thomas Davey and William Sorell. These two predecessors had led lives of notorious irregularity, and the strictly moral Arthur was determined to re-establish the rule of law and a sense of decorum as the norms of behaviour for government employees in the colony.

He was also determined to wipe out cohabitation of settlers with the female convicts, and the heavy drinking and sexual immorality that were common among the convicts themselves. A complete reorganisation of the convict system provided the means for Arthur to begin cleaning up the settlement—in keeping with his excitable and passionate adherence to the dictates of evangelical Christianity.

The administrative reforms undertaken by the 'new broom' at Government House received the enthusiastic endorsement of the authorities in Britain because the reforms fitted into the broad thrust of developing policy that had, as its over-riding aim, to restore the deterrent effect of a sentence of transportation to Australia. The British believed that such a sentence had lost much of its inhibiting effect because it was well known in England that the Australian colonies provided lower-class criminals with a breadth of opportunities for bettering themselves that was unavailable in the home country. Furthermore, it was also widely believed that the life of a convict was not one of suffering and torment, but rather one of comparative ease and comfort, where the criminal was better fed, better clothed, and better housed than he or she could ever have hoped to be in Britain as free labourers.

The centre-piece of George Arthur's reforms lay in a relentless and almost mechanical precision that characterised a convict's progress through his time in servitude. A series of classifications were introduced into the convict system, and a felon's behaviour determined whether he or she moved steadily through the different levels to increasingly easier treatment and greater amounts of freedom, or retrogressed down the levels—where treatment became progressively more ferocious as the convict descended. The final stages of this process for well-behaved and dutiful prisoners was the issue of a ticket-of-leave under which the convict was released into the wider community, although still under probation, and still liable to be returned to the prison system if further crimes were committed. This could be followed by a conditional pardon—which effectively removed all restrictions other than that the felons could not leave the convict colony until the period of their original sentence had been served. The ultimate condition was the free or absolute pardon—which restored all the civil rights of a freeborn English citizen. At the other extreme of the spectrum lay the descent into the colonies of secondary punishment—such as Port Arthur—in which conditions of life were made almost unendurable, and in which brutal and barbaric punishments were widely inflicted on the hapless inhabitants. Only about five per cent of serving convicts ever made it to these hell holes, but the mere threat of them normally proved sufficient to bring the most recalcitrant and rebellious convict to heel. It was Arthur's intention that the convicts' own behaviour would determine the treatment that they received, and, in this way, he hoped to create an incentive for their good behaviour.

George Arthur.
(Archives Office of Tasmania)

Obviously, such a scheme could work only if there was an efficient and comprehensive system of convict records, and it was in the creation of this information data-base that the Black Books made their appearance. These were the extensive records of every individual convict's passage through Arthur's prison system, from the time of arrival in Van Diemen's Land, where the physical description of the individual was carefully inscribed, together with: a report of their trial and a record of the sentence; a report from the ship's Surgeon of their conduct on the voyage out; and a thorough charting of their movement through every stage of the classification scheme to the end of the period of servitude. Nor did the records stop with the release of the prisoner, for every subsequent infraction of the law that brought a former convict to the attention of the colonial authorities would continue to be entered into that person's record in the Black Books—which were kept up to date until the death of the subject.

The administrative characteristics of George Arthur can be delineated very comprehensively when we study the detail of his reforms of the convict system during his time in Van Diemen's Land. To begin with, there was his absolute thoroughness and attention to detail. Allied to this was a deliberate policy of concentrating all administrative power in his own hands. Arthur exercised a degree of personal control over his colony that would have been quite impossible in the larger mother-colony of New South Wales. Moreover, Arthur created a most efficient machinery for the gathering of information on all aspects of life in the rural areas of Van Diemen's Land. He established nine police districts, each under the supervision of a stipendiary magistrate, and each with a force of mounted police who were directly answerable to the governor via weekly written reports on the conduct of the convicts and ticket-of-leave holders in their districts. These convict constables also reported on the behaviour of the convicts' employers—much to the chagrin of the free population who resented the reflection on their conduct which such reporting represented. In order to gain full control over the justice system, and to co-ordinate and make consistent sentences handed down by the courts, Arthur reorganised the previous system of local magistrates and justices of the peace. He replaced this with a new arrangement involving stipendiary magistrates who were dependant on the administration for the payment of their salaries—and who were therefore unlikely to challenge the authority of the central government.

When Arthur arrived in Van Diemen's Land in 1824, the population of the colony numbered about twelve-and-a-half thousand Europeans, of whom almost half were still convicts. By the time of his departure in 1836, the free population alone had risen to more than 18 000, and the prison population had also dramatically increased by a similar proportion. The close superintendence—which Arthur's system demanded—made it virtually impossible for his successors to maintain the degree of personal control that had become the distinguishing characteristic of his time in the colony. To do so would have required a level of devotion to duty that most colonial governors just did not possess, and the growth of the settlement made the control of a single individual over all aspects of daily life (as had been exercised by George Arthur) both impossible and inadvisable to continue.

Nevertheless, it was this personal control and meticulous record-keeping—epitomised by the Black Books—upon which was rooted Sir George Arthur's high reputation with the Colonial Office in London, and he is one of the very few governors of Australia's convict colonies who went on to a future career in the colonial service. Australia destroyed the health and the reputations of most colonial governors in the convict period, but Arthur was the exception to this general rule. After leaving Australia, Arthur became Lieutenant-Governor of Upper Canada (1837–41), and, following that, he was appointed Governor of the Bombay Presidency (1842–6). He was further rewarded with a baronetcy. He died in England in 1854 with the army rank of Lieutenant-General. The rewards seem little enough for a lifetime of duty and service. In all his years of colonial service between 1814 and 1846, George Arthur had spent only three years at home.

13

James Stirling and the Pinjarra Massacre

How did James Stirling manage to become Governor of Western Australia at the young age of 37 years? He also became the only Governor in the history of colonial Australia to plan and participate in a massacre. Why would he do such a thing?

James Stirling was born in 1791 at Drumpellier, in Lanarkshire, Scotland. At twelve years of age, he joined the Royal Navy and saw action against the French and their Spanish allies during the wars against Napoleon. The young lad showed promise, and in 1812, following the entry into the war of the United States, he received his first command as master of HMS *Brazen*, which he was ordered to sail to America to attack the forts at the mouth of the Mississippi in the Gulf of Mexico. The newly commissioned lieutenant was still only nineteen years old. By war's end in 1815, James Stirling had been promoted to the rank of post-Captain and had also been retired ashore on half-pay like most of the navy's now-redundant officers. There, with all his brother officers, he went onto the list to await his turn to command one of the vessels still in service in the small peace-time Royal Navy. It was not until late 1826 that Stirling's name came to the top of the list, and then he was given command of HMS *Success* which the Admiralty sent on a voyage to New South Wales to assist in moving the tropical trading settlement of Fort Dundas on Melville Island to a new location on the mainland at Port Essington, on the Cobourg Peninsula in the far north of Australia.

When he arrived in Sydney early in 1827, Stirling discovered that he had reached Australia in the season when the northern monsoons made his projected voyage north too dangerous, and he also encountered a French vessel which had just completed an exploration of the coastline of Western Australia in the vicinity of the mouth of the Swan River. Stirling was reluctant to sit cooling his heels in Sydney after waiting so long for a ship to command, and he proposed to the Governor of New South Wales, Ralph Darling, that the *Success* undertake a voyage to the same region in order to investigate the reasons for the French enthusiasm. Darling agreed, and, in March 1827, James Stirling spent two weeks examining the area in the company of Charles Fraser, the New South Wales' government botanist. Stirling fell in love with the exotic beauty of the place, and wrote a report for the British Government in which he recommended the immediate settlement of Western Australia to forestall the French, and requested that, in the event of any such decision, he be considered for the position of governor.

After two years of intense lobbying, the British decided to act on Stirling's recommendation, and, to his great delight, he found himself nominated to be the Lieutenant-Governor of the new colony of Western Australia. It may well have seemed to the ambitious naval officer that he had attained the apogee of his career at the comparatively young age of 37 when he proclaimed, in June 1829, that the new colony had officially come into existence. The problem was, however, that this infant settlement had been brought into being without consultation with the Aboriginal inhabitants of the region, who considered the country to be theirs by right of immemorial occupation. James Stirling's ambition was to bring him into headlong conflict with the local native people, and, as happened elsewhere in Australia, such a collision would be resolved only in blood.

By the end of 1829, approximately 1300 settlers had landed in the new colony, and relationships with the local tribespeople had already begun to break down into hostility. The problems in Western Australia were the same as those encountered by Europeans throughout the continent, and can be traced to a cultural gulf relating to land ownership and political organisation between the two races. No matter how much communication and negotiation occurred, the fundamental differences proved too great for either understanding or compromise. All the conflict of later years flows directly from the European failure to recognise that Aboriginal societies did not conform to the British preconceptions of primitive societies' being somewhere on a continuing and rising gradient that culminated in the industrial society of nineteenth-century Britain. From such a cultural position, all native societies which they encountered anywhere in the world could be evaluated on the basis of the distance they still had to travel between their present condition and the ideal represented by industrial Britain. That societies like those operating in Aboriginal Australia could exist—in which there was no identifiable political structure, and which did not possess any chiefs or headmen capable of negotiating an agreement that would be binding on all members of their people—proved to be completely beyond the comprehension of the British. James Stirling was not at all unusual in sharing this incomprehension. Moreover, the settlers were unaware that the Aborigines had a spiritual connection with the land that gave a shape and a meaning to existence that was far beyond the European concept of land—as an exploitable commodity that could be traded. The scene was set for tragedy.

For the most part, the Aborigines were away inland when the colonists arrived in 1829, so there was little conflict until they returned during the spring and summer of 1830 and attempted to resume their traditional practices of fire-stick farming. But the land that they attempted to burn was, by this time, carrying the

Artist's impression of frontier conflict between whites and Aborigines. Romantic representations like this failed to convey the ambush of Aboriginal encampments that formed the main tactic adopted by Stirling at Pinjarra, and which was replicated Australia-wide by land-hungry settlers.

James Stirling, the first Governor of Western Australia.

61

European crops so necessary for the almost starving settlement, and the dry grass was necessary to feed the livestock that the colonists had brought with them. Europeans refused to permit the Aborigines to set fires. Also, to complicate matters, personal relationships between the races began to decline. The Aboriginal custom of sharing resources was not understood, and settlers began to accuse the natives of being lazy thieves who preferred to steal the colonists' flour and crops of fruit and vegetables, rather than do an honest day's work. Shots were fired and spears were thrown. The spiral into violence had begun.

The most prominent of the Aboriginal leaders were Yagan (the son of Midgegooroo of the Wajuk people) and Calyute (of the Pinjarup tribe). After a series of incidents, Yagan was declared an outlaw by James Stirling, and a price of twenty pounds was offered for his capture. Eventually he was caught, and Stirling had him brought to trial for his attacks on the settlers. At the trial, Yagan was defended by a colonist named Robert Lyons who based his defence on the claim that Yagan was not a criminal but a patriot defending his country against an invader. He was therefore a prisoner-of-war, and entitled to be treated as such. Lyons argued his case successfully, but Yagan escaped from custody and took to the bush. In 1833, Yagan's brother, Domjun, was shot by a settler, and his head was removed and displayed as a trophy. In revenge, Yagan speared and killed two Europeans named Velvick. Stirling then offered a reward for Yagan and his father, Midgegooroo, 'dead or alive', and Midgegooroo was captured and executed by a firing squad. Three weeks later, Yagan was shot by a teenage settler for the reward money. His head was removed and smoked in order to preserve it for transmission to England as a curio. The escalation continued.

Calyute posed an even bigger problem for Stirling because he (Calyute) led his people on well-organised raids against the settlers, and the Governor feared that Calyute was growing into a leader of sufficient stature to unite all the separate Aboriginal tribes under his leadership. In that event, they would then be in a position to drive the colonists into the sea. It was in order to pre-empt this possibility that Stirling's experience as a military man came to the fore. He decided to strike first, and carefully planned a military-style attack on the encampment of Calyute and the Pinjarup people. James Stirling organised a corps of mounted police under Captain Ellis. They were all hand-picked men who were ex-soldiers or experienced bushmen well experienced in the ways of Aborigines.

On 28 October 1834, James Stirling and a force of twenty-four heavily armed men caught Calyute in a deadly dawn ambush. The massacre was carefully planned to kill the maximum number of Aborigines. The camp was rushed from the rear by a party of men who opened fire on the sleeping families. The survivors, panicked by the gunfire, fled towards the Murray River on the far side of the camp, but, when they reached the river, they found Stirling and another party of his men waiting in ambush for them. The slaughter resumed, and those Aborigines who jumped into the river to escape, or who floated away wounded, ran into a third armed group which Stirling had stationed downriver with the express purpose of shooting the wounded. The Europeans claimed to have shot fifteen Aborigines at the Pinjarra Massacre, but Aboriginal tradition puts the death toll at more than eighty, many of whom were women and children. In an ambush of this sort, in the early-dawn moments, there was no way that the Europeans— even had they wanted to—could have distinguished women and children from the warriors when they opened fire on the camp.

The British Government did not recall James Stirling for this horrific event. Rather, they issued a mild dressing-down to the Lieutenant-Governor, and permitted him to remain in office for a further four years. Even when James Stirling left Western Australia in 1838, he remained unpunished for this heinous crime. He returned to service in the Royal Navy which despatched him to commands in the Mediterranean until 1850. Later, he became naval commander-in-chief of the East India squadron, and died in Surrey in 1865 with the rank of full admiral. At no time can it be shown that Stirling's career or reputation suffered in any serious way from his activities in orchestrating and taking personal command of the punitive expedition which resulted in the Pinjarra Massacre. It remains probably the worst of the crimes against humanity perpetrated by British officials in the Australian colonies.

14

Brown Bess—Queen of the Frontier

Who or what was 'Brown Bess'? How did 'Brown Bess' play a pivotal role in relations between blacks and whites in colonial Australia? And what is a 'flash in the pan' anyway?

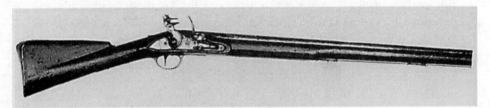

The 'Brown Bess' British military musket.

'Brown Bess' is the nick-name given by generations of British soldiers and settlers to the British military musket. Although the musket came into widespread use from the sixteenth century in Europe, and abroad as a part of European expansion to the new world, the firearm at this time was the inefficient and clumsy matchlock. This gun required the musketeer to carry a smouldering fuse with him into battle. He had to manually touch this to the charge of gunpowder in order to get the musket to discharge. It was slow, unreliable, and (in overseas conditions such as the forests of North America) fairly ineffective against humans—although it was a good killer of larger game-animals such as the moose. During the eighteenth century, the matchlock was replaced by the far more effective flintlock musket and pistol, and, by the time Australia was settled by Europeans, the weapon most widely in use was 'Brown Bess'—the flintlock musket.

The gap in technology—between the spears and woomeras of the Aborigines on the one hand, and the flintlock firearms of the incoming colonists on the other—has usually been interpreted as one of the main reasons for the Aboriginal failure to confront the invasion successfully. But, when we study the mechanism of the Brown Bess and accounts of its use in Australian conditions, we begin to see that explanations based on the alleged technological superiority of the Europeans might need to be reconsidered and somewhat modified.

A musket was prepared for firing by first pouring a charge of gunpowder down the barrel. Then a wad of cloth was rammed down the barrel to contain the charge in a compacted condition. Next a musket-ball (or a number of smaller projectiles) was rammed down the barrel of the gun until it rested alongside the wadding. This was normally quite a tight fit—to make sure that the ball did not roll out of the barrel before the weapon could be fired—and ramming it down the barrel therefore required the ramrod to force it down the smooth bore, and thus position it adjacent to the charge. Above the primary charge of black powder was a tiny hole in the barrel, and above this was a small metal plate (or pan) which held an igniting charge of gunpowder. This igniting charge was set off when a spring-loaded hammer was tripped. This hammer held (in its jaws) a flint, and, when the trigger was pulled, the hammer dashed the flint against a striker plate—thereby releasing a shower of sparks which fell into the pan below, and started the powder burning. The burning powder dropped through the hole into the barrel below it, thereby causing the main propelling charge to explode and propel the musket ball out the end of the barrel and towards its target.

Over the years, 'Brown Bess' proved to be a fearful weapon in the hands of a skilled soldier on a European field of battle. This was partly because battle tactics evolved into a situation where masses of infantrymen, on both sides, lined up in serried ranks and marched forward towards the enemy. One result of this practice was that volley-fire by muskets took a dreadful toll of the advancing armies. An experienced and battle-hardened soldier could sometimes load and fire his musket three times in the space of a minute—although, in the heat and excitement of battle, loading and firing once-a-minute would probably have been more normal. A proficient musketeer could be relied upon to hit his mark reasonably often, at ranges between 50 and 100 metres. Distances greater than this were often beyond the effective reach of the weapon, although musket balls would often cause random deaths over far greater distances during the heat of battle.

A measure of the damage capable of being inflicted by the musket in a European conflict can be gauged from the Battle of Waterloo in 1815, where the first volley fired by the English forces into Napoleon's advancing Old Guard killed about three hundred men.

The flintlock mechanism has contributed a number of terms to the language that are still common today—although most people who use them are unaware of their origins. For example, the 'Brown Bess' would sometimes set the small amount of powder in the pan alight, but would fail to ignite the propulsive charge in the main barrel. This became known as a 'flash in the pan'. Another feature of the musket was the time-lag between the burning of the powder in the pan, and the explosion in the barrel that actually fired off the projectile. These few seconds became known as the 'hang-fire'. Other terms still in common usage are the exhortations to 'keep your powder dry', and 'don't shoot 'til you see the whites of their eyes'.

In colonial Australian conditions, the 'Brown Bess' soon demonstrated several serious deficiencies. First, the military weapon was too long for effective use in the bush. Colonists could cut down the barrels of their guns, but they sacrificed accuracy when they did this. Secondly, the soldiers found that the damp conditions made the muskets unreliable if they were left primed for any length of time before being fired. The gunpowder in the barrel would not ignite when it was moist, and on many occasions in the early years of the colonies, muskets misfired and left the Europeans in situations of great danger. A good example of this can be seen in the spearing of Arthur Phillip, the first Governor, at Manly in 1790. Phillip was speared through the right shoulder by an Aborigine who picked up the spear from the ground with his toes, brought it to hand in one smooth movement, fitted it into the woomera and hurled the spear to hit the Governor— all before Phillip had time to take any evasive action. After their leader had been hit, four marines who were advancing to his rescue pulled the triggers on their muskets, and produced four misfires. Other marines did get their muskets to fire, and Phillip was evacuated amid an exchange of spears and gunfire. But the case does highlight the dangerous unreliability of the flintlock mechanism.

A further weakness which the colonists discovered lay in the time it took to reload a 'Brown Bess' in bush conditions—especially when they were under attack and trying to dodge three-metre spears flying in their direction. In Van Diemen's Land, Mosquito—one of the leaders of the Aboriginal resistance— developed tactics to take account of this. One of the tribe, often a female, would abuse and taunt the besieged colonists to provoke them into firing their weapons, and the warriors would then rush the colonists before they had time to reload. Similar tactics were also used to kill large numbers of sheep and cattle that were being overlanded to South Australia from New South Wales in the early 1840s.

However, the most important shortcoming of the flintlock musket was that it proved to be quite inaccurate against agile and running warriors, who specialised in the tactics of ambush and guerilla fighting. By the time that settlers in the bush had realised that they were being attacked, their assailants were no longer present. They threw their spears and disappeared—very effective tactics against flintlock muskets. In an effort to take account of this weakness in their technology, the colonists developed strategies of ambush where volley-firing into massed Aborigines again rendered the musket into a formidable killing-tool. In the 1820s, in the Bathurst district of New South Wales, British soldiers deliberately left stores of food out in the open as bait to attract the local Aborigines. The soldiers meanwhile hid in a nearby hut, and, when they had decoyed the Aborigines into a consolidated group around the food, they opened fire and killed many of them. In the 1830s in Western Australia, the Governor led a party of armed men who crept up on an Aboriginal encampment and opened fire indiscriminately at dawn on the sleeping natives. Similar attacks became the norm on the pastoral frontiers, where settlers tried to establish situations where muskets could be used in volley-firing or concentrated firing into groups of Aborigines—rather than being used against individual Aborigines in the bush where the advantage clearly lay with the Aborigines. The effectiveness of the 'Brown Bess' was also magnified (in this type of close-quarters' slaughter) by loading it with shot rather than with a single musket-ball. All sorts of old ironmongery was used in this way—even old nails and bits of wire—and it proved a most efficient way of killing human beings.

By the 1860s, the age of the 'Brown Bess' had passed, and settlers were equipped with breech-loading rifles which effectively ended any possibility of armed Aboriginal resistance to the loss of their country. The conflict and hostilities continued, but it was now a hopelessly one-sided contest; and, by the second half of the nineteenth century, the technological advantage genuinely had passed, at last, to the Europeans. We can see this comprehensively demonstrated in Queensland in 1884, when the Kalkadoon tribe stood and fought like Europeans rather than like the shadowy guerillas they had hitherto been. On this occasion, the Aborigines formed ranks and charged straight down a hill—known as Battle Mountain ever since—into the teeth of the rifles carried by the native police and their British officers. Again and again, they reformed their ranks and charged—only to be mown down in a hail of gunfire. Spears were now no match for European carbines, and the flower of the Kalkadoon people was destroyed in this single confrontation. The balance of advantage, which had been more evenly poised in the age of 'Brown Bess', had passed irretrievably to the whites, and no amount of bravery by Aborigines could alter that basic fact.

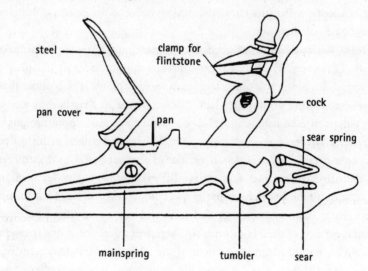

Diagram of the flintlock mechanism which put its users at a disadvantage in the Australian bush.

15

Samuel Marsden—Loathed in New South Wales; Loved in New Zealand

How can one man be known both as 'the flogging parson of Parramatta' and 'great-heart Marsden'? Why was the Reverend Samuel Marsden revered by contemporaries in New Zealand, and reviled by contemporaries in New South Wales?

Samuel Marsden was born at Farsley in Yorkshire, and educated at Hull and Cambridge for service in the Church of England. He came from a lowly background, and never entirely lost the common resonances in his speech. His education was sponsored by the Elland Society, which concentrated on providing promising members of the poorer classes with the education necessary for them to embrace the life of an English curate. He was recommended by William Wilberforce—an associate of the society—for appointment to the new penal colony of New South Wales in 1793, just a few weeks after he had been ordained. Marsden, accompanied by his wife Eliza, arrived in New South Wales in 1794 to take up his appointment as Assistant Chaplain to the Reverend Richard Johnson—who had sailed as Chaplain with the first fleet. The newly arrived assistant was given a residence at Parramatta, which was to become the centre of his clerical, legal, and pastoral activities.

In 1800, Richard Johnson returned to England, and Marsden became Acting Chaplain. However, he did not receive formal appointment as Chaplain until 1810, despite his being the only clergyman in the colony. It is possible that this delay reflected some doubts and lack of confidence in Marsden by the high-church Anglican establishment which controlled colonial appointments. As a churchman, Marsden favoured the low-church evangelicalism of his roots, and cleaved to a literal scriptural fundamentalism that rendered him intolerant of other denominations. He was quite illiberal in his attitudes and in his administration of the law in his capacity as a colonial magistrate. That almost half his flock were Roman Catholics and Irish did not cause him to temper his dislike of their race, or their faith, with any degree of tolerance or understanding—and it is in his hatred and mistreatment of the Irish that Marsden's reputation as an arch-hypocrite was established. This imputation was strengthened in the Chaplain's apparent inability to see the potential for conflict between his dual roles as magistrate and clergyman to the convicts.

In 1800, the authorities in New South Wales received word—from their network of informers among the convicts—that a rising was planned by the Irish. Samuel Marsden used his powers as a magistrate to order the flogging of one of the suspects—a man named Paddy Galvin—in an effort to force him to inform on his countrymen. Galvin was flogged with a cat-o'-nine-tails until his back had been reduced to raw meat. He was then flogged on the buttocks until they were in a similar condition. Finally, the scourger flogged the backs of his calves—but all to no avail. Paddy Galvin made it plain that he would die rather than pass information on to the authorities about his fellow Irish. This incident reveals that Marsden was prepared to misuse his powers as a magistrate and to subject a man—who was entitled to be presumed innocent until proven guilty— to torture in an effort to make him reveal information. The entire proceedings were illegal under English law, even in a penal colony.

But even when he acted within the law, Marsden behaved with a savagery that incurred the hatred of the convicts. He appeared to believe that the Word of God could be forced into a man through cruelty, and so free was he in ordering floggings for those who appeared before him in court, that he became known as 'the flogging parson of Parramatta'. The incongruity that was so clearly perceived by the convicts—that the man who preached the virtues of the gentle Jesus on a Sunday should hand out such savage punishments on the following day—was never recognised by Samuel Marsden himself, but it goes far towards explaining the contemporary opinion that he was a hypocrite who did not practise what he preached.

Samuel Marsden was similarly unsuccessful in other areas of his religious life—but none more so than in his total failure to Christianise the Aborigines. Despite repeated attempts over a period of almost twenty years, Marsden did not succeed in securing a single Aboriginal conversion. Far from seeing this as something of which to be ashamed, Marsden interpreted it as evidence that the Aborigines were so irredeemably stupid that they could not recognise the truth— even when it was placed before them.

Indeed, it was only in his farming avocations in New South Wales that the Reverend Samuel Marsden can be said to have made an unequivocal success, and he is rightly honoured as one of the earliest pioneers of the fine-wool industry.

In contrast to the overwhelmingly negative perceptions of the man in Australia, the name of the Reverend Samuel Marsden is highly revered in New Zealand, and he is referred to there as 'great-heart Marsden'. There is no doubting the courage that Marsden demonstrated in the two decades before formal British annexation of New Zealand—which occurred in 1840. During these two decades, Marsden made repeated voyages as a missionary to the Maori tribes. At this time,

Reverend Samuel Marsden. (Archives Office of Tasmania)

the two islands of New Zealand were in chaos as Maori tribes waged war against one another over territory and resources. The Maoris were feared as one of the finest warrior peoples that the British had encountered anywhere in the world. From the end of the eighteenth century, Maori war-leaders had increasingly obtained firearms from European traders, and the incessant warfare provided a very useful training for their use in battle. Maoris were also known to practise cannibalism. So, when Samuel Marsden turned his attention to evangelising the Maoris and establishing permanent missions among that warlike people, he was not taking any easy option, but one fraught with danger and difficulty.

Marsden's personal bravery was recognised by the Maoris who honoured him for it. But, more importantly, the Maoris (unlike the Australian Aborigines) embraced Christianity with great enthusiasm. By the final decades of the nineteenth century, almost ninety per cent of the Maoris had become Christians, and they venerated the man who had first brought that religion to them. Furthermore, they admired Marsden's attempts to protect them from the worst of the effects of unregulated white settlement from New South Wales. Marsden became an enthusiast for British annexation because he believed that only the mantle offered by properly enforced British law would provide the breathing-space necessary for the Maoris to come to terms with the massive and irreversible changes to their world brought by the Europeans. The Maoris never doubted that he had their best interests at heart.

Finally, Marsden is admired because he was responsible for first producing the Maori languages in written form. Prior to Marsden's missionary work, Maori society was functionally illiterate. It was Samuel Marsden's ambition to make the Scriptures available to the New Zealanders in their own language, and it was this ambition that produced the great breakthrough to literacy. The Maoris quickly recognised the benefits that a written form of their language would confer, and they became—and have always remained—very keen on literacy. Indeed, today, any New Zealander can elect to write his assignments, and take his university exams, in the Maori language. That right, which is enshrined in the New Zealand constitution, can be traced back to the efforts of the Reverend Samuel Marsden to turn the Maoris into Christians.

So we are faced with the conundrum—that a man disparaged by contemporaries and succeeding generations of Australians as a base hypocrite, was (and is) highly esteemed and respected by contemporaries and succeeding generations across the Tasman Sea. The epithets 'flogging parson of Parramatta', and 'great-heart Marsden', reflect the complexity of one of the most enigmatic and unfathomable characters of Australia's colonial past. It may never be possible, and perhaps we should not even try, to bring these apparently contradictory *dramatis personae* into congruence.

The Reverend Samuel Marsden died at Windsor, near Sydney, in 1838.

16

The Duke of Edinburgh's Braces

How did the Duke of Edinburgh's braces affect the course of Australian history (not to mention the course of the Duke's personal history!)? What unexpected souvenirs did the prince take home with him to England? And was there an Irish conspiracy behind the sensational events at Clontarf in Sydney in 1868?

In 1867, Prince Alfred Ernest Albert, Duke of Edinburgh, the twenty-three-year-old second son of Queen Victoria, landed in Adelaide from his ship HMS *Galatea*, to begin a tour of the Australian colonies. The prince was a personable young man, and, as the first member of Britain's royal family to visit this part of the world, his arrival triggered off paroxysms of hysterical loyalty wherever he went. The colonists put up gorgeous illuminations to celebrate his presence among them, and he was forced to attend endless dinners, and to respond to interminable loyal speeches and toasts, as his progress through the Australian colonies continued. Most newspapers in the different colonies went into rapturous frenzies of adulation, and the Duke's activities and comments on what he encountered were reported in the most minute detail. The Duke visited all the Australian colonies—apart from Western Australia—during the six months of his travels, and in every colony he encountered an identical reaction of forelock-tugging and grovelling from the large majority of the colonial populations.

There was, however, an undercurrent of muted and not-so-muted criticism from a small proportion of the predominantly Irish and working-class population, who were either ideologically opposed to the pretensions of royal superiority, or who regarded the English presence in Ireland as an occupation by a foreign military power. In their publications, the Duke's wanderings in Australia were deemed to be invariably accompanied by massive slaughter of the local wildlife (as his delight in shooting was well attested), and to be accompanied by an equally enthusiastic resort by the prince to the services of prostitutes (for his eye for a comely wench was similarly well known). During Alfred's time in Melbourne, for example, his tour of the local bordellos was conducted under the watchful supervision of a senior Victorian detective.

Nevertheless, such censures represented a tiny minority of the colonial population, although the involvement of the Irish did cause some concern for the prince's safety. This concern flowed from an abortive rising in Ireland by the

Prince Alfred, Duke of Edinburgh, second son of Queen Victoria (left); and his would-be assassin. (Taken from Jack Cato, *The Story of the Camera in Australia*, Melbourne, 1955)

Fenian movement (that had been quashed by the English before it could take place earlier in 1867), and from a campaign of terrorism that the Fenian Brotherhood had unleashed in England that same year. Indeed, during Alfred's time in Melbourne in 1868, a public feast for the poor had degenerated into a riot, and wild rumours had swept the city that a team of Fenian assassins—intent on murdering the Duke—was in the colony. Moreover, there had been gunfire when a group of Protestant Orangemen had opened fire on a crowd of Roman Catholic demonstrators outside the Melbourne Protestant Hall, and three young men had fallen wounded to the pavement, one of whom later died from his injuries. This had been reported in the press as a Fenian outrage, which neatly reversed the responsibility and pandered to majority sectarian prejudices.

Among the Irish-born population of Australia at this time, was a thirty-five-year-old colonist named Henry James O'Farrell. Born in Dublin, the youngest of eleven children, O'Farrell had arrived in Australia in 1841 when the family emigrated, only to find the trauma of migration compounded the following year by the death of his mother. The family prospered in their new country, and, in 1850, the devout young man undertook preliminary training to become a Roman Catholic priest. Apparently he began to exhibit signs of mental instability during his training, and, after two years, was persuaded to take a break from his studies, although he was ordained a deacon in 1852.

Henry O'Farrell travelled in Europe for two years, and returned to Australia during the goldrush in 1855, where he renounced his priestly vocation and joined his cousin in a successful business dealing in hay and corn in Ballarat. O'Farrell's father had died the previous year, and, in his will, had left the bulk of his estate to Bishop Goold, the Roman Catholic Bishop of Melbourne. These legacies had been paid to Goold before it was discovered that the deceased estate had more debts than assets. Henry's elder brother Peter O'Farrell, a lawyer, claimed to have explained the situation to Bishop Goold, who nevertheless refused to pay back any of the legacies, and who left the debts to be handled by the surviving family. Such behaviour may have lain behind Henry's refusal to continue his studies for the priesthood, and it certainly did little to improve his mental state.

Henry took two further heavy blows over the next decade, becoming hopelessly addicted to alcohol to the point where he started to throw fits, and in developing all the classic persecution complexes of a paranoid personality. His family had him locked up for short periods of time, and he laboured under the delusion that the staff of the institution were trying to poison him. He also demonstrated many other signs of excitability and psychotic behaviour. The police began to watch him because he had threatened a former business partner with violence, and had also expressed an intention to kill himself. As the decade of the 1860s unfolded, Henry's business failed, his brother Peter—claiming that Bishop Goold had driven him bankrupt—fled the colony in a blaze of publicity, and the politics of Ireland began to prey increasingly upon Henry's mind. The departure of his elder brother in 1864 seemed to have affected him the most, and his behaviour deteriorated steadily, until, by 1867, he had become a deeply disturbed and seriously deranged man.

The enormous publicity generated by Prince Alfred's rambles around Australia, and the undercurrent of anti-Roman Catholic sectarianism and anti-Irish racism displayed by the organs of the popular press, combined to convince Henry James O'Farrell that he had a mission from the Fenian Brotherhood to strike a blow for Ireland by assassinating the Duke. Despite an intensive police investigation, no evidence was ever unearthed that would support a connection between O'Farrell and the Fenians, and it seems clear that it was just another hallucination suffered by a very sick man. But O'Farrell determined to act upon his delusion, and began deliberately to plan Prince Alfred's murder.

On 12 March 1868, the prince attended a gala picnic at Clontarf, about ten kilometres from Sydney on the northern side of Sydney Harbour. The Duke stepped ashore from the steam launch at the picnic ground to join a large crowd of well-to-do people who had paid a pound a ticket for the privilege of attending the event, which was to include an example of an Aboriginal corroboree put on by 300 Aborigines especially assembled for the occasion. As the young prince walked through the crowd, Henry James O'Farrell slipped behind him, drew a pistol, and shot him in the back. The prince fell forward, and O'Farrell pulled the trigger a second time, but the revolver misfired. A further shot was fired, but by this time O'Farrell had been attacked by the crowd, and the last bullet missed Prince Alfred and hit one of the would-be rescuers in the foot. O'Farrell then disappeared under the weight of an infuriated and hysterical crowd that was intent on lynching him on the spot. It was with the greatest difficulty that the police and soldiers, who were accompanying the Duke, were able to rescue the would-be assassin and hustle him, bruised and bleeding, aboard a boat and across the harbour into the safety of Darlinghurst gaol.

Prince Alfred was removed on an improvised litter to Government House, where medical examination revealed that the bullet had missed the spine and all vital organs, and had lodged a few centimetres from his breastbone. The Duke's heavy braces had received a direct hit, and had taken most of the force out of the bullet which had then been further slowed by glancing off a rib on its passage through the prince's body. It seemed clear that it was the braces that had saved the young man from considerable internal damage.

Several days later, the Duke of Edinburgh showed his own personal courage when he submitted to the surgical removal of the bullet—without anaesthetic and seated on a chair. The surgeons were assisted by two of Florence Nightingale's nurses who had just arrived in the colony. As the prince gripped the arms of the chair, the surgeons made an incision in his right breast and quickly extracted the bullet with forceps. It was described as being a rough slug about the size of a small thimble. Aside from a momentary paleness, the prince bore his ordeal with equanimity and courage. It was reported that he examined the bullet and engaged the surgeons in conversation after the operation.

A fully fledged security alert was undertaken by the embarrassed colonial authorities, and O'Farrell's claims to have been part of a Fenian plot provided the Minister of Police, Henry Parkes, with a useful scapegoat to divert attention from the police failure to provide adequate protection for the royal guest. A tirade of virulent anti-Irish propaganda flooded the daily press, and Parkes deliberately inflamed the situation for his own political advantage by announcing that he had uncovered incontrovertible proof that O'Farrell had not acted alone, but had been part of a conspiracy of disaffected Irish Fenians to destroy a member of the English royal family. In response, Irish and Roman Catholic colonists fell over themselves to proclaim their loyalty to Queen Victoria, and their abhorrence of Fenianism. The colonial Roman Catholic clergy, led by Archbishop Polding in New South Wales, denounced the sectarianism of the local papers which held the entire Roman Catholic community responsible for the actions of a lone fanatic—and effusions of allegiance and fidelity became the order of the day in all Roman Catholic or Irish publications.

Henry James O'Farrell remained in close confinement until his trial towards the end of March on a charge of attempted murder—a crime punishable by death. While in gaol, he had been extensively interviewed by Henry Parkes, with a reporter from a Sydney newspaper, who was an experienced short-hand exponent, hidden behind a door to take down a record of all that was said. However, despite all Parkes' efforts, he could not get O'Farrell to temper, with any degree of reality, his imaginative and deluded flights of fancy regarding conspiracies—Fenian or otherwise—to attempt the murder of the prince. The trial itself was little more than a formality, and there seems little doubt that, in the climate of opinion at the time, there was no way O'Farrell could have received a fair hearing. All the evidence of his insanity and long-term mental instability counted for naught, and although his defence attorney fully recounted the prisoner's financial worries, his religious mania, his heavy drinking and his threats of suicide, the jury found him guilty as charged.

A petition for clemency was then prepared by O'Farrell's sister in which further evidence of his madness was presented. To his great credit, the petition was supported by Prince Alfred himself who suggested that the trial had been brought on with undue haste, and who further pointed out that the crime of attempted murder was no longer a capital offence in Britain. It was all to no avail, and the unfortunate man was hanged on 21 April at Darlinghurst gaol. The night before his execution, a calm and composed O'Farrell had written a dying declaration which he entrusted to the prison chaplain, Father Michael Dwyer, with instructions that it was not to be opened until after his death. Part of this declaration reads as follows:

> ... I had no foundation for saying there was a Fenian organisation in New
> South Wales. From continually thinking and talking of what I may still be
> allowed to call 'the wrongs of Ireland', I became excited and filled with
> enthusiasm on the subject. And it was when under the influence of these
> feelings that I attempted to perpetrate the deed for which I am most justly
> called upon to suffer.[5]

All the available evidence supports the view that O'Farrell was here telling the truth, and that Parkes had manufactured a conspiracy out of thin air and a maniac's ravings.

The final chapter in this bizarre story rests where we began—with Prince Alfred. When his ship finally sailed out of Sydney Harbour, the young prince took with him some strange curios. These consisted of the pistols carried by his would-be assassin on that fatal day at Clontarf, together with the bullet that the surgeons had removed from his right breast several days later. These had been carefully mounted in a special lined-and-polished cedar box, and were probably among the more macabre souvenirs ever to make the long voyage from Australia back to the home country.

17

The Catalpa Rescue

What was the Catalpa rescue? How did this audacious escapade in Australia almost cause a war between Britain and the United States of America? And why did the frustrated colonial authorities unsuccessfully attempt to ban the singing of a ballad commemorating the event?

As a result of the death by starvation of well over a million people in Ireland during the years of the great potato famine, and the forced emigration of several millions more to the Americas and Australia, the seeds of Irish hatred of England were planted in all quarters of the globe. Irish nationalism received enormous support from expatriate Irish migrants and their children, who were brought up on their parents' tales of the wrongs suffered by Ireland at the hands of the perfidious English. In Australia, this resentment was grafted on to the bitterness engendered by the belief that Irish convicts were not really criminals at all, but were patriots fighting against an occupying military power, and that, in this country, the Irish felons had been singled out for especially brutal treatment on the basis of their race and religion. After all, rebels from the Irish rising of 1798 were among the earliest arrivals in convict Australia, and, when a smaller rebellion occurred in 1848 during the worst of the famine, it surprised nobody that these rebels would also end up as convicts in Australia. The fight for Irish freedom was waged with the resources and backing of the new world as well as the blood and sinew of the old.

In 1858, the Fenian movement had its genesis in Dublin and in the United States. It was another reincarnation of the old Irish revolutionary pursuit of driving the English out of Ireland—a dream that had been a national preoccupation since the time of Oliver Cromwell. On this occasion, the movement was assisted by generous helpings of American money and arms, provided by members of the large Irish migrant community who had prospered in their new home. In Ireland, the movement proclaimed itself as the Irish Revolutionary Brotherhood, and in America it was known as the Fenian Brotherhood. In the event, it was the American name which stuck, and the Fenians became the bogey-men of the second half of the nineteenth century— especially in the somewhat fevered imaginations of newspaper editors throughout Britain and the empire, who were inclined to see Fenian conspiracies in the most improbable places.

In the United States, the growth of the Fenian movement seemed to moderate during the years of the civil war. Fenians fought on both sides of that conflict. But by war's end, the unforeseen outcome was that there existed in America thousands of Irish expatriates who had a background of military training and who were battle-hardened veterans. They determined to use their experience and their financial resources to help free their homeland from the hated English. Under the romantic leadership of the Irish revolutionary James Stephens, the Fenians determined to carry the fight to England, wherever English power could be found anywhere in the world. The revolution had been exported.

An early measure of the dangers posed by this development was gained in 1865, when the Dublin police swooped on the Fenian newspaper and arrested many Fenians, together with a quantity of documentation of revolutionary intent. (According to the documentation, the army was to be suborned, and Irish soldiers were to be involved in an armed rising.) Furthermore, the authorities arrested a number of American citizens who were in Ireland to train the local Fenians in preparation for the rebellion. The Americans were quietly expelled, and the locals were tried on charges of sedition. Sixty-two received sentences of transportation to the convict colony of Western Australia.

For the next two years, the news was full of accounts of Fenian outrages. In 1867, the Fenians organised an invasion of Canada from the United States. A force of several thousand Fenians had stormed across the Niagara River into Canada, where they had fought a brief and successful battle with a British force at Ridgeway, before retreating back into the United States. Police in England and Ireland were shot, magistrates and Irish landlords assassinated, agrarian outrages—including the burning of houses and crops, and the maiming and killing of valuable livestock—became common. It was even rumoured that the Fenians had purchased and equipped a warship to sink British shipping on the oceans of the world.

It was in this climate of opinion—exacerbated by the horror caused by the attempted assassination of the Duke of Edinburgh in Australia during his tour in 1867—that the Fenian convicts arrived in Western Australia. It would be fair to say that they received severe treatment from the local convict authorities—who regarded them as thugs and cut-throats to be handled with considerable caution and great watchfulness. In 1871, two of the Fenian prisoners, James Wilson and Martin Hogan, wrote to the headquarters of the movement in America complaining of their harsh treatment, and requesting rescue. The letters aroused great sympathy, and the leadership decided to mount a rescue mission to the isolated convict colony—a mission which, it was planned, would release the convicts and inflict a public humiliation on England at the same time.

A 202-ton whaler named the *Catalpa* was purchased for US$5250 in America.

The ship was a sailing vessel under the command of Captain George Anthony, who was American (not Irish) in origin. In all, the Fenians raised over US$19 000 to finance the expedition to deliver six of their adherents from the hands of their British captors in Western Australia, and the commitment of the American branch of the brotherhood cannot be doubted. The cover for the attempt was to be a whaling voyage by the *Catalpa*. This would provide a persuasive reason for the vessel's being in Australian waters—which were often visited by whalers from all the countries involved in the trade. The captain was a young twenty-nine-year-old whaler from Nantucket, who knew the ulterior motives behind the voyage. In the matter of the rescue, Anthony would be under the command of the Fenian John Breslin who was slipped aboard as a crewman with one other Fenian comrade. Aside from these three, the rest of the crew were experienced whalers who were quite unaware of the political nature of this particular journey—the fact was that the Fenian organisers were relying on a successful capture of whales to finance the loans which they had taken out to mount the expedition.

In April 1875, the *Catalpa* weighed anchor and the voyage began. It was a slow ship, and, since the real reason for the trip had not been shared with the crew before they began, Captain Anthony actually went on a successful search for whales. The whale oil sold at the end of the expedition realised over $11 000. By March 1876, the *Catalpa* had reached Bunbury on the southern coastline of Western Australia, and there contact was made with Fenian agents who had travelled to Western Australia to co-ordinate the escape of the convicts. Arrangements were finalised for the convicts to rendezvous with the *Catalpa* off the port of Rockingham in a small boat. The Fenian, John Breslin, travelled to Fremantle, only to find that it was occupied by a British naval gunboat making its annual visit to the colony. They decided to wait until the gunboat had departed before embarking on the rescue, because a schooner-rigged gunboat could easily pursue and capture a slow sailing vessel like the *Catalpa*. Once the gunboat had set sail for Adelaide, the plans for the escape were put into effect.

The six convicts, in the meantime, went about their daily routines and awaited the signal from John Breslin. It was arranged that the *Catalpa* would pick up the convicts and Breslin on Easter Monday 17 April 1876, while the rest of the colonists were distracted (or so the rescuers hoped) by the annual regatta. All six prisoners successfully slipped away and galloped to Rockingham, about twenty-eight kilometres south of Fremantle, where Captain Anthony and a small crew were waiting with one of *Catalpa's* whale boats to pick them up. The escape did not go unobserved, however, and the whale boat had travelled only a short distance before concerted attempts were under way to recapture the escapers and their liberators. Police cutters carrying armed constables were despatched from Fremantle, Bunbury, and Vasse to row after the fleeing men; and a steam-powered vessel, the *Georgette*, was commandeered by the colonial authorities, who lashed a nine-pound artillery field-piece to its prow. The *Georgette* then joined in the pursuit.

In the event, the Fenian escape was reduced to a frantic boat-race as the fleeing convicts rowed for dear life towards their rescue ship, while the pursuers closed in on them with great rapidity. Finally, the Fenians reached the *Catalpa* less than four hundred metres ahead of the police cutter, which could only watch in frustration as the *Catalpa* crowded on sail and stood out to sea. But the steamer *Georgette* was closing in fast, and it could sink the whaling vessel with the greatest of ease. The commanding officer had received authority from the Governor to open fire on the fleeing ship if that was the only way he could succeed in recapturing the escapers.

By 8.00 a.m. on the following morning, the *Georgette* had pulled alongside the *Catalpa* and ordered it to heave-to and prepare to receive a boarding party. Breslin ordered Captain Anthony to ignore the order, whereupon the British vessel fired a cannon shot across the bows of the *Catalpa* and ordered it once again to heave-to or it would be sunk. Breslin ordered that the Stars and Stripes flag be raised, and Captain Anthony hailed the *Georgette* with the following terse but dramatic message:

> That's the American flag; I am on the high seas; my flag protects me; if you fire on this ship you fire on the American flag.[6]

The *Georgette* was in a most invidious position. It was beyond doubt that the two vessels were well into international waters. To use artillery against an American ship on the high seas might well be seen as an act of war. On the other hand, the steamer had received orders to recapture the escapers. The commanding officer was not prepared, in the final analysis to open fire on an American ship, and after several more fruitless attempts to bluff the *Catalpa* into heaving-to and surrendering, the steamer was forced to turn away and set course for Fremantle. The jubilant Fenians continued on their voyage to America, where they were received with rapturous enthusiasm by the American-Irish. In Dublin, Cork, and other centres in Ireland, news of the release was signalised with torch-light processions and the burning of effigies of the British Prime Minister Benjamin Disraeli. In Western Australia, the escape was soon celebrated by a ballad sung in the streets and taverns of Perth and Fremantle, which so annoyed the authorities, that it was banned, and a public notice was issued that anyone caught singing it would be punished for an offence against the Treason–Felony Act. As we would expect, such a ruling only made the ballad more popular, and it became a classic of Irish-Australian folklore that is still occasionally sung today.

CATALPA

A noble whale-ship and commander, called the *Catalpa* they say,
Came out to Western Australia, and took six poor Fenians away.

> *Chorus:*
> So come all you screw warders and gaolers,
> Remember Perth Regatta Day;
> Take care of the rest of your Fenians,
> Or the Yankees will steal them away.

Seven long years had they served here, and seven long more had to stay,
For defending their country, Ould Ireland, for that they were banished away.

> *(Chorus)*

You kept them in Western Australia till their hair began to turn grey,
When a Yank from the States of America came out here and stole them away.

> *(Chorus)*

Now all the Perth boats were a-racing, and making short tacks for the spot;
But the Yankee she tacked into Fremantle and took the best prize of the lot.

> *(Chorus)*

The *Georgette*, armed with bold warriors, went out the poor Yanks to arrest;
But she hoisted her star-spangled banner, saying, 'You'll not board me, I guess'.

> *(Chorus)*

So remember those six Fenians colonial and sing o'er these few verses with skill,
And remember the Yankees that stole them, and the home that they left on the hill.

> *(Chorus)*

Now they've landed safe in America, and there they'll be able to cry,
'Hoist up the green flag and shamrock, hurrah for Ould Ireland we'll die'.

18

The Spies Who Came to Sydney Cove

What was the secret life of Governor Arthur Phillip? How did international espionage play a central role in Australia's early colonial history? And when is a scientific expedition not a scientific expedition?

The territorial expansion of the great powers of Europe in the eighteenth and the nineteenth centuries—and the intense imperial rivalries between these powers as they fought for advantage over one another—provide the often-neglected background to the official annexation of the eastern seaboard by James Cook in 1770, and the first British settlement in Australia, led by Arthur Phillip, in 1788. Britain had been at war, off and on, with her traditional enemies—France and Spain—for hundreds of years. Ever since the Elizabethan age, British national security had clearly been recognised as relying heavily on the navy, on the so-called 'wooden walls of England'. English naval supremacy was the cornerstone of the foreign policy of all British governments, and the ability of the British Admiralty to confront the nation's enemies—anywhere in the world—provided a source of much satisfaction to politicians and commoners alike.

The navy prided itself on being the 'Senior Service', and tended to look down upon the army as inferior and of little consequence. The importance of the navy was recognised by the government early in the eighteenth century when the Admiralty was granted a permanent seat in Cabinet, whereas the army did not attain a similar level of influence until the final years of that century. Moreover, the Admiralty was accustomed to thinking in global strategic terms— a most necessary outlook for a country which possessed vast overseas territories that had to be defended. The Lords of the Admiralty maintained fleets and squadrons of the Royal Navy in all the oceans of the world, and there was no quarter of the earth which was beyond the global strategic 'reach' of the British navy. The logistics of sustaining the manpower and equipment demands of its far-flung fleets also involved the Admiralty in the development of a strategic world-view or 'big picture', in which the intentions of Britain's rivals, and the anticipation of potential trouble-spots or threats to national security, played as big a part as did British purposes. Inevitably, the collection of intelligence— concerning the naval preparedness and expansionary ambitions of the other European powers—became part of the Admiralty's brief. How else could it offer reliable advice and accurate strategic assessments to British governments?

Almost by force of circumstances, therefore, the British Admiralty developed and operated a sophisticated intelligence-gathering capability. From the mid-eighteenth century this organisation grew into the first modern spy network. The Admiralty had paid-agents in all the main naval ports of its rival powers, and even of its allies. Their job was to report on naval movements and ship-building programs. In addition, the naval-intelligence network ran agents in England, to intercept and open mail addressed to the officials of foreign governments, to shadow such officials when they moved into the wider British community, and to report on whom they met and what they spoke about. In short, the Admiralty controlled most of Britain's espionage and counter-espionage operations.

So extensive and far-reaching was this influence that the Admiralty even had suborned clerical officials in most of the important departments of the French and Spanish administrations, and by the end of the eighteenth century, there was practically no decision involving naval or military movements made in either France or Spain of which the British Government was uninformed. For example, in 1778, the British knew the terms of the alliance between France and Spain within forty-eight hours of its being signed. In addition to this network of local agents, the Admiralty also employed its own team of senior special-service operatives, who would be sent into the field on missions of particular urgency or sensitivity. These men would be highly skilled in the arts of intelligence-gathering and strategic assessment. They would also be accomplished linguists and able to submerge into the populations of France (or other target countries), where they could pass as natives and not attract unwelcome attention.

All the European great powers were involved in similar intelligence-gathering practices, although there seems little doubt that none of their attempts matched the professional expertise and acumen of the British service. Moreover, we can see the way in which the imperial rivalries worked in this region of the world from the time of Cook's first voyage in 1768. It is important to remember that the Spanish monarchy claimed the whole of the Pacific as a closed sea, and all its coasts and islands as Spanish territory. In 1766, the British Government had rejected Spain's pretensions to close off the Southern Seas to British shipping, and had clearly informed the Spanish that Britain was prepared to fight a war over the issue. So it comes as no surprise to find that when the British Ambassador to the Court of Spain applied, at the beginning of 1768, for a passport to admit Cook's ship to Spanish ports on the Californian coast—as the vessel proceeded into the Pacific in order to observe the transit of Venus from one of the South Sea islands—the response was a frosty refusal. The Spanish Government announced that it was repugnant to the policy of Spain to admit foreigners to their American ports, unless driven there by emergency; especially if the applicant for entry was a person fitted to make observations that could facilitate an attack on the ports

Alexandro Malaspina. (Taken from Robert J. King, *The Secret History of the Convict Colony: Alexandro Malaspina's Report on the British Settlement of New South Wales,* Sydney, 1990. Original held by Museo Naval, Madrid)

Arthur Phillip, first governor of New South Wales. (Taken from M. Barnard Eldershaw, *Phillip of Australia: An Account of the Settlement at Sydney Cove,* Sydney, 1938. Original held by the National Portrait Gallery, London)

during time of war. Since it was James Cook who had charted the St Lawrence River in Canada—and who had then piloted General Wolfe's successful expedition up the river to capture Quebec from the French during the earlier Seven Years War—Spanish concerns about the possibility of Cook's making observations and drawing tactical conclusions on behalf of the British Admiralty were not so far-fetched. However, the time had passed when the Spanish could successfully maintain an interdiction on other Europeans entering the Pacific.

The French, Spain's ally, had already embarked upon a series of explorations in the South Seas. In 1768, Cook left on his first voyage of exploration, and, in that same year, a French expedition under Bougainville set out for the Pacific and arrived at Tahiti slightly behind Cook. Spain worried that Britain might establish a base in the Pacific, and sent an expedition to the South Seas in 1770 to check on the English discoveries and to see whether the southern continent might be found. In 1772, a second Spanish expedition was despatched to ensure that no English settlement had been made, and, in 1774, another Spanish voyage was mounted from South America to explore Tahiti and to claim it for Spain.

When the Spanish heard of the preparations being made for Cook's third navigation of the Pacific in 1776, the Spanish Government instructed the Viceroy of Mexico to arrest Cook and to charge him with violating the Spanish Laws of

Francois Peron.

Nicholas Baudin.

the Indies if he should touch at any of the Spanish ports in the Pacific—and similar orders were issued to the Viceroy of Peru. Spanish fears of British intentions were shown to have been well founded when Cook officially annexed the east coast of Australia in 1770 on behalf of the British King, George III, and followed this up by annexing Norfolk Island in 1774.

When the decision was made by the British Government to establish a convict colony in New South Wales, strategic considerations were of paramount importance, and the man chosen to lead the expedition was Arthur Phillip, one of the Admiralty's senior intelligence operatives. Arthur Phillip had been born in London in 1738, the son of a German-born language teacher and an English-woman who had previously been married to a naval officer (then deceased). Phillip had been educated in the navy which he joined as a young man. He saw action in the Seven Years War where he was commended for his bravery at the siege of Havana. It is not clear whether it was Phillip's courage, or his inherited abilities as a linguist, that brought him to the attention of the more shadowy department of intelligence-gathering in the Admiralty, but, for the rest of his professional life, Phillip would combine spying with his mainstream naval career.

Phillip was not well-off financially, and he found the opportunities for advancement rather limited during the peace which followed the Seven Years

War. Consequently, he took advantage of an opportunity to take service with the Portuguese Navy between the years 1774 and 1778. Portugal had been an ally of Britain's in most of the wars against Spain, and the Portuguese had good reason to fear Spanish ambitions to relieve them (the Portuguese) of their South American colonies. Phillip received the Admiralty's blessing on his service for the King of Portugal, and took part in the small-scale war between Spain and Portugal in South America—which was fought over who should have possession of the Río Grande area. While engaged on this account, Phillip nevertheless set about gathering useful information on the fortifications and armaments maintained by both Spain and Portugal in South America. He also charted the harbours and the coastline of the area, and noted which harbours were unfrequented and offered supplies of wood and water.

When France joined in the American War of Independence on the side of the rebellious colonists in 1778, Phillip's Portuguese sojourn came to an end. He rejoined the Royal Navy, taking with him his detailed knowledge of the strategic possibilities available for British exploitation in South America. From 1779—when Spain also came into the war on the side of the colonists—the British began to contemplate an expedition to attack the Spanish colonies in South America, and Phillip's charts and advice were earnestly sought. In 1781 Phillip provided copies of his charts of the South American coastline and of his recommended ports to the government, only requesting that he be remembered as their originator should they be called upon while he was at sea on other business. Little is known about the nature of this particular 'business', but it is an intriguing possibility that, from 1781 to 1782, Phillip was involved in a clandestine mission in South American waters preparing for a British invasion of Spanish America. One tradition is that Phillip was involved in conveying a shipload of Portuguese convicts to the Portuguese colony of Brazil. It may well be that such a cover was used to disguise Phillip's real intention of helping to prepare the ground for a successful British military expedition. All that we do know is that, at the end of 1781, Arthur Phillip was promoted to the rank of post-captain, and that such promotions were given as a reward for particularly meritorious service. Since the service he rendered was not while he was afloat in a British naval squadron, it seems more than likely that it had been in the intelligence area.

In 1784, Arthur Phillip was sent by the British authorities on a mission to France where he was instructed to visit the naval port of Toulon, and check out some very disturbing reports that agents on the ground had been sending back to Britain. These related to a massive increase in ship-building, with six new ships of the line on the stocks for the French Navy, and with between sixteen ships of the line, and up to twenty frigates, already in port. The information coming in to the Admiralty informed the British that French officials hoped to have thirty battleships ready to put to sea by January 1785. To the British, such preparations could mean only one thing—that an attempt was being planned by their inveterate enemy to drive them from their last stronghold in the Far East, the jewel-in-the-crown, India. Without the wealth of India, it would be impossible for Britain to recover and rebuild her shattered strength following the calamitous losses of the American War of Independence. The survival of Britain as a great power was at stake.

Admiralty records indicate that Phillip remained abroad for almost the full year of 1785. His reports from Toulon, and from the other French naval ports, showed that France was on a war-footing—with ships and stores so well stocked that a significant fleet could be readied for sea in a short period of time. The records also show that, during this time, he was paid over three hundred pounds of secret-service money. When he returned to England in 1786, it was to take command of the first colony ever established by a European government (previous colonies having been established by private entrepreneurs)—a colony of enormous strategic significance in the Pacific, where it could serve as a supplier of naval stores to British fleets in Indian waters, and as a strategic outlier to help protect and maintain British India.

Therefore, when Arthur Phillip sailed into Sydney Harbour as commander of the first fleet in 1788, he described the site in strategic terms as: '... the finest harbour in the world, in which a thousand sail of the line may ride in the most perfect security'.[7]

Phillip's assessment was echoed by the spies sent by Britain's rivals when they, in their turn, reported on the new settlement. The first espionage expedition of which we have some record was organised in September 1788—just a few months after Phillip had landed his convicts and had begun work to establish the colony. The Spanish Government decided to send an expedition to investigate Botany Bay settlement (as it was known), and placed Don Alexandro Malaspina in command. Like Cook's earlier expeditions, its stated purpose was to make scientific and geographical discoveries, but—like many such voyages—its real purpose was espionage. Malaspina's report on New South Wales highlighted the danger which the British now posed to Spanish America. He completely refuted the British Government's proffered explanation of the reasons for settlement, and felt that the British plea of overcrowded English prisons was unacceptable. He concluded that the real motives involved Britain's pressing economic problems, and the expected renewal of war among the nations of Europe. In that eventuality, a military expedition could quite easily be assembled and despatched from Australia to lay waste the Spanish colonies. Moreover, Malaspina also saw that New South Wales posed a threat to Spanish control over the trade of its American empire. A British colony in the region could not be prevented from trading with Chile, even if the Spanish had the power to attempt it.

The strategic threat posed by New South Wales to the position of France also did not go unremarked. When the Anglo–French wars broke out again (between Britain and revolutionary France, and later between Britain and Napoleonic France), the little settlement of New South Wales lived in incessant expectation of a French attack. When Napoleon sent the French navigator Nicholas Baudin with two ships to explore the great south land, they were equipped with a passport which allowed them to pursue their scientific investigations without interference from combatants on either side of the raging war. Thus, when Baudin and his expedition showed up in Port Jackson in 1802, they were generously received and fêted by Governor King and the British garrison. The botanist attached to the voyage, Francois Peron, reported to the French Governor of Mauritius that he had taken full advantage of the open-hearted hospitality in Sydney to do some spying and intelligence-gathering. Peron reported that his botanical expeditions in the vicinity had been pretexts to enable him to spy out the land and to gauge Port Jackson's defences. He recommended the immediate destruction of the colony because of the strategic dangers it posed to French ambitions in the Far East: 'My opinion ... is that it should be destroyed as soon as possible ... Today we could destroy it easily. We shall not be able to do so in twenty-five years' time.'[8]

Louis de Freycinet, the surveyor attached to Baudin's expedition, concurred with this assessment when he wrote that the conquest of the colony, if undertaken immediately, would be quite easy to accomplish.

And so we have to take account of an element of the early history of European Australia—an element that is still little appreciated. This country was caught up in the battle of the great powers of Europe for global supremacy, and although the role it played was a minor one, there is no doubt that Australia had a place in the big picture that the Lords of the Admiralty, and the governments of Britain's traditional foes, took into account when they calculated the strategic global balance of advantage among themselves.

By the end of the Napoleonic wars in 1815, the British navy had succeeded in largely wiping the French and Spanish fleets off the oceans of the world, and the strategic balance was tilted in Britain's favour for almost one hundred years. The long period of comparative peace for the remainder of the nineteenth century allowed Australia to develop its subsidiary function as a penal colony, rather than to continue to fulfil its primary role as the strategic outlier originally intended. Our position in the Admiralty's 'big picture' faded into the background—and largely out of memory.

We forgot, until quite recently, that while Australia was founded *by* the convicts, it was not necessarily founded *for* the convicts.

19

Mad Tom Davey

Why was Governor Thomas Davey known irreverently as 'Mad Tom'? Why didn't Lachlan Macquarie trust him? And what was the greatest sin that could be committed in the eyes of colonial society?

Among the extensive gallery of eccentric and unusual characters that makes up such a significant proportion of colonial Australian history, few come any stranger than Thomas Davey, professional soldier and Lieutenant-Governor of Van Diemen's Land between 1811 and 1816.

Thomas Davey was born in 1758 in Devon, England, and joined the Royal Marines as a second lieutenant in 1778. He saw active service during the American War of Independence—serving in North America, and later in the West Indies when France joined the hostilities. By 1787, Davey had been promoted to first lieutenant, and he joined the marines accompanying the first fleet under Captain Arthur Phillip to New South Wales. According to family legend attested-to by his wife, Davey was the first European from the first fleet to land on Australian soil. He was also one of the last group of marines to leave New South Wales in 1792 when he returned to England following the arrival of the final draft of the New South Wales Corps. Promoted to captain in 1795, Davey saw additional active service in the French wars where he distinguished himself. He was appointed brevet major in 1808, and was confirmed in the rank the following year.

In 1810, David Collins—Lieutenant-Governor of Van Diemen's Land—died in Hobart, and, as soon as the news reached England, Thomas Davey applied for the vacancy. Davey's patron, Lord Harrowby, was then a member of the Cabinet, and he secured the position for his client in 1811. Thomas Davey's commission united, under his rule, all the settlements in Van Diemen's Land which had previously been separately administered, although—as had been the case since the island colony had first been settled—the Lieutenant-Governor remained junior to, and under the direct authority of, the Governor of New South Wales, the austere and God-fearing Scotsman, Lachlan Macquarie.

Thomas Davey arrived in Sydney in October 1812, accompanied by his wife, Margaret, and his daughter, Lucy Margaretta—but his reputation had preceded him. Governor Macquarie had received an extraordinary letter from Henry Goulburn (the British Under-Secretary of State in the Colonial Office) which warned him that there were serious flaws in Thomas Davey's character. Apparently

Davey had contracted substantial debts which he had paid with regimental funds while paymaster in the marines, and the British Government had garnisheed his salary of eight hundred pounds a year until the debt had been recovered. By 1814 the debt must have been repaid, because, in that year, Lieutenant-Governor Major Thomas Davey was promoted to the rank of lieutenant-colonel in the marines, and put on the half-pay list, where he would stay—like all colonial officials seconded from military or naval service—until he returned to active duty. But the upshot was that a convict colony was about to receive, as its ruler, a man whose behaviour seemed to make him more suited to be there as an inmate rather than as its administrator! Davey's patron, Lord Harrowby, was clearly prepared to foist upon the hapless inhabitants of Van Diemen's Land a most unsuitable vice-regal representative.

When Thomas Davey and his family arrived in New South Wales, Governor Macquarie was quick to condemn Davey for behaviour which Macquarie described as exhibiting both frivolity and low buffoonery. Most of this can be attributed to the fact that Thomas Davey demonstrated a considerable capacity to consume alcoholic beverages—sufficient even to startle a cosmopolitan and widely travelled Scotsman.

Davey's wartime heroism counted for nothing apparently, and Macquarie's instructions to Davey—about how he was to conduct his administration in Van Diemen's Land—embodied attempts to protect the public funds from the anticipated depredations of which Macquarie had been forewarned by Henry Goulburn. Davey was forbidden to draw bills on the British Treasury without Macquarie's permission, or to make grants of land, to charter ships, or to enter into contracts.

The rot set in from the time Thomas Davey and his family finally arrived in Hobart on 4 February 1813. The day was warm, so Davey removed his coat and landed from the ship in his shirt sleeves—an unheard-of departure from protocol in the stuffy and status-conscious convict colony. The situation only deteriorated from there. His first demand was for rum—a requirement from which he did not desist until his departure from the colony. Indeed, the eccentricities of the Lieutenant-Governor's behaviour soon became the subject of gossip in Van Diemen's Land, and the subject of displeasure and disapproval from Governor Macquarie in Sydney. The locals called him 'Mad Tom' or 'The Mad Governor', and he spent most of his time carousing at the *Bird in Hand* tavern—with convicts as his drinking companions.

Rather than bother himself with the intricacies of government, Thomas Davey habitually walked the streets in his shirt sleeves, greeted all and sundry by their Christian names or their nick-names, dropped in for a drink at any house that took his fancy, openly conducted liaisons with convict women—and treated his

Thomas Davey.
(Archives Office of Tasmania)

critics with humorous contempt. When affected by liquor, he displayed a taste for rough practical jokes that had already earned the censure of Lachlan Macquarie. On one occasion, Davey invited some of the prominent free citizens of Hobart to dine with him at Government House. When it also became plain that Davey intended to include former convicts among his dinner guests, all the respectable folk declined to participate. Davey invited them a second time—making it clear this time that no emancipists or former convicts would be sitting at his table— and the respectable citizens graciously accepted the renewed invitation. When they arrived, they found the Lieutenant-Governor seated alone at a table groaning with tasty joints and other dishes. As they were about to begin the feast, the convicts who had been excluded from the dinner by the social pretensions of the respectable, suddenly burst into the dining room and commandeered the victuals. These they carried off with wild shouts of glee, accompanied by the sound of Davey's laughter. The settlers retired in disarray, and, at the door, the Lieutenant-Governor directed them to a local public house where, he informed them, a reasonably tolerable meal could be obtained!

The profligacy and promiscuity of Thomas Davey were enough to horrify

Governor Macquarie in Sydney—especially as Macquarie had a real regard and respect for Davey's hapless wife and daughter, who continued to live with the Lieutenant-Governor, and who would, therefore, have been confronted on a daily basis by the gross irregularities of their husband and father's behaviour. Thomas Davey also revealed himself to be corrupt in his public life, where he sanctioned and connived at the smuggling of spirits—thereby providing the pretext for the authorities to dispose of him.

Accordingly, in 1815, Governor Macquarie recommended to the Colonial Office in London that Thomas Davey be recalled—but so slow were communications between Australia and the United Kingdom at this time, that it was not until 1817 that Davey handed over to his successor, Colonel Sorell.

Thomas Davey received a very large land grant in Van Diemen's Land, but he proved to be as unsuccessful a farmer as he had been an administrator. In 1821 he left his wife and daughter in the colony and returned to England to try to straighten out his affairs. He died in England in 1823, intestate, leaving an estate valued at only twenty pounds. In 1821, Macquarie had ordered a grant of 1000 acres of land to provide for the maintenance of Davey's family, and he had further directed that Sorell victual them from the public store for a twelve-month period. He could do no more. The Admiralty ruled that Davey's loyal and long-suffering wife was not entitled to any pension on her husband's account. She died in Hobart in 1827—a poor but much respected lady.

Mad Tom's conduct was intolerable in colonial Australia because he crossed the social divide between 'came-free' respectability and 'came-in-chains' felonry. A hard-drinking, oafish military man could be readily accommodated in a convict colony, provided he did nothing to blur the essential social distinctions which insisted that colonial status should be dependent on civil condition on arrival—rather than on actual behaviour in the colony. It was not his financial improprieties which brought down Macquarie's wrath upon the head of Thomas Davey—many governors in colonial Australia were equally guilty—although corruption did furnish the excuse for his replacement. Nor was it Thomas Davey's drinking and buffoonery that became the cause of his dismissal—for drunken and intemperate deportment was also the mark of many vice-regal representatives in the colonial period. His real offence was social, and basically lay in the fact that his companions of choice had been convicts.

It is one of the nice ironies of Australian history, that Lachlan Macquarie—who was responsible for Thomas Davey's downfall in remote Hobart—would be destroyed, in his turn, in New South Wales six years later, for the same underlying reason.

20
Walers and Gunners

What was a 'Waler'? And what was a Gunner? As well as wool, wheat and gold, 'Walers' and 'Gunners' were important exports from Australia in the nineteenth century. Why was this so? And what do the Wells of Beersheba have to do with all of this?

Early in the nineteenth century, an export trade began between the colony of New South Wales and the British Empire in India—a trade which made the Australian colony of vital and continuing importance to the maintenance of the British Raj.

When we think of Australia's traditional nineteenth-century exports, wool, wheat, and gold usually come to mind. Yet exports of Australian working horses constituted an important and expanding market for a highly esteemed commodity from the 1830s onwards, and these animals went on to become the mainstay of the Indian Army's cavalry for more than a century. The stock was shipped to the British Army to replace horses that had died, become worn out, or been killed in battle—and therefore they became known as 'remounts'.

The horses came originally from New South Wales, and hence received the name of 'Walers', a name which became so widely used that it developed into a generic term to cover all Australian-bred remounts for the British Army in India, irrespective of the actual part of Australia in which they had been bred. Since, at various times in the nineteenth century, the colony of New South Wales comprised territories which later came into independent existence as the colonies of Van Diemen's Land, Western Australia, South Australia, Victoria, Queensland, and the Northern Territory, the generic term was not entirely inappropriate.

Walers were a composite of English thoroughbred and Arab bloodlines mixed with colonial Australian stock. Like Banjo Patterson's famous pony in the classic poem *The Man From Snowy River*, Walers were usually about three-quarters thoroughbred with the other quarter made up of various strains of local bloodlines—depending on the function the horses would be expected to perform. For example, if the object was to produce a stronger breed for use by the brigades of Horse Artillery to pull heavy artillery pieces rapidly round a battle field, then the Clydesdale would be introduced to make up the quarter of the non-thoroughbred bloodline. This variation became known as 'Gunners', and the speed and mobility of the British horse-drawn artillery in India became legendary.

Men of the original Light Horse of the AIF 1914, mounted on Walers. (Taken from C.E.W. Bean, *Official History of Australia in the War of 1914-18,* vol. xii, Photographic Record of the War, Sydney, 1938)

For ordinary mounted cavalry, the Australian 'Walers' stockhorse proved almost perfect. Both Gunners and Walers enjoyed an amazing reputation in India for their endurance, strength and adaptability, and hundreds of thousands of these wonderful horses served with distinction in the British armies in India.

There were local breeds and Arab horses in India, but they proved quite unsuitable as cavalry mounts. For serious cavalry purposes, horses had to be imported from England, or from the other parts of the British Empire. In part, this was due to local Indian circumstances. The rural areas of India were not fenced, and all the available arable land was subjected to intensive agricultural activity. This meant that all horses—even developing young foals—normally had to be hobbled or tethered when not in use. The result of such a practice was to produce an adverse effect on the gait and chest development of young Indian horses, to say nothing of the major dietary deficiencies to which horses were subjected on the sub-continent.

On the other hand, Australian horses grew to perfection on rich open pastures, well watered and with plenty of limestone to produce calcium for good bone development. Some of the best Walers came from the high country where mountainous broken ground and fallen timber taught foals at an early age to lift up their feet to avoid a sharp and hurtful blow to the ankle or shin. The wide open pastures also allowed them to gallop freely from their earliest days, and these conditions combined to produce the deep powerful chest and high-stepping gait that made Walers so superbly equipped for cavalry duty in the rugged frontier districts and the inhospitable inland regions of the Raj.

If the strength and endurance of Walers and Gunners made them the favoured horses of the Indian Army, it was also partly because they were heavier built than the local horses. Indian and Arab breeds were too lightly framed for heavy European dragoons with full military accoutrements. The specifications of the Indian Army for cavalry remounts insisted that the horses be capable effectively of carrying 17 stone (108 kg) in weight.

Where Walers and Gunners really shone, however, was in their ability to subsist and to cover enormous distances day after day on forage feed alone. In contrast, English thoroughbreds—although strong enough to carry the weight of a mounted dragoon or an Indian cavalryman—proved unable to survive without grain feed which had to be carried wherever they went. This greatly restricted their utility and flexibility when the army campaigned in the various wars and frontier engagements of the nineteenth century.

The advantages of the Australian environment combined with selective breeding practices to produce a very superior type of horse. The pre-eminence of the Waler was quickly recognised in India, and, when used as race horses, they were handicapped as though they were English thoroughbreds. When the quasi-military sports of polo and pig-sticking were included with the daily ritual of riding for exercise, the use of Walers made them ubiquitous as the main steed of choice throughout India. The trade with India continued after the replacement of horses by mechanised transport, because the Waler was still the most prized mount for the sport of polo—and as a general riding hack for the remaining British and upper-class Indian administrators.

The horse also had an important role to play all over rural Australia and in Australian military history.

After federation in 1901, Australian troops took their beloved Walers with them into the battle fields of the Middle East during World War I, where approximately 30 000 Australian troops served in the Light Horse—notably in Palestine and Syria. Known as the Desert Column, the Australian Light Horse took part in one of the last major cavalry charges of the modern era when they attacked the Turkish forces at Beersheba—their inland base. Beersheba had to be captured before nightfall or both men and horses would be without water after an arduous desert crossing. The wells of Beersheba have become an icon in the larger history of the Waler, as the Light Horsemen charged into Beersheba through artillery, machine-gun, and finally rifle fire, and took the town and its wells—where they watered themselves and their horses. One of the saddest moments in the whole war came when it was time to return home to Australia and the word came that the horses had to be left behind. Rather than leave their Walers to the not-so-tender mercies of the local Egyptian and Arab inhabitants—who treated their donkeys and horses with great cruelty—the Light Horsemen preferred to shoot their horses, and this was done en masse following the Walers' last parade.

21
Michael Howe—Governor of the Ranges

Michael Howe was Australia's first real bushranger. What was the secret of this audacious outlaw's ability to evade capture for so long? What did he say in a letter which so infuriated and humiliated the Governor of Van Diemen's Land? And why did Mary Cockerell turn on her former lover?

The first appearance of bushrangers in Van Diemen's Land occurred within the first year of settlement in 1803, when the convicts began to abscond almost as soon as Europeans had arrived. Supplies were short, and the possibility of starvation led masters to send their assigned convict servants out into the bush to look for food. They even armed them with muskets and equipped them with dogs. Many of these men became convict bolters who lived a life of precarious freedom in the bush and refused to return to servitude—preferring to eke out a living from the sale of kangaroo meat, and through robbery. There were no courts capable of inflicting the death penalty at this time in Van Diemen's Land, and the local authorities had no machinery at hand to deal with outlawry of this sort.

The bushrangers soon developed links with the local community, and built up a network of spies and informants who kept them apprised of the attempts to capture them. In addition, over time, quite a lot of people gained from their relationships with the criminals in the bush. The sale and circulation of stolen property throughout the colony, together with the profits to be gained from illegally 'fencing' stolen goods, made many colonists reluctant to report the bushrangers—especially as they became famous for the brutal way in which they took reprisals against known informers.

In the years following the arrival of the Europeans, the style of these armed bandits altered, such that they became gangs of thugs in the bush who engaged in systematic robbery of farms and houses, and acquired an image of romantic rebellion against authority. In addition, a majority of the inhabitants of a convict settlement rejoiced to see the police baffled—even if the inhabitants obtained no direct personal advantage from the bushrangers' activities.

The career of Michael Howe (1788–1818)—sometimes known as the first of the bushrangers—illustrates the romantic gloss with which those at the lowest levels of colonial society imbued the attacks of the bushrangers upon the property owners and the authorities. Howe was a young man with a long record of desertion. He first joined and then deserted from the merchant navy, then he joined and deserted the Royal Navy, and, finally, the British Army. He was convicted at York of highway robbery, and arrived in Van Diemen's Land in 1812 with a seven-year sentence. His proclivities for desertion had not abated, for the following year Michael Howe deserted his assigned master in Hobart, and took to the bush. In the next five years, his name became so inseparably connected in the public mind with bushranging—and with a daring defiance of the lawful authorities—that he became something of a hero in the eyes of the wider convict society.

In the bush, Michael Howe soon joined a large gang of bushrangers, numbering more than twenty in total, and, being a natural leader, he was soon one of the most prominent of the gang members. In May 1814, Governor Macquarie in Sydney attempted to deal with the growing lawlessness in Van Diemen's Land by offering a period of general amnesty on all crimes short of murder. He hoped, by doing this, to entice the bushrangers out of the bush, and to encourage them to rejoin the wider colonial community. Unfortunately, the amnesty period stretched from May to December 1814, and Macquarie's offer made conditions much worse, because it appeared that the bushrangers had been given a six-month period to do as they liked—and that any crimes they committed during that time would be covered by the amnesty. It seemed like a licence to commit crime.

Howe and his gang became increasingly bold in their activities during these months—to the point where the gang actually attacked a party of soldiers who had captured two bolters and were bringing them in. As the men camped for the night, the bushrangers struck. They released the two prisoners to join their gang, and confiscated all the soldiers' arms. When the authorities finally succeeded in tracking down one of the gang's hideouts, they seized from the camp enough ammunition and firearms to equip a platoon of infantry.

Nor was it only the army who suffered such humiliation at the hands of Michael Howe. In one daring operation, in 1815, the gang raided the district of New Norfolk—the colony's third-largest settlement—where they visited every single house and exacted tribute. The Lieutenant-Governor, Thomas Davey, seemed to attract special attention from the Howe Gang, and Davey's farm was twice attacked and robbed—with the audacious bushranger sending his compliments to the Lieutenant-Governor. Michael Howe also sent a letter to Davey—written in blood—in which he complained of the harassment of himself and his gang by the authorities, and threatened to shoot the Lieutenant-Governor if he did not change his ways. In this letter, Howe titled himself 'Governor of the Ranges', and titled Davey as merely 'Governor of the Town'. It was a great and calculated insult, and was intended to rub the hapless Davey's nose in the fact that Michael Howe actually controlled more of the colony of Van Diemen's Land than did the vice-regal representative of the British Government.

Thomas Davey was provoked into declaring martial law, much to the chagrin of his superior, Governor Macquarie, in Sydney, who cancelled the proclamation as soon as he heard of it—on the grounds that such a declaration was beyond the powers of the Lieutenant-Governor and was therefore illegal. Nevertheless, in the martial-law period, Davey and his supporters were able to capture a number of bushrangers whom they tried before a military court and then sentenced to death. Davey displayed their remains as some sort of ghastly trophy by publicly gibbeting them in chains near the Hobart wharf. Some of these executions were carried out in a particularly crude fashion, with the men being left to strangle at the end of a rope rather than having their necks broken in a proper hanging drop. Michael Howe, however, was not one of them.

In 1817, a party of soldiers—perhaps acting on a tip-off from a disaffected member of the gang who hoped to claim the one-hundred pound reward now offered for Michael Howe—discovered the bushranger and his constant companion, an Aboriginal girl named Mary Cockerell, alone in a hideout on the edge of a swamp. The two fugitives ran for their lives, with the soldiers in hot pursuit. The fugitives had been forced to leave behind their muskets, and all their gear, as they ran for the safety of the bush. Mary Cockerell began to fall behind, and, when Michael Howe stopped to look back, it appeared that she was on the

Flogging a convict, from the book *The Fell Tyrant, or the Suffering Convict* published in London in 1836. Men like Michael Howe became bolters and bushrangers to avoid such treatment.

point of being taken. Howe turned and opened fire on her with his pistol. He later claimed that he was shooting at the men chasing her, but it did appear as though he was shooting directly at her—perhaps because she knew too much to be allowed to fall into the hands of the authorities alive. Mary was wounded by this gunfire, and felt sure that her former lover had deliberately tried to kill her. Accordingly, once she had recovered from her injuries, she joined the police and led them to all the hidden lairs and caches of equipment that the gang had secreted throughout Van Diemen's Land.

The hunters were closing in on their quarry by systematically blocking-off his supply routes and communications. The scope of Howe's enterprise can be gauged by the fact that, at a single one of the hideouts which Mary betrayed to the authorities, they found a flock of fifty sheep that the bushranger had put aside in case they needed a meat supply when life on the road did not produce sufficient for the gang to eat. For her own protection, Mary Cockerell was sent by the government to Sydney. It was the only way that they could be sure that she was beyond the reach of Michael Howe.

As the noose tightened around the 'Governor of the Ranges', he negotiated directly with Lieutenant-Governor Sorell, and arranged to surrender to the government in return for providing the authorities with information about the gang which he had now abandoned. Howe believed that his location with Mary had been betrayed by members of his gang, and that he could no longer trust such treacherous associates. He surrendered in April 1817, and was taken to Hobart to be interrogated or debriefed by the authorities. In Hobart, Michael Howe provided a wealth of information to the police that they already knew, and very little that was either new or useful. In fact, he had trumped the government once again.

It was at this stage that his love of freedom and the life of the bushman outweighed his common sense. Despite the relative safety of his position, he just could not bear to be a prisoner again, and to be subject to the galling regimen of prison routines. He cut and ran for the bush.

The government responded by doubling the reward offered on Michael Howe to two hundred pounds—plus a free pardon and a return passage to England—for any prisoner or assigned servant who would betray the fugitive. This reward resulted in two further attempts to capture the bushranger—in the first of which he freed himself and killed both his captors. In the second attempt, it seems clear that no genuine effort was made to take Michael Howe alive. Perhaps he was judged to be just too dangerous. At any event, in October 1818, a man by the name of Jack (or Thomas) Worrall decoyed Michael Howe out of hiding by offering new supplies of ammunition for the lone bushranger. Howe was, by this time, living in complete solitude in the vicinity of the Shannon River. Hunted by everybody, he had embraced a hermit-like existence. He was clothed entirely in kangaroo skins, heavily bearded, and mentally unstable. He had made a small book which he had covered with kangaroo skin, and in which he wrote in animal blood an account of the dreams that troubled him when he slept. Many of these presaged his own violent death. He had also drawn-up a list of seeds that he wanted to obtain and plant around his hideout.

The lure of a new supply of ammunition drew the suspicious Michael Howe into the open, and Worrall and his partner ran him down and battered him to death. This marked the end of Australia's first real bushranger, and the end of the first era of Australian bushranging.

22

Lola Montez versus Henry Seekamp

Lola Montez was the notorious strumpet who enlivened the Victorian goldfields by her presence. Why did she attack the only man to be imprisoned for his part in the Eureka rebellion? Why was it considered a hazardous occupation to be married to Lola? And what was so shocking about Lola's 'spider dance' anyway?

Lola Montez became probably the most notorious woman in the world during the goldrush years around the middle of the nineteenth century. Her notoriety spanned three continents, and her name brought sniffs of disapproval from the higher levels of polite society in Britain and Europe, North America, and Australia. On the other hand, wherever she went, she proved to be enormously popular among the men of the lower classes. The gold diggers of California and Victoria were so enthused that they could be described almost as devotees.

Such celebrity could not have been foreseen in 1818 when she was born in Limerick, Ireland—of a professional soldier, Ensign Edward Gilbert, and his fourteen-year-old wife who claimed to be descended from Spanish nobility. It was probably from her mother that the young girl inherited the darker colouring that was to enable her, in later life, to claim that she had Creole blood in her veins. This was not necessarily a bad thing for a stage career, because it made her exotic, and since Napoleon's Empress Josephine had also been Creole, it was a background that did not appear to be considered socially unacceptable.

She was christened Maria Dolores Eliza Rosanna Gilbert—and the name alone suggests an interesting combination of British and Spanish bloodlines. Her father died when she was six, and her mother remarried a more senior army officer—Major John Craigie. Maria received an education at boarding schools in England and France as befitted a young lady, but when her mother arranged a marriage for her in her nineteenth year—to a wealthy but aged judge—the first signs of her fiery spirit emerged. She eloped with a young army officer—Lieutenant Thomas James—who married her in Ireland and then took her to India with him. In 1839, her husband ran away with another woman in India, and the abandoned wife returned to England alone. Apparently, she had not been too lonely on the voyage, because her husband obtained a judicial separation from her on the grounds that she had committed adultery aboard ship. A judicial separation meant that the couple had agreed to live apart, and that the husband

Lola Montez as a young woman. By all accounts, Lola was well past this prime by the time she appeared in the Australian colonies.

was no longer responsible for his wife's debts; but they were still legally wed.

Maria travelled to Spain, where she trained as a dancer, and took the stage name Donna Lola Montez. She made her stage debut at Her Majesty's Theatre in London during 1843, but she was recognised as the wayward wife of Lieutenant James, and was hissed off the stage. Lola then fled to Europe, and embarked on a career as an exotic dancer in Warsaw, Paris, and elsewhere. Her dancing was considered shocking and suggestively lewd—and her private life seemed equally discreditable. Lola enjoyed the protection of, and became the mistress of, both Franz Liszt and Alexandre Dumas—who were only two among many others.

When her then-current protector was killed in a duel in March 1845, Lola decamped to Munich, posing as a Spanish noblewoman. There she met the ageing King Ludvig I of Bavaria whom she bedazzled to the point where he fell totally under her spell. The besotted Ludvig purchased a house for his lady-love, and settled a generous annuity on her. In return, she betrayed him and took a number of additional sexual partners. As her influence over the king grew, she began to meddle in Bavarian politics, and ministries rose and fell at her whim. On 25 August 1847—to the horror of the Bavarian nobility and most of the respectable middle classes—Ludvig raised her to the ranks of the aristocracy, creating her Countess Marie von Lansfeld. Within six months, street riots broke out against her influence, and in February 1848—the year of European revolutions—infuriated mobs marched on Ludvig's palace and demanded Lola's expulsion from the country. The devastated Ludvig gave way, in the face of irrefutable evidence of her common background and her amours, but insisted on abdicating the throne.

The following year, Lola went through a bigamous marriage ceremony in London with yet another young officer—this one named George Heald—and was arrested and charged with bigamy a few weeks later. Released on bail, she and Heald fled to the continent, where Heald conveniently drowned the next year. Lola thereupon returned to the stage, and enjoyed a triumphal tour of Europe and America—in which she carried a cow-hide whip and sometimes a pistol—and became caught up in innumerable assaults, scandals, and law-suits.

In San Francisco, she first introduced her notorious 'spider dance' which thereafter was to be her signature performance. It was the last word in erotic dancing at that time, and provoked a frenzy of disapproval from the more censoriously inclined. The fact that she also smoked cigars and enthusiastically enjoyed the pleasures of the flesh, did nothing to help her reputation. In San Francisco, she participated in yet another bigamous marriage ceremony—this time with a local newspaper owner. Shortly after, this man was petitioning for a divorce on the grounds of her infidelity with a local doctor. The doctor was soon found shot dead in nearby hills. Drama seemed to follow Lola wherever she went.

In 1855, the lure of the Australian goldrushes drew Lola to this country, and she undertook another of her successful tours. She received a rapturous welcome in Adelaide, Melbourne and Sydney, although her scandalous reputation led the ladies of Melbourne society to boycott the Theatre Royale as long as Lola was appearing there on stage. But, when she reached the Victorian diggings, her reception from the goldminers was tumultuous. She offered a number of melodramatic pieces and comedy sketches as part of her act, but it was the spider dance that her largely male audience had come to see. Although age and lifestyle had ravaged her once-famous beauty, she was still a striking woman, and a local diarist described her in the following terms:

> There is no mistaking the leading 'star' when she makes her appearance. She has evidently inherited the best points of her aristocratic (sic) father and her handsome Creole mother. One has only to look at her magnificent dark, flashing eyes, her willowy form, and traces of former beauty, and her lithe active movements, to see that one is in the presence of a very remarkable woman, and it is not hard to believe that she should have been able to bewitch a king and cost him his throne.[9]

Lola's spider dance so delighted the miners that they responded enthusiastically when she invited them to show their appreciation of her performance by showering her on stage with gold nuggets and coins. And it was her very popularity that caused her to come into conflict with Henry Seekamp, the editor of the *Ballarat Times*.

Henry Seekamp was one of the most influential men on the Victorian goldfields. His newspaper became a crusading supporter of the goldminers in their struggle against the corrupt goldfields' administration, and in the miners' campaign against the hated mining licence system, which obliged every miner— no matter how successful or unsuccessful he had been—to purchase a mining licence each month in advance. Failure to present the licence on demand resulted in a fine, or even a gaol sentence. So closely involved was Henry Seekamp with the radical miners, that he was arrested in 1855 at the time of the rising at the Eureka Stockade, and charged with sedition. The support he extended to the miners through the columns of his newspaper led the jury to find him guilty at his trial, and he became the only man ever to be gaoled for his part in the rising. He had described the actions of the police and troops at Eureka as a 'foul massacre', and the authorities determined to make an example of him. He served only three months of his sentence, before being recommended for mercy and released.

So, in 1856, Henry Seekamp was a person of note and was considerably admired on the goldfields. However, he soon found that when he attacked Lola Montez for the immorality of her spider dance, his eminent position counted for naught. His punishment and humiliation was both public and extended.

Once the *Ballarat Times* published its denunciation of the spider dance, Lola Montez began to search for the editor, breathing fire and determined to avenge the insult. She finally ran the unfortunate Seekamp to ground in a local tavern where she subjected him to a tirade of furious abuse, and then attacked him with a horsewhip in front of the delighted patrons. When Seekamp attempted to defend himself, the miners refused to allow him to retaliate with his fists, and the poor man was driven through the public bar and then out into the street, as the infuriated Lola belaboured him with her whip. She did not halt her attack just because they were now in a public thoroughfare, and the beating continued as the hapless Seekamp took what evasive action he could. Eventually, the two combatants ended up in the public bar of another tavern across the road, and there Seekamp seized a whip from a bystander, and began to repay Lola in her own coin. The battle surged back into the street once again, where Henry Seekamp was finally disarmed by the diggers before he could do any real harm to their favourite. Lola was also too tired to continue the assault, and retired from the field with full honours. Her spirited rejoinder to Henry Seekamp's editorial certainly did little to diminish her standing with her public on the goldfields. When, a week later, the intrepid editor published yet another uncomplimentary attack on her, Lola responded by swearing-out a warrant for his arrest on a charge of criminal libel, although, when the case came up for trial, she failed to appear.

Lola did not always win her battles, however, and a few weeks later she fought another titanic struggle with the wife of her goldfields' impresario. On this occasion she came off decidedly second-best, needing a full month to recover. Henry Seekamp's newspaper reported the fracas as a dispute concerning a short payment by Mr Crossby to Lola, which led the artiste to make some disparaging remarks about the honesty of the gentleman in the presence of his wife:

> ... Whereupon Mrs Crossby immediately commenced striking Madame with a heavy whip, which she broke in the struggle, then seizing Madame by the hair, beat her most unmercifully about the head and neck, so much so, that it rendered Madame totally unable to appear on the stage according to public announcements.[10]

Lola sailed from Australia later in 1856, and returned to America. On the voyage she lost the latest of her bigamous 'husbands'—who disappeared overboard at sea. Perhaps Henry Seekamp was fortunate that he received nothing more than a beating, for people who crossed Lola Montez seemed to be awfully accident-prone. Back in the United States, Lola's star had waned, and a number of attempted comebacks to the stage failed. She was no longer well, and was beginning to show obvious signs of the tertiary syphilis that eventually took her life in 1861. The rages that overwhelmed her during her sojourn in Australia may quite possibly have a medical explanation. She died at the age of forty-two, and was laid to rest most respectably in Greenwood cemetery, Brooklyn, as Mrs Eliza Gilbert.

Melbourne Punch, the satirical magazine, immortalised the Montez versus Seekamp bout in a long poem entitled *The Battle of Ballarat*, part of which appears opposite.

THE BATTLE OF BALLARAT

And, therewith arm'd, she sallied forth
Erle Seekamp to defy;
Her little mouth compressed in wrath,
While fire flashed from her eye.

'Come forth, come forth, thou vap'ring Erle,
Thou scribe, so rude and rash,
And yield thee to the punishment
Of Lola Montes' lash.'...

Erle Seekamp grasp'd his riding-whip,
(For he was armed also),
And with sharp words and haughty mien
Did thus defiance throw: loud,

'I'll do the best that do I may,
Whilst I have power to stand:
Whilst I have power to wield my whip
I'll fight with heart and hand.'

Then, in a struggle dread and dire,
The combatants did close,
And on each other rain'd a shower
Of swift and stinging blows.

Erle Seekamp's face, bore bloody trace
Of Lola Montes' lash;
Her shoulders fair, if they were bare,
Would show a crimson gash.

Ah me! it was a grief to see
So pitiful a sight,
Like lions wode, they laid on lode,
And made a cruel fight.

They fought until they both did smoke
And glow like furnace red,
I wis the Erle and Lola too,
For breath were sore bested.

They flung their whips aside, anon,
And tore each other's hair,
'Gainst which the crowd rais'd protest loud,
And swore it wasn't fair...

The fight did last from half-past five,
'Till setting of the sun;
For when they rang the evening bell,
The battle scarce was done.

The rumour ran on Ballarat,
The doughty Erle was slain;
These tidings spread along the road,
That is y'clept the Main ...

Howbeit, it did haply chance
No deadly blow was strook;
And from the field of combat, both
Alive, though faint, were took.

23

A 'Mill' on Sydney's North Shore

When nineteenth-century newspapers referred to a 'mill', what was the object of their attention? Why were such 'mills' the cause of considerable concern to the authorities? And what does it mean to say that a man is not 'up to scratch'?

When the Sydney newspaper, the *Monitor*, informed its readers on 15 November 1827 that there would be a 'Mill' take place in the suburbs north of Sydney Harbour, it was not referring to the grinding of wheat into flour. The word 'mill' was, in fact, a slang term—and was part of an entire sub-species of language that had emerged in England during the second half of the eighteenth century and that had flowered during the Regency period. It applied specifically to the illegal activity of bare-knuckle prize-fighting, and probably reflected a style of fighting that was characterised by a furious flailing of the fists that looked for all the world like the sails on a windmill rapidly turning in a strong breeze.

When the first fleet arrived in New South Wales in 1788, its members brought with them all aspects of their original culture—and an interest in gambling and prize-fighting was a part of this culture. The English art of boxing was as much admired then as are the various systems of Asian martial arts in the modern era; and the British prided themselves on settling their differences in a manly fashion in the 'good old English way'—rather than indulging in what they regarded as the cowardly and typically continental resort to the dagger.

At the beginning of the first edition of the nineteenth-century classic work on British pugilism, *Boxiana*, published in 1813, this traditional English method of self-defence is presented as a distinguishing feature that demonstrated the superiority of the English over the other peoples of Europe.

> *An Englishman will take his part,*
> *With courage prime and noble heart;*
> *Either forgive, or resent offence—*
> *And bang-up in his own defence.*
> *No sword or dagger—nor deadly list—*
> *And rise or fall but by his fist!*
> *The battle o'er—all made amends,*
> *By shaking hands, becoming friends.*
>
> John Bull

Gaming and betting always accompanied a 'mill' in England, and the prize-money awarded to the winner of a bout was only a small fraction of the amount wagered on the outcome. For example, in 1750, the Duke of Cumberland attended a prize-fight between the champion, Jack Broughton, and a young challenger, and the Duke lost several thousand pounds in wagers on Broughton. At the other end of the social spectrum, the lower orders would bet in amounts as small as a few pence. But the practice of gambling on fights between men or animals was widespread in England and affected all levels of society—despite the fact that prize-fighting was illegal and was deplored by the churches. Thus, the men and women of the first fleet brought with them popular attitudes towards gaming and betting that were not endorsed by the colonial authorities, but were nevertheless a part of popular recreation in the home culture, and there are very early references to a mania for gambling among the convicts, who were known to hazard their clothes and rations in games of cards, dice, and coin throwing.

In a convict colony like New South Wales, the magistrates were very unhappy about the popularity of prize-fighting, because a good 'mill' could be expected to draw quite large crowds, the members of which would be betting and drinking heavily. This situation carried the risk that a breach of the peace could well be expected. In the first decades of the colony, there was the additional concern that such a large assembly of men might provide cover for the organisation of a convict rising. There were also well-placed fears that large congregations of the lower orders would attract criminals like pickpockets and touts—to say nothing about the high possibility that unsuccessful gamblers might waylay the successful on their way home, with robberies and violence following.

So, although we know that there had been prize-fighting in Australia from the earliest days of settlement, it is not until 1814 that we have the first recorded prize-fight—between two convicts named John Parton and Charles Sefton. The bout lasted more than fifty rounds, and went for over one-and-a-half hours of hard fighting. With Parton's victory, the first Australian boxing champion emerged.

The fights were conducted according to the rules drawn up in 1743 by the then English champion Jack Broughton. Broughton's rules applied in all championship bouts until the modern era when the rules were revised and brought up to date by the Marquis of Queensbury. Under Broughton's rules, fights often lasted for hours because there were no limits on the numbers of rounds to be contested, and the combatants fought until one of them was unable to toe the line in the middle of the ring at the commencement of the next round. Rounds lasted until a knock-down or a wrestling throw, or until a boxer went down on one knee as a result of receiving a blow. Once one of these eventualities occurred, the boxers' seconds had thirty seconds to get their men up to the scratch-mark in the middle. Failure to toe-the-scratch meant the loss of the bout. Hence the

Depiction of a typical bout of bare-knuckle prize-fighting. Although drawn from English sources, such events were widespread throughout the Australian colonies.

colloquialisms that people fought 'toe-to-toe', or that a man did not feel 'up-to-scratch'.

By the 1820s, a generation of locally born 'currency' lads had begun to emerge, and the authorities in the colony deplored the fact that the young native-born men seemed to be just as enamoured with prize-fighting as were their British-born parents. The colonial boxing contests did not attract the sums of money that had become common in Britain, and the fighters often contested a purse of as little as fifty pounds, but there was widespread betting on the outcomes, and the fighters often got their friends or connections to place bets on their behalf. The local newspapers followed a deeply ambivalent practice of deploring the interest of the 'currency' population in such a violent sport as prize-fighting, but of also informing their readers of the time and location of forthcoming bouts, and reporting their outcomes. The local events were popular and well attended, especially when the fight could be presented as a contest which invoked wider questions of patriotism and identity—by pitching boxers who represented the native-born population against the British import. The purses reflected the increasing wealth of the population, and, by the 1830s, had reached the level of 500–1000 pounds a fight.

Moreover, the emergence of local champions led them inevitably to want to pursue their chosen occupation in England—the home of their sport—and in the 1840s the first Australian-born boxing champion appeared in Britain. His name was Isaac Gorrick, and, when he first presented himself as an Australian

John 'Black' Perry, one of the most feared colonial pugilists in Australia, in fighting stance.

native-born boxer, he found that nobody would believe him—because he was not black! Gorrick sounds as though he was quite a showman, and fought under the name of Bungaree to confound the expectations of the English. He appropriated the name from a well-known Sydney Aboriginal identity who was recognised by the colonial authorities as the chief of the Broken Bay tribe, and who often welcomed visitors to Sydney by wearing colourful scraps of British military uniforms, and boarding vessels as they sailed into Sydney Harbour. Isaac

Gorrick also produced the first Australian flag, for he adorned his corner of the ring with a flag of light sky-blue on which brilliant yellow corn-cobs were depicted. The corn-cobs probably represented the rising generation of native-born colonists, who were referred to by the name of 'corn-stalks' in New South Wales. On the flag was displayed the motto: *Advance Australia! Who'd Have Thought It!*

Gorrick proved to be far more effective as a promoter than as a fighter, and unfortunately, the story does not have a happy outcome—for when Bungaree was matched against an English fighter of moderate abilities named Broome, he was soundly thrashed in a bout that lasted less than an hour.

Six years later, another local boxer of renown named Bill Sparkes travelled to Britain in search of fame and reputation. He also lost his fight, but, in this case, there was no doubting the man's courage, as he slipped and broke his arm during the contest, but fought on for a further six rounds before his seconds ended the bout in the teeth of his objections.

In the 1840s, the free-and-easy rules established by Broughton were modified to outlaw head-butting, gouging, and kicking—and a greater measure of decorum made the fight game more acceptable and increasingly popular with the 'respectable' members of the colonial population. Once the transportation of convicts to New South Wales ceased after 1840, the moral strictures against gambling lost much of their force. Whereas it might previously have been argued that prize-fighting, and the betting that accompanied it, led to convicts wasting their time, neglecting their duties, and possibly stealing—when they might have been employed more productively in learning habits of hard work and deference to overseers and other figures of authority—the locally born non-convict and ex-convict population could not be bullied out of their belief that the enjoyment of games of chance and contests between men or animals—and wagering on the outcome of such contests—were all part of the rights that free people were entitled to exercise in a free society. Since the gentry supported and exercised these same rights in the area of horse-racing—and had done so since the earliest days of the colony—the double-standard quietly disappeared, and prize-fighting grew to be accepted as a genuine recreational pastime and spectator sport. This process of increasing respectability accelerated after 1872, when Scottish nobleman John Sholto Douglas, the 8th Marquis of Queensbury, sponsored a new boxing code of conduct which has been used, with minor variations, throughout the world ever since.

24

Sydney and the Second Coming— the Star Amphitheatre at Balmoral

Why was Sydney selected for the Second Coming of Christ? Who was the mysterious 'Great Teacher' and how was he to manifest his authority? Why was an amphitheatre built facing Sydney Heads? And how true were the reports of the *Truth* newspaper?

One consequence of the post-World War I disillusionment with the pre-war world was the growth, in some spiritually-minded people, of a conviction that the suffering of the war must have been some form of divinely inspired purgatorial experience—and a necessary part of God's plan to purify the earth and prepare it for the Second Coming of Jesus Christ. This expectation had been foretold in the Scriptures, and anticipated as imminent since the days of the apostles. As part of this wider search for meaning in the horrors of the immediate past, the religious revivalistic fervour, and the growth of atheistic communism, constituted the opposite ends of the same spectrum.

Among the enthusiastically Christian groups eager for the Second Coming, was a rather strange organisation that had developed a body of doctrine that amounted to an amalgamation of misunderstood and oversimplified Hinduism, with an esoteric and eccentric variant of Christianity. Known as the Theosophical Society, the organisation had come into existence during the final decades of the nineteenth century, and had spread all around the world. It founded its teaching authority on the claim of its designer—a crafty Russian woman named Helena Petrovna Blavatsky—to be in personal contact with a group of spiritual masters who guided the evolution of mankind from secret hideaways in the Himalayas. The organisation had over thirty lodges in Australia, with a total membership that hovered around 1500, and this country was depicted as possessing a great spiritual destiny, because it was to be the location for the next great leap forward in the spiritual evolution of humanity, and the home of a new spiritually advanced sub-race of mankind.

Theosophists believed that a new 'Great Teacher' of humanity—in the tradition of Buddha, Zoroaster and Christ—would take birth around the turn of the twentieth century, and would reveal himself and his mission to the world in the first few decades of the new epoch. They were convinced, by the successors of

Madame Blavatsky, that a young Indian boy named Jiddu Krishnamurti had been chosen by the Himalayan masters to be the physical vehicle through which the great teacher would incarnate. One of Blavatsky's successors, Charles Leadbeater, had taken up residence in Australia in 1914, and his dynamic personality and proselytising activities—which included the establishment of the Sydney radio station 2GB—had led to a rapid expansion in the number of converts to the hybrid religion, and to the expectation (vigorously promoted by Leadbeater) that Krishnamurti would manifest his real divinity in this country.

It is easy to see how the Theosophical anticipation built on, and was strengthened by, its similarity to the more millennial of the Christian expectations. The messianic enthusiasts among the Theosophists formed an organisation specifically to prepare for the great event. Known as the Order of the Star of the East, it artfully merged the identities of Jesus Christ and their awaited 'World Teacher' Krishnamurti, to the point where the Sydney newspaper the *Truth* could inform its readers that Leadbeater had promised that the Second Coming would take place in Sydney. The newspaper embroidered the story by incorrectly claiming that it was widely expected, within the Theosophical movement, that Christ's Second Coming—in the person of Krishnamurti—would include a demonstration of his power by walking on the water through the heads of Sydney Harbour. In 1922, the Order of the Star of the East decided to build a large amphitheatre on three blocks of land on the foreshore of Sydney Harbour in the suburb of Balmoral, at which their Messiah could address his Australian devotees. They believed that Krishnamurti would reveal his true nature and his divine mission on a visit to Sydney, planned to take place during 1925; and they wanted to secure front-row seats.

Between 1923 and 1924, sympathisers collected and spent at least 20 000 pounds in the construction of a giant Greek amphitheatre facing east into the Pacific. Frenzied calls for money went out to the Theosophical faithful, so that the edifice could be completed in time. People were able to book their seats in advance, and seating plans of the 'Star Amphitheatre'—as it was known—were prepared. Individuals were invited to select a place by marking clearly—on the copy of the plan which they had been sent—their preferred section, row and seat. They were to forward this, together with their money, to Leadbeater's organisation in Sydney. Choice seats—those among the elect—did not come cheaply. The capacity of the amphitheatre was about 2500, and the price of a place varied from 10 pounds (at the top of the 26 tiers of seating) to 100 pounds (for a seat near the arena). Owners of seats could have their names engraved on them, and the seats could be passed on in people's wills.

The theological mishmash on which Theosophy was based had been well demonstrated in 1923 at the turning of the first sod of the new complex—

Following a London custom which was adopted in the building of the Albert Hall, we are offering Founders' Seats, though in a modified form, at the prices marked on the accompanying plan.

Select your seat, mark it thus (X) on the plan, sign your name and address (writing very clearly), and forward the plan with or without deposit or cash to Dr. Rocke, The Manor, Mosman, Sydney.

Should you wish to keep the plan, send instead the following details:—Section, row, number of seat.

Seats filled in are already sold. You may select a seat in any part of the house, there is no need to keep to your country's section, since if your choice elsewhere proved to be already allotted we would then give you the seat nearest to that spot.

From the splendid support already received we know that all who can will help the Amphitheatre to materialise by taking the best seats.

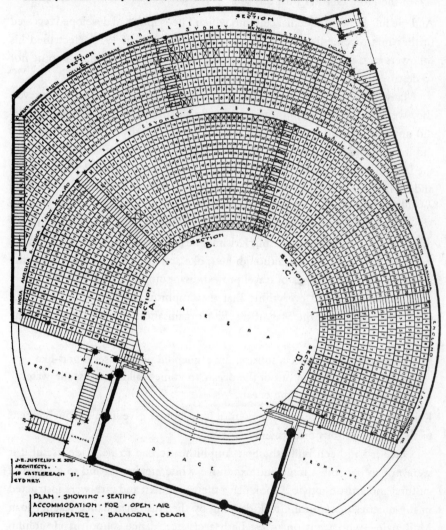

Diagram of the seating arrangements for the ordering of seats at the Star Amphitheatre.
(Theosophical Society of Australia)

which was to come complete with arena, library and tea-room—when Lead-beater proclaimed:

> In the name of all the Buddhas, past and future, in the Name of the Great
> Master of the Wisdom, and in the Name of the Father, and of the Son, and
> of the Holy Ghost, I turn this sod.[11]

And the full-blown millennial cult into which Theosophy had developed received further reinforcement when Krishnamurti, at the end of 1925, electrified his followers by using the first personal pronoun and announcing that: 'I come not to destroy but to build'.[12]

Many Theosophists believed that the Second Coming had begun. However, they were doomed to disillusionment, for Krishnamurti's 1925 tour of Australia did not produce the yearned-for disclosure of his divinity to his followers, nor did it lead to any miraculous walking-on-water as the more credulous among the faithful may have hoped. Nevertheless, at public meetings in Perth, Adelaide and Melbourne, Krishnamurti received plots of land from the local Theosophists on which buildings could be erected in the future to assist in the work of the World Teacher. When he and his entourage arrived in Sydney at the beginning of April, expectations ran high, but Krishnamurti appeared to avoid having much to do with Leadbeater, and, although he spoke at a number of gatherings at the amphitheatre, his methods of travel proved disappointingly conventional.

The *Truth* mocked everything that the amphitheatre represented, and the extravagant claims of the Star of the East organisation, when it described the edifice as:

> A splendid place to see a sunrise, and a splendid place to see a god-like
> form rise like the sun out of the ocean, to come walking across the water
> to see the assembly of the ocean.[13]

Krishnamurti did not leave Sydney until June, but he gave little encouragement to those seeking for portents and marvels.

Once it had been built, the Star Amphitheatre had to be made useful if it were not to become a huge and expensive white elephant—and so a range of cultural and artistic activities took place there. Women and girls were instructed in the niceties of classical Greek dancing by the Australian dance teacher Joan McKenzie—who went on to establish a classical dance school in Honolulu. Plays and choral concerts were also tried to mixed success, although, in the long run, the amphitheatre did not fulfil Theosophists' hopes of becoming a viable theatrical venue. The Star Amphitheatre passed into the hands of the Roman Catholic Church, and was eventually demolished in 1951 and replaced by a block of units—after proving to be a great and continuing source of embarrassment to its founders.

The combination of the great depression and Krishnamurti's renunciation of the part of World Teacher—thus rejecting the role for which the Theosophical Society had been training him since early childhood—led to a collapse in the organisation's membership and finances. In January 1927, the President of the Theosophical Society, Annie Besant, had announced to the press that her adopted son Krishnamurti was, indeed, the long-awaited World Teacher. In 1930, Krishnamurti resigned from the Theosophical Society on the grounds that truth could never be found in any organisation, but only by and through the individual effort of each seeker. He also confirmed that the unsophisticated and simple-minded amalgamation of eastern and western spiritual traditions in Theosophy had produced a doctrine that he found essentially unintelligible.

In Australia, the organisation declined dramatically following Krishnamurti's defection—although it still continues to exist today, and operates lodges and spiritual bookshops in most Australian capital cities. Today, it is a pale shadow of the vital and vibrant religion that once so enthusiastically articulated the millennial aspirations of a war-torn generation for a better and more spiritual world. The Star Amphitheatre, and its role in the Second Coming, has become something of an urban myth, and is nowadays usually, most unjustly, attributed to the Seventh Day Adventists. The unsubstantiated assertions of a scurrilous scandal-sheet like the *Truth* have resulted in a distorted rendition of the story. It was certainly an example of an adventist expectation that was widely shared by a number of religious organisations and fringe groups, but the sole responsibility for it, and the disappointment it engendered, is shared by the international leadership of the Theosophical Society, and the Australian members of its offshoot, the Order of the Star of the East.

The Star Amphitheatre, Balmoral, Sydney. (Theosophical Society of Australia)

25

Ned Kelly and the Kelly Outbreak

Ned Kelly is Australia's most famous outlaw. Why has his legend developed into one of mythological proportions? Why do the career, capture, and execution of this man continue to capture the imagination of generations of Australians? And what role did *Music* play in the Siege of Glenrowan?

The story of Ned Kelly and his gang of outlaws has become part of Australian folklore. The courage of the man won him great admiration among the rural poor in Victoria and New South Wales, where the expression 'as game as Ned Kelly', passed into common usage. But his enduring fame can be properly explained only by recognising that Ned and his gang reflected something very deep in the Australian psyche—and that the tale of the Kelly gang touched and vibrated a deeper chord in frontier society than that superficially represented by the story of a group of violent criminals at odds with the police.

Ned Kelly's life, and the manner of his death, provided the raw material for the Kelly legend; but a myth requires more than this. The mythological status still accorded to Ned Kelly rests firmly on the fact that, even during his life, Ned represented far more than just a criminal on the run. Ned and his gang knowingly became spokesmen for a profound discontent with the conditions of life for those at the lowest levels of the rural community—the selectors and their children who attempted to wrest a living from impossibly small holdings of marginal land that often proved to be insufficient, even for subsistence farming.

Because the authorities recognised this representative quality, Ned was hounded by those authorities and the corrupt rural police who protected the interests of the rich pastoralists at the expense of the selector community. It was because of the persecution of his family that this petty stock thief became, in time, the far more formidable figure of the social bandit—a man at war with those who exercised such arbitrary authority in his world. The charisma and dominance of Ned Kelly the personality, meant that the other members of his gang were always of minor importance, and even today they remain shadowy figures remembered only because of their association with their leader who has retained the larger-than-life standing he gained in his short but spectacular existence.

Edward (Ned) Kelly was born in 1855 in Victoria, the son of Red Kelly—a former Irish convict who had served his time in Van Diemen's Land; and of his wife, Ellen Quinn—whose family came from the ranks of the impoverished selector class, and had already incurred such a reputation for stock theft that they were subject to almost constant police attention. From his early teens, Ned was on the fringes of the rural underworld. He partnered a bushranger named Harry Power until Power's capture; he seemed to be caught up in the flourishing trade in stolen livestock with his uncles from the Quinn family; and he had developed into a tall and well-built young man who was a formidable bare-knuckle fighter. He had also been recognised by the police as a 'flash' type who needed to be brought down a peg or two. In 1871, after a number of minor brushes with the law—involving obscene language and assault on a constable—Ned was imprisoned for horse stealing on false evidence sworn by a corrupt local policeman. The sixteen-year-old was sentenced to three years hard labour in Melbourne's Pentridge Prison. The rankling sense of injustice can be seen to originate here.

We need to understand the social and political conditions in rural Victoria, if we are to comprehend the consequences of the police resort to perjury to rid themselves of a trouble-maker. The four Victorian Selection Acts of the 1860s had brought a rapid growth in population in the north-eastern region of the colony. The district of Benalla—in which the Kellys lived—had doubled the number of its residents, so that, by the early 1870s, the population stood at 10 000. The Acts also brought much marginal land into agricultural production, and wheat, oats, hay and potatoes were marketed as a result. The downside of the selection process, however, was the creation of deep social antagonisms. The wealthy pastoralists had previously enjoyed uninterrupted possession of the land, and had run their livestock without hindrance. The arrival of a community of impoverished small farmers left the pastoralists feeling resentful and angry. When these farmers, to feed themselves, sometimes stole a sheep from the hundreds of thousands of sheep the pastoralists ran, or stole cattle to sell in markets over the borders in New South Wales or South Australia, the pastoralists argued that the selectors were a criminal class with no respect for the law—a criminal class who would respond only to tough and aggressive treatment from the authorities.

Pastoralists enlisted the poorly paid rural police as their allies in a campaign of harassment directed against the selector community. The pastoralists paid rewards for arrests of selectors on charges of stock theft, and the reward was paid irrespective of whether the charge was upheld later in a court of law. The police were armed, and the appearance of the mounted troopers reminded the largely Irish selectors of the hated Royal Irish Constabulary—which acted as an army of occupation back home in Ireland. The links between pastoralists and the police were so close at this time that the police were little more than the agents of the large landholders. The selectors found that they obtained rough justice indeed when they came

'Free Selection' as seen by *Melbourne Punch* in 1870. Many selectors, including the Kelly family, lived lives of squalid poverty. Such conditions proved fertile ground for resentment against authority. The Kelly outbreak was the most dramatic example of a much wider anger felt by selectors.

before the local magistrates, who tended to be pastoralists themselves, and who uncritically accepted perjured evidence from the local members of the police force—if it led to the conviction of a local trouble-maker like Ned Kelly.

There are a number of parallels between the wild youthful rebellion of Ned Kelly and his peers, and the wildness and lawlessness of today's urban youth—especially in the area of personal transport. In Ned Kelly's time, it was as socially important for a youth to possess a good horse, as it is today for a youth to have a fast car. Those too poor to buy such a horse sometimes stole one—just as today the theft of motor vehicles is largely comprised of young men taking vehicles for joyriding. There was also a thriving market in stolen horses, with its own underground distribution methods. This seems to be very similar to the stolen car industry that operates in most large cities—even mirroring the alteration of horses' brands with the manufacture of new number-plates.

The police persecution of his mother and his family turned Ned Kelly from a small-time hoodlum to a social bandit. In 1878, Ned and his brother, Dan, became involved in an altercation with a policeman over that constable's unwelcome attentions to their sister. The brothers claimed that they returned to the family home one afternoon to find their sister being sexually harassed and assaulted. In the confrontation that followed, the policeman swore that Ned had drawn a pistol and fired at him. Ned always said that what had happened was that he had given the constable a thorough hiding with his fists, and that the pistol story was a fabrication. Whatever the truth, it was beyond doubt that a charge of assaulting a policeman with a pistol would result in a very long term in prison. Ned and Dan Kelly fled to the bush where they were soon joined by two of their friends in Joe Byrne and Steve Hart. The Kelly Gang had assembled.

Their rise to national notoriety and legendary status began in October 1878 when the police sent out a party of armed troopers to capture the gang. This party boasted of their intention to shoot Ned Kelly dead when they caught up with him. Ned ambushed the troopers at Stringybark Creek, and three of them were killed. The selector community kept Ned informed of all police movements, and provided the gang with food and supplies. The bushmanship of the outlaws was superb, and, in their own local terrain, the gang proved far too adept for parties of mounted troopers. The death of the policemen was viewed by many in the district as a blow struck against the agents of tyranny.

Ned and the gang then raided the bank at Euroa in Victoria in December, before crossing the border into New South Wales in February 1879, and capturing the town of Jerilderie. In both these endeavours, Ned showed an awareness of his role as spokesman for the downtrodden—by building a bonfire in the street and burning all the mortgage documents which they found in the banks' safes. The proceeds of the robberies also found their way into the hands of many Kelly

SOONER OR LATER.
THE UNERRING ARM OF JUSTICE

The capture of Ned Kelly by the long arm of the law, as seen by *Melbourne Punch*.

sympathisers among the selector population, and the records show that outstanding debts were suddenly paid off in cash by the most unlikely people over the following few months. Moreover, the gang's behaviour was gentlemanly, and they treated everyone they encountered with courtesy and good humour. Even their victims commented on what a fine group of men they were, while their continued humiliation of the troopers in the bush made them heroes in the eyes of their peers. For the next sixteen months, the gang hid in the Strathbogie Ranges in northern Victoria, and their status continued to grow as they eluded all police attempts to take them.

The bubble burst at Glenrowan, when Ned determined to take the initiative and create a situation where he would lure a trainload of troopers from Melbourne, derail their train, and ambush the occupants. There is evidence that he also intended to declare an independent Republic of Northern Victoria at this time, and to assemble an army of armed supporters to defend the new country. The siege at Glenrowan got out of control when Ned permitted the local schoolmaster to leave the Glenrowan Hotel—in which the gang had imprisoned the town population—in order that the schoolmaster might attend to his sick wife. The schoolmaster broke his parole and flagged down the train before it reached the section of track which the gang had pulled up. The troops disembarked and

Ned Kelly on the eve of his execution at 26 years of age. (Taken from Alan Sierp, *Colonial Life in Victoria: Fifty Years of Photography*, Adelaide, 1972)

Redmond Barry, the Irish-born judge who presided over the mis-trial of Ned Kelly and passed the death sentence on the outlaw. (Taken from Sierp, *Colonial Life in Victoria*)

made their way in the darkness to the Glenrowan Hotel, where they encountered the gang wearing the heavy home-made armour which they had manufactured out of ploughshares. Ned and the gang had believed that the armour would render them impervious to the fire from the police, but the armour extended only to the waist, and did not cover their arms, although their heads were encased in heavy metal helmets. It was a huge tactical mistake, for Ned had sacrificed his most effective weapon—mobility—in order to make a static defence against overwhelming odds and firepower.

In the initial exchange of gunfire in front of the hotel, Ned received a severe wound to his right hand and elbow, and a rifle bullet tore through his big toe and out the back of his right heel. The other members were also wounded. The gang retreated into the hotel, and a full-scale siege ensued. The legend of Ned's bravery gained further lustre during the siege, as he slipped out of the hotel to warn his supporters not to come to his aid, and to disperse before the authorities recognised any of them. He then passed out from loss of blood. When he came to, the fight was still raging, and Ned lurched out of the bush to the rear of the attackers—looking like an apparition from hell in the dull dawn light which was wreathed with the smoke and fog of battle. His armour was covered with a cloak, and he banged a pistol on the breastplate of his armour and challenged the police to come and fight him. He began to walk towards the police lines and directly into a hail of gunfire. Eventually, he was brought down by a shotgun blast to the legs, and was captured by the police. The other three members of his gang were killed during the siege or in the fire that later burned the hotel to the ground.

When questioned by reporters from Melbourne—who had accompanied the police to Glenrowan—about why he had not made his escape from such an obviously lost cause when he regained consciousness in the bush, Ned replied simply: 'A man would be a nice sort of dingo to walk out on his mates'.[14]

Nor was the possibility of escape merely academic. During his final shootout with the police, Ned's horse—a grey mare named *Music*, of which he was enormously fond and which was, in her turn, devoted to him—galloped into the gunfire and came looking for him. She found him, and the badly wounded outlaw—he was shot twenty-eight times—could have mounted her and escaped. But witnesses noticed that, as Music galloped towards him, Ned waved her away, and a police marksman then shot her down. A second time, however, she struggled to her feet and came to him through the battle, and once again Ned Kelly waved her away—whereupon she galloped out of the siege and into the legend.

At his trial, Ned received the sort of summary justice that he had always expected. The judge, Sir Redmond Barry, misdirected the jury—to the point that a later Chief Justice of Victoria was to claim that the trial had been a travesty, and that Ned Kelly had been the victim of unfair judicial procedures. He received a sentence of death, and, despite a petition for mercy carrying 60 000 signatures, he was hanged at Pentridge Prison on 11 November 1880. His mother, also serving time in Pentridge, visited him in the condemned cell. Her advice to him was reported to be: 'Mind you die like a Kelly, son'.[15]

He took the admonition to heart, mounted the scaffold unaided, and, just before the drop, he uttered the words: 'Such is life ... OR ... I suppose it had to come to this'.[16]

He was twenty-six years of age.

Ned Kelly has passed into the mythology of outback Australia as a symbol of the rural poor, the champion of the underdog, and the protector of the defenceless. He epitomised those characteristics of the bushman that were most widely admired—loyalty to one's mates whatever the cost, bravery and courage in the face of adversity, resourcefulness and the ability to survive by one's wits, disdain for the police as creatures of the rich, and living and dying by a code of honour that was beyond the reach of his social superiors.

26

Aboriginal Sorcery—Singing a Man to Death in Northern Australia

What was the connection between a land-based spirituality and a powerful sorcery in Aboriginal Australia? How was a person 'sung to death'? And why did European Australians appear to be immune to such magic?

In traditional Aboriginal culture in the northern regions of Australia, there are two levels of reality. First, there is the world of day-to-day experience—which is perceivable with our physical senses. Secondly, there is the Dreaming—which dates back to the time before time began; which is experienced with the subtle psychic senses; and which originated and interpenetrates the physical plane.

Aboriginal culture conceptualises itself in an abiding relationship with both of these levels of being. According to Aboriginal spirituality the sacred speech learnt at initiation provides the practitioner with access to the supernatural powers responsible for the Dreamtime creative process.

In the beginning was the Word, and the Word was with God, and the Word was God.

This verse from the Gospel according to St John articulates the connection in Western culture between speech and the act of creation. In traditional Aboriginal culture a similar truth is propounded. Aborigines believe that the sacred speech of the Ancestral Beings was responsible for giving form and life to the earth. The world existed only as a group of potential possibilities until the great Spirit Ancestors awoke and brought our world into existence.

The Ancestors slumbered dormant beneath the earth's crust through the ages. On the morning of the first day, the Sun—feeling the urge to take birth—burst through the surface and bathed the land with nurturing warmth. This aroused the Ancestral Beings who emerged from the earth and initiated creation by calling out the name of each animal, plant and geographical feature. With each step they called into being a new aspect of the world, and they journeyed over huge distances. When creation was completed the Spirit Ancestors returned to rest beneath the earth's surface where they remain today.

These great Ancestral Beings were not human, although they sometimes took human (and sometimes animal) shapes. They were vast unbounded vibratory bodies or fields of energy. The naming-act stabilised this energy in a particular form. The name therefore vibrates with the inner essence of the creative power, and the inner nature of the thing created. The web of song or energy-grid which brought the world into being, and which maintains it in existence, is known as 'songlines', and, together, the songlines embody the creative energies of the many different Ancestral Beings. Although the Ancestors have returned beneath the earth, they have left residues of their powerful boundless energy vibrating in the world. Sometimes this has a physical location, and such a place becomes a sacred site, but otherwise the songlines connect the earth and everything on and beneath its surface into a sacred relationship. This links together humanity, earth and its creatures, and the cosmos—like beads on a shared thread of life-force. For Aborigines the earth is not inert, but is vibrating ceaselessly with the undiminished potency of these slumbering spiritual powers.

Furthermore, the songlines provide a sort of psychic map to a shared cosmos, linking places and people together in indissoluble relation with one another. Some modern scientists claim that words are a structural part of a neural pattern concerning the world. When a word is uttered, the brain constructs an image of the corresponding object or quality. In a similar sort of way, Aboriginal society recognises the esoteric power of words, especially of names, as providing access to fields of energy established by the Ancestral Beings. Ngarinyin elder, David Mowaljarli, from the north-west of Western Australia puts it simply when he says, 'Words carry the spirit, you know?' For example, it is forbidden to speak the name of a dead person because the name could summon the ghost of the departed. Speech and chanting therefore vibrate with power—especially when sacred words are used—because they replicate the vibration and tune into the awesome potency of these primordial energies.

In Aboriginal Australia, from the moment of birth, babies received the first of a series of revelations concerning themselves and their relationship to the world. The midwives took the newly born infants and wrapped a piece of the umbilical cords around the children's throats. This symbolised a spiritual connection which permitted the young ones to be taught the language of sacred knowledge linking them with their progenitors—the Ancestral Beings. Next, the midwives would breathe into the children's nostrils the sacred totemic names of the children—which connected them forever to the place where they were born and to the totemic spirits of their clans. It was believed that babies were born from the earth itself and that the physical mother merely provided the medium through which the spirit took birth. For this reason, the relationship with the land—and particularly the energy fields of the birthing site—transcended the relationship with the physical parents. As a further symbol of this connection with the powers inherent in the land, the placentas were usually buried at the birthing site.

Top: 'Bone–pointing ritual enacted by two Clever Men'. (Baldwin Spencer and F.J. Gillen, *Across Australia*, London, 1912)

Bottom: 'Clever Man extracting evil magic from a victim'. (G.H. Knibbs (ed.) *Federal Handbook prepared for the Eighty-Fourth Meeting of the British Association of the Advancement of Science*, Melbourne, 1914)

For the remainder of their lives, Aboriginal persons would undergo successive levels of initiation—some involuntary and unavoidable; but others purely voluntary—in which a new sacred language was passed on and deeper and more profound levels of understanding were imparted. Each initiation brought a new language—or an extension of vocabulary—to enable these mysteries to be crystallised, and both the creative and destructive potentialities of words were clearly recognised.

On Mornington Island, for example, a man undergoing initiation into the ranks of the sorcerers was taught an entirely distinct and different language from that in daily use; and the Lardil tribe possessed three different languages—each one used for different occasions. Aborigines feared and respected the fully initiated 'Clever Men' or Kadaitcha Men—very rare and powerful sorcerers—because they possessed the knowledge to unleash death and destruction, or to bring about miraculous healing, by using the power of speech to key into the energy fields left by the Ancestors, and to project that power into any person they chose. The secret lay in special incantations which gave them power over the spirits of the living and the dead. It was not necessary for the targets to be physically present for a Clever Man to produce a powerful impact upon them.

A sorcerer from Mornington Island described his powers in the following way:

> See that man sitting over there? I sing or chant a curse at him—it doesn't matter whether I can see him or not—and I point the bone at him as I sing. If that song is right the man will feel as though a bullet or stone hit his body. The pain will get worse every day until he fades away to skin and bone and dies.[17]

There are four principal elements involved in singing a person to death in the bone-pointing ritual:

- The first and most important is that the song be chanted correctly. Only a precisely modulated chant will enable the Clever Man to access the energy field and empower his curse.
- The second is the bone itself. The bones of birds are most effective, although human or animal bones can also be used. There are occasional accounts of this ritual in which a sharpened stick replaces the bone.
- The third aspect is the string of human hair attached to the hand-held end of the bone. This can be used to increase the force of the curse when the sorcerer has an assistant kneel behind him holding the end of the string while the Clever Man points the bone/stick in the direction of the victim. Both sorcerer and assistant chant the song and thereby magnify the virulence of the curse.

- The fourth component is a lump of wax or a stone attached to the handled end of the bone by the hair-string. The bone/stick usually acts as a projecting agent which focuses the supernatural energy, and discharges the psychic essence of the stone or wax into the body of the victim where it infects the blood.

The chanting by the sorcerer taps into the force-field of the songlines, and transforms this non-physical power into an energy source which is used to 'fire' the psychic projectile. The victim sickens with fevers and pain, and, unless the singing is withdrawn by the sorcerer, or another Clever Man counteracts the singing with a protective ritual, the death of the victim occurs in a short space of time. Europeans have often put this down to auto-suggestion, but there is no doubting the effectiveness of singing somebody to death. We are fortunate to have an account of this ritual from a prospective victim who survived due to the timely intervention of a friendly sorcerer:

> My skin was hot. My stomach felt as though it would soon come to the boil. My limbs trembled ... My heart palpitated, my head ached, and I sweated profusely ... Until the moment when I first felt ill I was happy and carefree. I was as healthy as any Aboriginal boy can be. I had no thought of violence or malevolence or death. Yet within a few minutes I was running a high fever and my stomach was boiling.
>
> I have been asked how such an illness can be attributed to auto-suggestion when I had been unaware of symptoms until the very moment I was struck down. I can say only that that is how it happened to me and has happened to others. I believe that a person who has been 'sung' knows about it instinctively and begins to react physically long before his conscious mind communicates the reaction to him ...
>
> The curse was upon me, insidiously destroying my mind and body. I would reject all food and water. I would defaecate where I lay. I would groan and grovel, twitching in an agony of muscular contraction until the day, perhaps a week, perhaps two weeks hence, when I would scream at the hideous picture in my mind, ignoring the equal horror of my physical degeneration, and die the most terrible of deaths.[18]

A person who is 'sung' usually dies. Occasionally, when the intended victim can be treated by European doctors, and also removed from the tribal environment, a recovery does take place. In more recent times, the power of the Clever Men seems to have diminished. For example, in the 1950s, a young tribesman named Lya Wulumu was 'sung' at Yirrkalla mission in north-eastern Arnhem Land following a complaint by his mother-in-law to the sorcerer about the young man's unfaithfulness to her daughter. Once Wulumu had realised that he had been 'sung', he developed complete paralysis, and, within hours, had lapsed into unconsciousness. The flying doctor transported Wulumu to Darwin where he was placed under the care of Dr Jim Tarleton Rayment. Wulumu's respiratory system collapsed and he had to be put into an iron lung. Every time he was removed his breathing stopped. Eventually Dr Rayment convinced the young man that modern European medicine was stronger than the rituals of a Clever Man, and Wulumu made a complete recovery, even returning to live on his tribal land.

Such recoveries may explain the relative decline of Aboriginal sorcerers, but it may also be that no Aborigines in this modern age are prepared to undergo the intense discipline and prolonged training necessary to become an Aboriginal man of high degree. There are no cases of Europeans succumbing to the singing and bone-pointing ritual, yet we also know that sorcery was directed at the whites during the colonial days, which suggests that a strong element of psychosomatic interaction at the subconscious or unconscious level may be necessary for the powers of the Aboriginal sorcerer to come fully into play.

27

Israel in the Kimberleys

How, when, and why did Australia almost become the site of the State of Israel? Who was Isaac Steinberg and how did he almost succeed in his enterprise? And why did he ultimately fail?

At Basel in Switzerland, in 1897, the first Zionist Congress was held. It passed a number of resolutions that have become known as the Baseler Program, and the final outcome of that program was the establishment of the modern State of Israel in 1948, to provide a homeland for the Jews who had survived the Nazi holocaust. But, at the time of the first Zionist Congress, a Jewish homeland in the country known as Palestine was by no means a foregone conclusion, and, in the decade prior to the outbreak of World War II, a proposal to locate a Jewish settlement in the Kimberley region of Western Australia received a great deal of support—both from within and outside Australia. Perhaps it was only the intervention of the war that stopped Israel from being established in this country rather than in the Middle East.

The congress in Basel had called for a home for the Jews to be located in Palestine, and, although they flirted with Uganda for a short time, from then on most Zionists worked towards the return of Jews to their original homeland. But not all Jews were Zionists, and there were many who accepted the need for a Jewish home wherever it could be established. They eventually formed the Jewish Territorialist Association, and, in opposition to Zionism, the Territorialists concentrated on establishing a Jewish homeland elsewhere in the world, which could be run as an independent state. In the late-nineteenth and early-twentieth centuries, Jewish settlers were set up as farmers by the Jewish philanthropist, Baron Maurice de Hirsch, in Argentina, Brazil, Canada, and the United States of America, but, rather than forming a new embryonic nation, the colonists abandoned their farms and melted into the cities of their new countries.

As part of this search for a homeland, the Territorialists approached the Australian Government in 1907 and in 1910, but on each occasion the proposal was rejected because no Australian government—either state or federal—would countenance the idea of an independent country existing in their territory.

Nevertheless, as conditions in Germany deteriorated for the Jews throughout the 1930s, the Territorialists resolved to try again. In London, in 1935, they formed the Freeland League for Jewish Territorial Colonisation, and determined

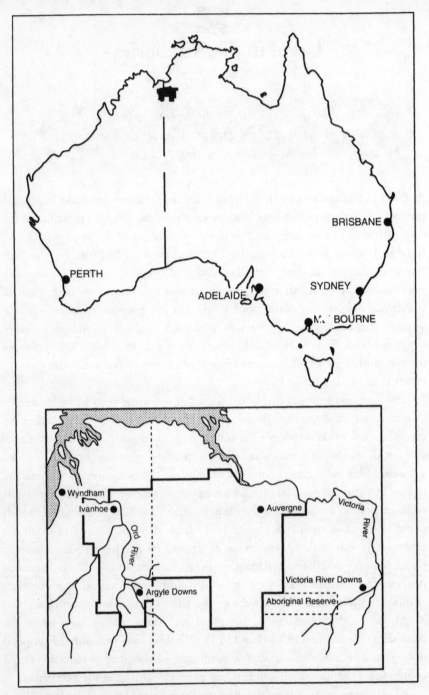

Area of the proposed Jewish Settlement. (Leon Gettler)

to build a Jewish colony in some unoccupied part of the world to act as a safe haven for their people. The new territory would have to satisfy four main criteria:

- First, it had to be empty or sparsely populated—as they did not want friction between the incoming Jewish settlers and the local population.
- Secondly, it had to have a tolerable climate, fertile soils, and adequate water resources.
- Thirdly, the host country had to be a democracy which would allow the settlers to prosper and develop without hindrance and obstruction.
- Finally, the host country had to be sufficiently large to be able to absorb thousands of Jewish refugees.

In May 1936, the Freeland League approached the Australian Minister for Trade, Earle Page, when he arrived in London, with a proposal to establish 10 000 Jewish families in northern Australia. Page was interested—because Australia had become very aware of the tenuous hold which the tiny population of Europeans in northern Australia actually possessed. The government was definitely interested in northern development for security reasons. Thus encouraged, the League persevered with its proposal, and had a number of meetings with the High Commissioner for Australia in London, the former Prime Minister, Sir Stanley Melbourne Bruce. By 1939, the deteriorating conditions in Europe, and the continued nibbles of interest from Australia, resulted in a visit to Australia by Dr Isaac Steinberg, one of the co-founders of the Freeland League.

One of the main reservations expressed by the Australian Government was its reluctance to permit the establishment of a foreign ghetto—which could result in future racial conflict between the incoming Jews and the homogeneous Anglo/Celtic population of Australia. One of the first enactments passed through the new Federal Parliament, in 1901, had been an Act to restrict the immigration of non-white settlers to Australia. This had been largely designed to keep out coloured folk—including Asians. However, in 1911, the restrictions had been quietly extended to include European migrants who were in the 'not-wanted-because-not-British' category. Russian Jews had been included in this group.

Isaac Steinberg therefore had his work cut out for him when he arrived in Australia, armed with letters of introduction—from prominent British politicians and businessmen—to the Australian Labor Party, and to the United Australia Party. Clearly, he hoped to appeal to both sides of the political divide, and the record shows that such aspirations were not ill-placed. Steinberg must have possessed enormous charisma, for he also obtained the support of the mainstream Christian churches in Australia for his proposed Jewish settlement in the Kimberleys—largely on humanitarian grounds. Most sensitive people were profoundly disturbed at what was being done to Jews in Hitler's Germany, and

Isaac Steinberg during the
1920s. (Leon Gettler)

church leaders were no more immune to this feeling than were their flocks. In addition, Isaac Steinberg himself had been a member of the Russian Socialist Revolutionary Party which formed a coalition with Lenin's Bolsheviks in 1917, and Steinberg had been Lenin's first Minister for Justice—before finding himself purged and imprisoned by the Bolsheviks in 1918, and deported altogether in 1923. Thus, his revolutionary credentials were also beyond doubt, and this swung the support of the trade-union movement behind his plans.

In Western Australia, the State Government under Premier Willcock enthusiastically touted the benefits of northern development—especially in the face of the aggressive and expansionist behaviour of Japan in Manchuria and in Chinese cities like Nanking. As far as Western Australia was concerned, the only serious question to be asked was: 'Are we going to have Jews or Japs?'. At the federal level, the Menzies' government was very sympathetic to Steinberg's blueprint, and hoped that a Jewish settlement would provide something of a bulwark against a Japanese invasion from the north.

In addition to the necessary political backing, Isaac Steinberg had also secured an agreement from the Durack family—who had opened up the Kimberley region as an extensive series of cattle runs more than fifty years earlier—that they and the other northern pastoralists would sell their vast holdings to the Freeland League for 200 000 pounds, and that the League would acquire all rights to the land, buildings, and cattle in the territory.

Everything seemed to be progressing towards the realisation of the League's dreams, but superficial appearances were deceptive. In fact, there was a groundswell of opposition to the planned Jewish colony—and it came from a variety of sources.

First, there were the bigots who opposed Steinberg simply because he was Jewish, and opposed the colony on the grounds that Australia would be flooded with people they described as Refujews. Secondly, there were those who pointed to the harshness of the Kimberley region, and doubted that inexperienced Jewish refugees would be able to survive there. After all, it was some of the toughest country in Australia, and had broken the hearts of many of the pioneers, and they at least had known what they were doing. There were also fears expressed that it would be impossible to quarantine the Jewish settlers to the Kimberleys. What was to stop them heading for the coastal cities once they had arrived in the north? Wasn't this what had happened in the earlier Jewish settlements in South and North America? Might not the Freeland League's plan result in a massive influx of European Jews into the capital cities of Australia?

Australia's premier anthropologist, A.P. Elkin, argued against the proposed settlement on the grounds that it would effectively obliterate the Aboriginal culture that had existed in the region for thousands of years. The Aborigines would be swamped under thousands of Jews, and their culture would disappear. Others argued that the country was too harsh for European women, and that it would be a great cruelty to force them to go there.

Finally, the (federal) Department of the Interior was extremely sceptical about demands for Jewish cultural autonomy and large-scale immigration, on the grounds that it would lead to the creation of 'a state within a state', and that, far from strengthening Australia, such a development could fatally undermine it.

In any event, the march of history overtook Isaac Steinberg before he could perfect his plans and bring them to fruition. In August 1939, the German Army roared into Poland, and the world dissolved into six years of horror and bloodshed. Settlement proposals for the Kimberleys were regarded as unimportant in the wartime emergency. After the war, the Australian Government favoured a policy of assimilation—under which newcomers would be encouraged to submerge their old identities and cultures in their new home. The government was no longer sympathetic to the preservation of cultures within a host culture, and Steinberg's plans could not be revived. Besides, the Zionist proposal for a Jewish homeland in Palestine now had the backing of most of the world's statesmen.

The day had passed for a proposal to locate Israel in Australia to be taken at all seriously.

28

Sarah Wentworth—the Whore of Sydney

How did the wife of the most important politician in colonial New South Wales come to find herself haunted by her own past? Why did sexist colonial society forgive her husband, but never his wife? What did the Governor's wife think of all of this? And does exile extinguish love for one's native land?

Sarah Wentworth became the wife of William Charles Wentworth—the most influential man in colonial society in New South Wales during the first half of the nineteenth century. Yet her life was anything but easy, and, in the end, both she and her husband chose to live out their final years in exile, rather than endure the slights and abuse aimed at them by Sydney's arriviste high society.

Sarah and William were both born illegitimate, the children of convict parents, and, although this was not at all uncommon in the colony in those days, it did mean that their behaviour forever would be scrutinised for evidence of whether or not they had inherited any predilection for criminal and immoral behaviour. The fact that they were the products of long-standing common-law relationships—rather than of a casual fling by their parents—apparently did not improve their suspect moral status.

In New South Wales, Francis Cox, blacksmith, and Fanny Morton, milliner, lived together for more than thirty years. They were unable to regularise their union, because Francis had left a wife behind in England when he had been transported in 1790. Therefore, when Sarah was born in 1805, she bore the badge of bastardy. Similarly, William, born in 1790, was the illegitimate son of a highwayman father, D'Arcy Wentworth—who had left England after plea-bargaining by his influential family to avoid a formal conviction—and Catherine Crowley, a convict girl. Catherine died after producing three children to D'Arcy Wentworth, who lived a life of considerable notoriety, and fathered a further eight children with another long-term partner in subsequent years.

In a looking-glass world like convict Sydney, only the most exemplary lives could outweigh such parentage—and William and Sarah proved anything but exemplary.

In 1824, William had returned from England, where he had been educated, and had become a barrister. Within a year he had made the acquaintance of Sarah Cox who worked as a milliner's apprentice in a shop near to where William

A formal Government House Ball, of the type from which Sarah Wentworth was excluded all her life in New South Wales.

had set up his practice. By 1825, when Sarah won a law suit for breach-of-promise against her fiancé John Payne, the two had already become lovers—although William did not let this stop him from representing Sarah in the legal action in which she described herself as a good and respectable girl. The successful prosecution for breach-of-promise created a sensation in the colony at the time, for it was the first case of its kind in colonial Australia. Sarah was awarded damages of 100 pounds for the damage to her reputation from the broken engagement, despite implications during the case that she was promiscuous.

In December 1825, Sarah gave birth to their first child—a daughter named Thomasine—in the house which William had rented for them in the suburb of Petersham. The baby was christened the following month as the child of Sarah Cox and William Charles Wentworth. More children followed. When William purchased the estate of 105 acres (42 hectares), including a house, stables, detached kitchen, dairy, gardens, and orchard, at Vaucluse—now known as *Vaucluse House*—in 1827, he installed Sarah as his mistress and partner, and she, heavily pregnant again, became the lady of the house. Their son was born at Vaucluse in December 1827. Two years later, Sarah and her children were still living at Vaucluse with Wentworth. She was expecting their third child when William amazed and scandalised Sydney society by marrying his mistress.

According to the moral standards of the time, there was nothing really wrong in Wentworth having a mistress. Gentlemen were expected to gather sexual experience before they married. Nor was it an unacceptable thing that he had acknowledged fathering children by his mistress. What was required in such circumstances was that he do 'the right thing', and make some financial provision for the children's futures. For Sarah also, the relationship did not spell social outlawry, as it was expected that a gentleman would settle a comfortable annuity on, or make a generous financial gift to, a former mistress when he had tired of her. Such a settlement meant that the woman became quite an attractive marriage prospect with a handsome dowry at the lower levels of society from which mistresses were usually drawn. What was completely unacceptable, was that a gentleman of wealth and education—such as William—should actually *marry* his mistress, the uneducated daughter of a blacksmith. In the eyes of polite society, Sarah would have been considered unmarriageable—given that she was living in sin as the ill-educated, dowerless daughter of two convicts. Sarah and William had violated one of the unwritten conventions of so-called 'respectable' society— and they would pay a heavy price for the rest of their lives.

Wentworth's philandering was notorious—in addition to fathering ten children by Sarah, he also acknowledged a clutch of other children with assorted women in Sydney. However, the double standards of the day meant that William could still be associated with by the male members of high society in business and club, while Sarah was ostracised—as *that damned whore*—by the female section of society, who refused ever to visit her, or to invite her to visit them. Sarah Wentworth lived a life of loneliness and isolation in her grand house at Vaucluse, and it made no difference that marriage had legitimised the relationship.

The design of the house itself reflected the social isolation imposed on the Wentworths. Most of the houses of that era were entered through an imposing entrance hall in which visitors had to wait while the family decided on how they were to be greeted, and what degree of familiarity would be appropriate. At suppers and balls, the host and hostess would greet their guests there before ushering them into the correct rooms for the night's entertainment. But *Vaucluse House*, when Sarah and William were in residence, was entered through a simple gate, and thence by crossing a courtyard—which took the visitor into the kitchen, the office, or the residential sections of the house. The architecture dispensed with the formal entrance, in a mute recognition of Sarah's status as a social pariah.

As her children grew, so the effects of this isolation developed and were compounded. Sarah was insufficiently well educated to take over the job of teaching her children, and they received their education at Sydney day schools. Moreover, the Wentworths had seven daughters, who would eventually expect to enjoy the same social activities as other young women of similar rank and means. Yet Sarah was excluded from all the social events of the colony, and was therefore unable to chaperone her daughters or introduce them into society where they could find suitable husbands. Girls from well-to-do families with social pretensions could do little in Sydney at that time that did not involve chaperones. They were usually kept in seclusion at home until they reached 17 or 18 years of age, when they made their debut in society at one of the regular balls held at Government House. There they would be presented to the Governor and would then be eligible to attend the other balls, parties, and entertainments held so that the sons and daughters of the gentry could meet one another, and marriage contracts could be negotiated by their parents or guardians. The focus of social life in New South Wales was Government House—the residence of the presiding vice-regal representative. In 1832, Eliza Darling, the former governor's wife, wrote to one of her correspondents describing the treatment meted out to Sarah Wentworth—and the moral and class reasons behind her continued exclusion:

> It was thought that people ought to be born and educated as gentlefolks before they should be admitted to Government House. Mr Wentworth himself—as a Barrister, educated at Oxford—might certainly have been asked, but his Wife, having lived with him for years, has only recently become his wife, and when we left, used to sit at a Stall selling Beef in consequence of the very low price of Cattle and Mr Wentworth having so many Thousands he had set up a butcher shop.[19]

When Governor Richard Bourke visited Vaucluse in February 1836, it provoked a tide of vicious gossip that he had had some formal contact with Sarah by dining with the Wentworths, and William was forced to publish a statement to restore the Governor's reputation, in which he acknowledged that the Governor had merely inspected the building works.

In New South Wales, the most prestigious social event of the year was the celebration of the monarch's birthday, and the premier event was the Queen's Birthday Ball hosted by the Governor and his lady at Government House. In 1846, the newly arrived Sir Charles Fitzroy sent out invitations for the gala event. Unfortunately, his son broke his leg in a fall, and Fitzroy was forced to postpone the ball. The delay afforded the local press time to discuss the guest list, and great exception was taken to the inclusion of people of doubtful reputation—especially Sarah Wentworth. By this time, William had become one of the most prominent political figures in the colony, and during the preceding decade he had been the acknowledged champion of the emancipated convicts and the native-born children they produced. In taking this stance he had made many enemies among the conservative 'exclusives', who prided themselves on family bloodlines that were free of convict taint. These people hid their snobbishness behind the screen of moral concern, and used the columns of the *Sydney Morning Herald* to launch a cowardly attack on Sarah Wentworth, in which everybody recognised the target, but to which William could not reply because they did not mention her by name:

> Damaged female characters ... albeit they had been completely and clerically repaired, should be uncompromisingly shut out ... Whenever a woman falls, she falls forever ... She becomes as it were socially dead ... There should be no statute of limitation enacted for the relief of female error. Should the reader have a wife or sister, he would not desire that she should be at any time introduced to a reformed lady of easy virtue, however romantic, peculiar or pitiable her individual case.[20]

Sarah's private world was also the scene of pain and rejection. In 1844, William and Sarah's eldest daughter, Thomasine, married a lawyer named Thomas John Fisher who was the nephew of William's former business partner Dr Robert Wardell. Fisher was caught between awe of William's political influence and fear of the social consequences of forming a matrimonial connection with the Wentworth family, and he refused before the wedding even to join the family for a dinner at *Vaucluse House*. Nonetheless, William and Sarah were extremely fond of Thomasine, and William gave her a splendid dowry in the form of land at Vaucluse, land in the city of Sydney, and more at Bathurst. Fisher responded, as soon as the wedding had been performed, by forbidding his wife any social contact with her parents at any time—in public or even in private. This ban lasted for twenty years, and the only contact Sarah had with her daughter was the occasional letter.

After enduring decades of humiliation, and following the death of her much-loved parents, Sarah and William determined to travel to England. Sarah hoped to be able to arrange good marriages for her other daughters in an environment where her past would not be continually flung in her face. In February 1853 she sailed for England accompanied by one son and six daughters. William joined them the following year.

Life on the other side of the world proved to be far less stressful. Sarah found that she could, at last, become the hostess that her role as William's wife dictated, and the Wentworths entertained widely in London and in Paris. They rented houses in a variety of fashionable locations in Britain and in Europe, so that their girls could obtain the education befitting their status as children of one of the wealthiest men in colonial Australia. Their girls attended schools, had governesses, and, in general, mixed with the daughters of the best families. The pall of oppressive restriction was lifted from Sarah, and she blossomed in the freer atmosphere.

In 1861, Sarah and William returned briefly to Australia, and on this visit

Sarah entertained—for the first and last time in her own country—when they gave a ball in Sydney, which was attended by the Governor and his wife, and by most of the members of the Legislature and their wives. She had finally lived down the taunts that she was nothing more than a 'whore'. Within a month, they sailed again for England, and never returned to their homeland which had been the scene of so much personal pain and humiliation. William died in 1872, and Sarah died eight years later in 1880.

Sarah never ceased to pine for Australia and to identify with the country of her birth. In England, she wrote sadly: 'Gumtrees cannot flourish in the snow'.[21]

29

The Rebellion at the Eureka Stockade

What were the reasons behind Australia's most important attempt at armed rebellion? Why were the rebels not punished by the courts when the rebellion had been quashed? Why were foreigners blamed for the rising? And who was the foreigner who produced that enduring symbol of radical Australian nationalism—the Eureka Flag?

Gold was first discovered in payable quantities at Bathurst, in New South Wales, in 1851—and the first Australian goldrush began. The goldrushes in California during 1848 and 1849 had captured the imagination of the world, and the news of further discoveries in Australia only served to heighten the already rampant tide of hysteria that was sweeping across Western Europe and Asia. Migrants from all the Australian colonies joined the influx of overseas immigrants drawn to New South Wales by the lure of gold; and the newly independent colony of Victoria—now separated from New South Wales—faced the alarming prospect of losing the bulk of its population, as men streamed north towards Bathurst.

The new colony of Victoria attempted to deal with this problem by offering rewards for the first payable goldfields discovered in its territory, and very soon prospectors announced the existence of the fabulously wealthy alluvial fields at Ballarat and Bendigo. People flooded into Victoria. The population leapt from 97 000 in 1851 to 168 000 in 1852, and thereafter it increased by about 60 000 a year for the next three years. By 1861, Victoria's population stood at well over half a million.

Such huge increases in population posed a genuine problem for the administrations of these two Australian colonies caught up in the goldrushes. How was law and order to be maintained on the goldfields, and how were the additional police and soldiers—to say nothing of goldfield administrators and their staff—to be recruited and paid? The authorities in both New South Wales and Victoria resolved to issue licences to the gold diggers. The revenue raised by this expedient would cover the additional costs of administration, while the payment of the licence fee by the diggers constituted a tacit acknowledgment by them of the Crown's legal right to ownership of all minerals found in British territories. Failure to possess a valid licence meant that the digger was effectively stealing crown property, and was liable to suffer criminal proceedings at law.

The moonscape terrain of the Ballarat goldfields. Such harsh conditions of life in the heat of an Australian summer may well have helped precipitate the Eureka insurgency. (Taken from Alan Sierp, *Colonial Life in Victoria: Fifty Years of Photography*, Adelaide, 1972)

The licence system caused great outrage among the miners:

- First, the licence had to be purchased in advance, and it cost one pound ten shillings per month—at a time when a rural labourer was paid only two pounds a month and keep. The price seemed extravagantly high to working-class men.
- Secondly, it had to be paid irrespective of the digger's success or lack of success in his search for gold. Miners who struck it rich found no problem paying the licence fee, but it became a definite cause of resentment among the majority who enjoyed only moderate or no success.

The licence system on the Victorian diggings was rendered even more explosive by the excessively low calibre of the police employed to enforce the law. Many of the officers had been recruited from the convict colony of Van Diemen's Land where they had been employed as overseers of convict work gangs, and many of the rank and file had actually served time as convicts. Stories abounded of their arrogance, corruption, and brutality, and the troopers—or 'Joes' as they were known to the miners—soon became the most hated people on the goldfields.

It was the policy of frequent licence-checking to which the diggers objected most vociferously. The law insisted that a miner must carry his licence on his person at all times, and produce it on demand to a duly authorised officer. This presented a difficulty, for the licences were made of paper, and the men often worked waist-deep in water, at the bottom of shafts that were up to 100 feet deep. They sometimes worked underground accumulating a load of gravel—or 'washing stuff'—which they then had to carry long distances to the nearest creek or river where they panned out the gold. The police specialised in stopping miners thus engaged and asking them to produce their licences. Men sometimes had to come to the top of their shafts—or 'ground' their heavy load of gravel— many times in a single day, thus wasting valuable time at the whim of corrupt men who were intent on reinforcing their authority through systematic intimidation. Failure to produce a licence because of working in water was no excuse. They were still hauled unceremoniously before the resident commissioner, who was also a magistrate, and fined—even if they actually possessed a licence which they kept in their tent to protect it against disintegration.

This state of affairs meant that extraordinary tensions were rising on the fields around Ballarat just as the alluvial gold began to show signs of running out. By 1854, there were ominous portents that the days of a single digger or a group of friends working in partnership were almost gone. A switch to deep-lead mining—with crushing plants and machinery requiring heavy capitalisation— was well under way, and gave an added sense of urgency to the efforts of the miners to change the hated licence system.

A series of public meetings was held in November 1854 by the miners at Ballarat to express their indignation over the licence system and the arrogant behaviour of the goldfields police. These meetings became expressions of a radical political program, in which the diggers demanded universal manhood suffrage for the Victorian legislature, and payment for members of Parliament. In this way, they hoped to be able to elect members to the Legislative Assembly from their own ranks who could represent their interests, and make the administration aware of the miners' point of view. A local issue of law and order—involving the trial of a publican and two employees on charges of murdering a digger at the Eureka Hotel—complicated matters, and gave added point to complaints about the corruption of the goldfield's administration. The men had been acquitted at a trial before a local magistrate who was notorious for accepting bribes, and the miners believed that the accused men had purchased their acquittal. Some of the men had burned down the hotel, and a few had been arrested and charged with incendiarism. Anger over the local concerns fuelled the volatility of the public meetings.

The large meetings were harangued by a strange assortment of would-be leaders. There were Americans, there was a German revolutionary named Frederic Vern, and an eccentric Italian follower of Garibaldi called Raffaello Carboni—and, of course, there were countless Irish immigrants, many of whom were imbued with a virulent hatred for England after the Great Famine of 1846–7. A Canadian digger—Charlie Ross from Toronto—together with his wife, produced a flag which was run up an eighty-foot pole on Bakery Hill where the meetings took place. All of a sudden, the disaffection began to take on a revolutionary appearance.

On 29 November, more than 10 000 miners assembled under the flag of the Southern Cross on Bakery Hill, and voted in favour of a motion proposed by the fire-eating Vern—that they all burn their licences in protest, and that they protect any digger who was threatened by the police for failure to produce a licence. This defiance, couched with threats of violence, brought roars of approval from the meeting. Revolvers and pistols were fired in the air and blazing licences were waved aloft.

The following morning, in a pig-headed response calculated to inflame the situation even further, the goldfields Commissioner, Robert Rede, ordered his troopers to conduct a licence hunt. The police were met with a volley of abuse and stones as they attempted to enter the field. Rede read the Riot Act and ordered the miners to disperse, and cavalrymen charged into the camp and arrested a number of diggers who were charged with failure to produce a licence. The troopers fired a volley of shots over the heads of the miners. To their surprise, a number of shots were fired in return from the seething camp. The police then retreated with their prisoners, while the miners assembled under their flag at Bakery Hill to discuss an appropriate answer to such extreme provocation.

There, an Irish miner named Peter Lalor galvanised the assembly when he mounted the stump and proclaimed 'Liberty'. Lalor came from a well-educated family in Ireland—he himself was an engineer—and he was well equipped to provide the leadership which the diggers had lacked to this point. He was a tall young man, just under six foot in height, with a beard and a scraggle of brown curly hair. More to the point, he spoke with a passion that mirrored the passion in the hearts of his receptive audience. With a rifle in his hand, Lalor called on volunteers to fall in, and he asked Carboni to tell those who could not understand English that, even if they did not own firearms, a piece of sharpened metal attached to a long stick would make a most effective pike. His Irish background was never more apparent than in that advice. The meeting then swore an oath, with Peter Lalor standing bare-headed and arm raised to the flag, that: 'We swear by the Southern Cross to stand truly by each other, and fight to defend our rights and liberties'.[22]

The diggers then withdrew to a nearby hill on the Eureka ore body mainly occupied by the Irish, where they erected a rough palisade of logs, over which they raised the Southern Cross flag. Then they took up positions behind the palisade to defy the police and the army.

There were 700–800 police and soldiers in the government camp at the beginning of the troubles on 1 December 1854, and a similar number of men in the insurgent camp—but the odds were anything but even in terms of experience and equipment. The miners did not own an impressive armoury, and those who were the possessors of firearms often had only one or two cartridges. As the Friday drew on and evening fell, men in the stockade began to slip away. Many were put off by the increasingly Irish nature of the affair. Three hundred miners from nearby Creswick, who had marched the eighteen kilometres behind a band playing the 'Marseillaise' that afternoon to join the rising, decided that they were not wanted and marched home again. Others were acutely aware of the stockaders' great shortage of arms and ammunition. And finally, as the cooler heads began to realise, the stockade signified a willingness to take up arms against the British Empire, and not many of them felt ready to take that fateful step. By Saturday night, there were fewer than 150 men left in the stockade, out of a goldfields' population in excess of 27 000 diggers.

It seemed obvious that the rebellion was fast running out of steam, and a couple more days of patient waiting by the authorities would have resulted in the whole episode becoming nothing more than an embarrassing memory for the miners. The problem was that, in the government camp, there were plenty who wanted desperately to inflict a humiliating defeat on the diggers. Robert Rede, for example, informed a local Roman Catholic priest—who tried to act as a go-between—that he regarded the agitation over licences as little more than a cloak to cover a democratic revolution.

Early in the morning of Sunday 3 December, more than 400 police and soldiers approached the stockade. When they were about 150 metres away, they encountered a ragged volley of fire from the defenders. In reply, the police and soldiers loosed two withering volleys of rifle fire, and then charged. After about ten minutes of hand-to-hand fighting, it was all over. The outnumbered stockaders were overwhelmed, their flag was hauled down, and the rebellion ended ignominiously. The troops behaved disgracefully at this point, bayoneting the wounded, and firing-off shots at random into the nearby mining camp, and into any tent that showed a light.

In its final form, the affair was largely confined to foreigners. The leaders were all born overseas, and all the casualties were foreign-born. Frederick Vern ran away when the attack began, but the others had stood up well under the pressure. Raffaello Carboni was captured at the stockade, and Peter Lalor escaped after receiving a severe wound in the left shoulder which necessitated the

Contemporary artist's depiction of the attack by government forces on the Eureka Stockade.
(Taken from Peter Coleman and Les Tanner, *Cartoons of Australian History*, Melbourne, 1967)

amputation of his left arm a few days later. Captain Charlie Ross, who produced the rebel flag of the Southern Cross, died beneath it in the battle. The rebel leaders were all of Irish, American, German, Italian, and Canadian origin, and most of the dead and wounded were Irish. There are no native-born colonists to be found among the leadership or the casualties at the Eureka rebellion. Vern and Carboni both left the country, and Peter Lalor went on to a career as a Member of the Victorian Parliament—with a rather conservative political outlook.

Only the Eureka Flag came out of the affair with increased and lasting stature, and it has become, fittingly, the flag of radical Australian nationalism that is instantly recognised by all Australians today. Canadian Charlie Ross produced an enduring symbol at Eureka, and symbols are the only positive outcome of that dramatic affray.

30

Australians in the Boxer Rebellion

When did Australians first take part in a military expedition against China? Why did they take up arms against the Chinese? How did inter-colonial rivalries shape the whole affair? And what is a 'Boxer' anyway?

By the final decades of the nineteenth century, the great powers of Europe and the United States of America had effectively divided China between themselves. Since the 1830s, when Britain had fought the first of a series of Opium Wars—to force her way into the markets of the celestial empire, and to balance the flow of trade by forcing a reluctant Chinese Government to accede to the importation of large quantities of opium—the inroads of the West had gathered pace. By the end of that century, all the main trading powers of the day—including the Japanese and the Germans—had large territorial trading concessions in China. The balance of trade was completely reversed, and, in addition to the export of Chinese silks, cottons and tea in exchange for opium, the Chinese authorities saw vast amounts of silver leaving the country. In addition, by the 1890s, the trading concessions had become spheres of influence in which any country which possessed such a sphere in China would, *de facto*, run its affairs. To a proud people like the Chinese, who regarded all foreigners as barbarians, this was a humiliating position.

A nationalistic anti-foreigner movement began in China's isolated northern provinces, where opposition focused on two things—the impact of Christian missionaries and the impact of railways.

The architecture of Christian churches, with their spires and tall crosses, was contrary to the art of *feng-shui*—in which structures were placed so as to be in harmony with the spirits of the land and of nature. Moreover, the missionaries established teaching hospitals and schools, where Chinese children were taught to despise their traditional ways and beliefs, and in which the Chinese culture was undermined and disparaged. The missionaries also intervened in local customs, particularly where these involved the exposure of unwanted babies—who were almost always female. These children were rescued by the missionaries and taken to orphanages where they were brought up as Christians, and often trained to be lay missionaries.

Railways also caused feelings of great uneasiness, because of the way in which the locomotives snorted and puffed across the landscape, blowing large clouds of steam and sparks into the atmosphere. The railway lines intruded on the *feng-*

shui, and the survey and construction of many new lines caused much uneasiness. What Chinese peasant wanted to have fire-breathing dragons introduced into his district by these foreign devils?

The response to these incursions into Chinese society was the development of a secret society in northern China known as the *I He Chuan* society. The name translated into 'Righteous Harmony Fists', and it was only a short step for local European missionaries to start calling them 'Boxers'. The name stuck.

Boxers became the cutting-edge of the anti-foreign movement in China, and, during the 1890s, they grew in strength and influence as they concentrated on slaughtering foreign missionaries and their Christian converts. The Dowager Empress and her government became sympathisers, and many local Chinese provincial administrators threw in their lot with the Boxers because they recognised that their empress supported the movement. At length, the Manchu Government declared war on the foreigners, and the Chinese Army joined the Boxers in an attack on the foreign legations in Peking in the middle of June 1900—where they bottled-up the Europeans (and the handful of troops they had with them for guard duties and protection) in a siege that lasted for 55 days. In the meantime, the Boxers rampaged across China, killing over 200 foreigners and thousands of Christians and others thought to be too sympathetic to the 'hairy barbarian round-eyes'.

On 9 June 1900, the British Commander-in-Chief of the China Station, Admiral Sir Edward Seymour, landed a mixed force of European sailors and marines comprising over 2000 men—of whom 900 were British, 500 were German, 300 were Russian, with the rest made up of a miscellany of contingents from American, French, Italian, Japanese and Austrian warships. The corps also had seven pieces of artillery and a number of machine guns. As this force began the long march towards Peking, it met the Chinese Army and was defeated—with heavy casualties—being then compelled to take up a defensive position in a fort north of Tientsin Harbour. The situation in the besieged legations had now become desperate, and, with communications cut and no relief able to get through, the Europeans expected that the legation populations would inevitably be captured, tortured, and slaughtered.

This was the dramatic situation to which the Australian colonies responded. The response was always going to be a naval one, because most of the colonial militia was already serving overseas in Britain's war against the Boers in South Africa, and it was proving increasingly difficult to recruit replacements for the South African campaign. The naval reserves, however, had originally volunteered for South African service and had been turned down—there not being all that much call for sailors in a land war against the Boers!

When the news reached Australia of the perilous position of the legations in

Peking, and the obvious need for the swift assembling of a military expedition to rescue or avenge them, the colonial governments quickly fell into line. The colony of Victoria offered a force first, and a keen sense of competition sprang up between the colonies to rival the Victorians. On 29 June, the Government of Victoria offered 200 well-trained naval men and officers, with two quick-firing guns to be despatched 'at our own expense'. Three days later, the South Australian Government offered their gunboat HMCS *Protector*—to be manned either by a British or a South Australian crew as the imperial authorities preferred—for service in the Chinese war. On 3 July the Government of New South Wales cabled Britain with an offer of the services of 300 officers and men of the colony's naval brigade, and Queensland proffered the use of her two antiquated gunboats. Within a week of the initial Victorian offer, all but the Queensland one had been accepted by the British—and the last-mentioned was rejected only on the grounds of the age and general decrepitude of the two vessels.

The Victorians proceeded at speed to assemble and prepare their force, and the South Australians readied their gunboat for an extended sea voyage to China, and arranged coaling stops and provisioning for the vessel's trip into a theatre of war. The *Adelaide Observer* congratulated itself on this opportunity for the colony to demonstrate its loyalty:

> For the first time in the history of British colonization, a self-governing province was sending 'to the front' a fully equipped ship of war to take its place in the fighting line with vessels of the Royal Navy.[23]

Only the New South Wales Government dragged its feet, and this was probably due to the fact that this government resented being seen to follow the lead of Victoria. In the New South Wales' Parliament, the Premier exposed his thinking on this question when he stated:

> I do not think it will stand to the credit of New South Wales if she, the mother colony of the group, on an occasion of this kind, stands back and allows other colonies to take the lead.[24]

The press took the same line, and the *Australian Star* newspaper editorialised that:

> If the Victorians and South Australians are to go, it is desirable that this colony should maintain its prestige and position with the Imperial authorities and the British public as the head of the Australians, and it will not do to fall back.[25]

The British Admiralty requisitioned the liner *Salamis*, then in Sydney, to become a troop-carrier for the combined expeditionary force from Victoria and New South Wales, and the Victorians mobilised their men in a most efficient fashion. By the end of June, the Victorian Government had received hundreds of

HMCS *Protector,* the South Australian gunboat just prior to her departure from Adelaide for the China War. (Taken from Bob Nicholls, *Bluejackets and Boxers: Australia's Naval Expedition to the Boxer Uprising,* Sydney, 1986)

Commander Creswell and his officers aboard HMCS *Protector* in Adelaide.

enthusiastic volunteers from the ranks of its colonial naval brigades, and in South Australia the permanent staff of the *Protector*—together with nearly the entire naval reserve, and even some outside enthusiasts—all offered to fill the 100 positions available.

The situation in New South Wales, however, was confused, and the ambivalence of the colony's government towards the entire proposition of a military force being sent to China was demonstrated by the laxity and delay in doing anything to hasten or back-up the offer of 300 men. The Premier's rhetoric had been nothing more than empty posturing. Indeed, when a parade was held on 11 July for the purpose of obtaining the volunteers from the colony's naval brigade, it produced only three officers and twenty-six men. A call for volunteers by private circular brought in another 60–70 men, and, by 2 August, only 201 naval men had come forward. Meanwhile, the Victorian force had been ready to start for at least three weeks, and the Victorian Government expressed its disenchantment with the dilatory performance of its New South Wales' counterpart. In the event, the numbers from New South Wales had to be made up from the ranks of the army, and it was not until 7 August 1900, that the combined contingents sailed out of Sydney Harbour aboard the *Salamis*, bound for China. The gunboat from South Australia set out under its own steam for the China Seas, and arrived in Sydney to recoal three days after the departure of the *Salamis*. The South Australian contingent never met up with the forces from the other two colonies, and served in a minor way as a small naval auxiliary in the British Fleet in Chinese waters.

The *Salamis* sailed into Hong Kong Harbour on 26 August, and the first news which the ship received was that the legations in Peking had already been relieved by a mixed-race military force of approximately 20 000 men, led by the British General Gaselee. The delay occasioned by the disorganisation of the New South Wales' Government had resulted in the Australians arriving too late to participate in the main action, and the volunteers were bitterly disappointed.

At that stage, however, nobody knew what the future course of events in China would be, and there was a real possibility of a punitive war to pay back the Chinese for their attack on European property and for the massacre of European missionaries and their flocks. So the men disembarked, and, after a series of misadventures—caused as much by their inexperience as by anything else—the Australians found themselves assigned to police duties in Peking and several other large cities in the defeated country. Here, they were responsible for the protection of their district from Boxer attempts at incendiarism, and for general law and order, with jurisdiction over the Chinese population. Aside from executing prisoners who were found to be Boxer supporters, the Australians saw no action against the Boxers, who just disappeared from view after the war had gone against them. The men from Australia found themselves organising the fire brigades, the cleaning, and the street-lighting of their districts—and searching for loot in the ruins of banks and government buildings. Since they had arrived so late, they found precious little plunder either, the Europeans, the Indians, and the Japanese forces having already picked the place clean.

The first death of an Australian in China did not occur until 6 October, when a private in the New South Wales' infantry died of influenza. The following month another private died from exhaustion caused by severe dysentery—and the New South Wales' staff doctor killed himself with an overdose of sleeping mixture!

As the winter drew ever closer, the British planned to withdraw their Indian Army troops from north China, and requested the Australian colonial governments to permit their contingents to stay until the arrival of the northern spring. The New South Wales' troops took up winter quarters in the Tientsin region, while the Victorians remained in Peking. In January 1901, a member of the New South Wales' contingent died of pleurisy, and one man was in hospital after having contracted smallpox. By the end of March, the Australians were ready to depart for home, although not all the men seemed to be anxious to return, and one able seaman committed suicide at the prospect.

The trip home was not without incident, and because some of the men developed illnesses on the voyage, their troop transport was not allowed to dock at Circular Quay in Sydney, where the naval brigade's brass band waited with their families to welcome them home. Instead, their ship was directed to the quarantine station, where one of the sick men was found to be suffering from the after-effects of smallpox. All the men had been inoculated when they left Australia, but the safety period was thought to be only six months, and they had been in China for several months longer than this. One of the sailors developed a case of smallpox during the quarantine period and died in hospital. The men who were passed fit to land finally arrived from the quarantine station on 3 May at Circular Quay, where they were met by the police band and went for a short march around that part of the city adjacent to the dock area. The Victorians received no welcome, and caught the train to Melbourne, where, due to the lateness of the hour, there was no official reception and they quietly rejoined their families—a parade inspected by the Duke of York being their only thanks.

The low-key return to Australia in 1901 reflected the ambivalence and the generally irresolute spirit behind the dispatch of the expeditionary forces the previous year. Inter-colonial rivalries, and the opportunity to blood their naval brigades in Asia—as the militias were being similarly blooded in South Africa—seemed to play as much a part in the respective decisions to offer military assistance to the mother country as did the colonies' willingness to play a part in the protection of the wider British Empire as their contribution towards the cost of imperial defence.

The Boxer Affair also showed that the colonial naval reserves could well provide the basis for a future Australian Navy, at the same time as it rendered the Australians acutely aware of the possibility of a prospective military threat from the rising warlike power of Japan. Australia became sensitive to the fact that Asia could become the storm-centre of the world and a long-term danger to Australian security. Henceforth, Britain came to regard Germany as the potential future enemy, whereas Australia increasingly began to focus on Japan as the source of possible threats in the years to come. The separate national interests of the different parts of the British Empire had begun to emerge, and Australia's long journey towards full independence—with its own blue-water fleet and strategic defence capability—had finally begun.

31

Charles Joseph La Trobe—a Most Unlikely Governor

What was the unlikely vocation of Charles La Trobe before his appointments as a Superintendent and a Lieutenant-Governor? Which well-known writer described La Trobe as 'a complete virtuoso'? Who was Sophie, and why was she unhappy? And what tragic news did La Trobe discover by chance when reading a newspaper?

Charles La Trobe (1801–75), was born in London, the son of a family of Huguenot origin. The family had migrated to England in 1688, and his father and grandfather had both been ordained clergymen in the small Protestant sect known as Moravians, for whom his father—rather appropriately named Christian—had worked as a missionary in Africa in 1815–16. Christian was also active in the campaign against slavery, and enjoyed some personal contact with the enormously influential leader of the abolitionist cause, William Wilberforce.

The family maintained its contacts with the continent, and Charles was educated in Switzerland, with the intention of continuing the family tradition and entering the ministry. He did not carry through this intention, however, and instead became a school teacher at a Moravian boys' boarding school in Manchester. Following this, he obtained an appointment as a tutor to a Swiss nobleman's family (who were also of Huguenot background) in 1824, and remained in this position for almost four years. In his spare time, he became quite an accomplished mountaineer and walker, climbing mountains without the help of guides or porters, and going on extended walking tours of Switzerland and Italy. This marked the beginning of a lifetime obsession with travel and visiting exotic places. It also represented the start of Charles La Trobe's career as a writer of travel stories. In 1829, he published his first such book in which he described Swiss scenery and manners, and, in 1832, his second book—on rambles in the Tyrol—came out. These works were lightweight but pleasant enough, and sufficiently well received to encourage their author to keep producing more of them. Between 1832 and 1834, the son of the family for whom he tutored embarked on an extensive tour of North America and Mexico, and Charles accompanied him. A two-volume account of his American adventures emerged in 1835, followed by a one-volume treatment of their Mexican sojourn the year after. It was during this trip to the Americas that the American writer Washington Irving, who accompanied the two travellers for six months, described La Trobe in the following terms:

> He was a man of a thousand occupations; a botanist, a geologist, a hunter of beetles and butterflies, a musical amateur, a sketcher of no mean pretensions; in short, a complete virtuoso; added to which he was an indefatigable, if not always a very successful, sportsman. Never had a man more irons in the fire; and, consequently, never was a man more busy or more cheerful.[26]

In 1835, at the age of 34, Charles proposed marriage to Sophie de Montmollin, a Swiss girl who was a relative of the young count whom La Trobe had tutored. He had some doubts concerning his acceptability and his slender means, but, with three published books to his name, and with more in prospect, he probably felt that he was in a position to offer marriage. The family accepted his proposal, and the young couple were wed in the British Legation at Berne in September 1835, according to the rites of the Church of England.

The following year, Lord Glenelg, the Secretary of State for the Colonies, appointed La Trobe to report to the British Government on the administration and use of the funds voted by Parliament—as part of the package in which slavery was finally abolished—which were expressly intended for the education of the former slave population of the West Indies. It seems likely that patronage flowing from his father's long association with the abolitionist cause was the key to this preferment, for there was little in Charles's career to this date to suggest his being the appropriate person for such an appointment.

In 1837, La Trobe submitted three detailed and extensive reports on Negro education in the West Indies—which he had visited alone because Sophie was expecting their first child. The baby was born in her family's home in Switzerland on 2 April 1837, only four weeks after La Trobe's departure, and he did not return from the West Indies until July 1838. This pattern was to recur over and over again for the remainder of their lives together, as La Trobe's wanderlust was continuously at odds with his undoubted affection for his wife and family. Sophie came, in time, to hate her husband's prolonged and repeated absences.

Lord Glenelg must have been impressed with La Trobe's reports, because, in January 1839, he offered La Trobe the position of Superintendent of the Port Phillip District of New South Wales. Port Phillip, although within the territory of New South Wales, had been colonised from across Bass Strait and Van Diemen's Land in 1836. The new settlement grew rapidly, and it had become obvious that it needed an administrator on the spot, because enterprise and development were being stifled as a result of having to wait for long periods for decisions on local concerns to arrive from Sydney. Once again, we have to point to patronage

Charles Joseph La Trobe. (Archives Office of Tasmania)

to explain the appointment of a man who did not possess the usual background of a colonial governor. La Trobe had no army or naval training, and little if any administrative experience, yet he was given the task of administering a new settlement and protecting its native population from the colonists in the rip-roaring days of its earliest development—quite a step up from writing travel yarns!

On 30 September 1839, Charles Joseph La Trobe—accompanied by his wife, his daughter, and two servants—arrived at Melbourne, after spending eight weeks in Sydney making contact with his superior Sir George Gipps, the Governor of New South Wales, and receiving a detailed briefing from Gipps on the state of affairs in the Port Phillip District. This marked the beginning of an increasingly warm and mutually supportive relationship between the two men, and there were clear signs of a warm father/son interaction that developed between them as the years went by. La Trobe was not ambitious to replace Gipps, and showed that he valued the experience and advice of his mentor. After all, up until this time, the only authority that La Trobe had exercised had been in a school room, and he was sensitive enough to recognise that he could learn a great deal from George Gipps.

The La Trobes were not well-off financially. In fact, while in Sydney the family had been forced to shift to a cheaper hotel to stretch their resources as far as possible. In addition, Sophie La Trobe enjoyed only indifferent health, causing her entertaining and visiting activities to be reduced. When they arrived in Melbourne, the La Trobes had erected a six-roomed prefabricated house—which they had brought with them from England—on land owned by the government, because Charles could not afford to purchase land in Melbourne on the rising local market. Eventually, Gipps authorised the auctioning of the land on which the La Trobes had squatted, and, in a gesture that demonstrates the respect Charles had already earned in the eyes of the locals for his fair-mindedness and genial disposition, the only person to bid on the twelve-and-a-half acres he wanted, was Charles himself. The market value of the land was about 300–400 pounds an acre, and Charles purchased his estate at the reserve price of only twenty pounds an acre. He had certainly got a bargain!

The La Trobes named their property *Jolimont* after the house in Switzerland where they had spent their honeymoon, and, although they added rooms and outbuildings as the years went by, it always remained an exceedingly modest residence. La Trobe lived a quiet social life in Melbourne. As a Superintendent, he did not have the burden of entertaining as extensively as was expected of a vice-regal representative—and Charles did not feel obliged to keep up appearances just to impress his fellow citizens. In a letter to his friend and publisher John Murray, Charles explained his situation:

> I had the common sense to start at once with the determination that whatever my supposed position and liabilities might be, so long as Her Majesty's Government neither gave me a house nor the means of keeping an open one, I would not pretend to do so to please the little world around me. A man with a fortune may spend it, and ruin himself, to please people, if he think proper; but having no fortune, I could not even do that.[27]

Sophie La Trobe's lack of facility in the English language might also have played some part in circumscribing the social life of the family, as well as the fact that she gave birth to a further two children during their stay in Melbourne—in addition to suffering a miscarriage with complications.

In the years before the Victorian goldrushes, La Trobe seemed content to remain subordinate to Gipps, and then to Sir Charles Fitzroy, in Sydney. He appeared to administer the Port Phillip District competently enough, although it is almost impossible to point to any particular development or initiative that he could claim as his own singular contribution to the rapidly expanding settlement. He spent much of his time indulging his love of travel, and his journals show that he made more than ninety trips away from home during his Victorian period. Much of this was not strictly necessary, as the personal presence of the Superintendent was not a prerequisite for any decision that he had to make. Sophie fretted greatly at these sometimes prolonged absences on the road, and always waited fearfully for him to return safe and sound. While he was away, she would pray for his safety, and, when he returned, her reaction provided ample evidence of the worry and mental agitation she suffered. Charles loved travel, and, in this case, it is possible that some of his trips were little more than excuses to escape the atmosphere of sickness and restriction at home.

The limitations of Charles Joseph La Trobe as an administrator began to emerge in the years after Port Phillip became the Colony of Victoria in 1850, and he himself became the new colony's first Lieutenant-Governor. He antagonised the British Colonial Office by giving in to colonial pressure in refusing to allow the convict transport *Randolph* to unload its cargo of convicts in Melbourne. In this decision alone, he may well have shipwrecked his career, for he was never offered another post after his return from Australia.

During the massive dislocation caused by the discovery of gold in Victoria, La Trobe can be described merely as coping adequately with the problems that emerged. He copied the licence system then operating in New South Wales, and, in so doing, may be said to have laid the groundwork for the rebellion at the Eureka Stockade several years after his departure. He reorganised the machinery of government to deal with the massive increase in work that was an inevitable consequence of the huge growth in the colony's population once the news of the gold discoveries reached the mother country, and he built up the police presence on the goldfields so that the Californian experience of anarchy and mayhem was not repeated in Australia.

By the end of 1852, La Trobe submitted his resignation to the Colonial Office. He had been in Australia for thirteen years, his eldest daughter had been sent back to Switzerland to be educated, and they had not seen her for five years; and Sophie was desperately homesick for her child and her family. Although the resignation was accepted, La Trobe was not relieved until 1854. In the interval, Sophie and the children preceded him to Europe. They would wait for him to rejoin them in Switzerland.

The period following the departure of his family was a hard one for La Trobe, and he missed his wife and children enormously. In October 1853 he wrote a long letter to Sophie in which his heartache and sense of loss are clearly enunciated:

You cannot imagine my dear wife how fully my mind has been occupied with you & my dear children. My dear wife yesterday & today I see you at every turn—on the beach on the hill, at the lighthouse, at the gate of our pretty cottage—the children run way down the steep pathway to the sand & calling out Papa! Papa! as in times past at Point Lonsdale ... In fact Jolimont itself is not more full of recollections—& perhaps these are the more vivid because I had some of my pleasantest days in Victoria here with you. May God bless you wherever you are.[28]

Some prescience may have been at work here, because Sophie was destined never to read her husband's endearments and expressions of affectionate love. A week before La Trobe was due to sail out of Australia and rejoin his family, he was perusing an English newspaper to catch up on the events at home. In the newspaper, he found, purely by accident, Sophie's death notice. Sophie had died in Switzerland in December 1853. She had spent all her married life waiting for Charles to come home after his travels, but this time she had not waited, and had embarked on the longest journey of all—without him.

Charles grimly served out his final week in Melbourne, and took ship a shattered man. He rejoined his children in Switzerland, and, a year later, he married his wife's widowed sister Rose. He never took another position in the colonial service, and even his plans to write an account of his time in Australia came to naught, as his eyesight failed, and he went blind long before his death in 1875. He is most remembered in Victoria today, by the university that bears his name, and as the provider of Melbourne's Botanical Gardens.

32

The First Labor Government in the World

Where, when, and how did the first Labor Government in the world take office? How long did it last? Who was Anderson Dawson, and why is he remembered as both a Labor hero and a Labor anti-hero? And why can we confidently say that—for Dawson at least—politics was no joke?

In Queensland, on the first day of December 1899, the first fully Labor government in the world was sworn in. It lasted only a number of days, but it electrified the Labour Movement, because it held out hope that all the dreams of reform—that had developed as a result of the great strikes and the great depression of the 1890s—were not merely pipe-dreams, and that the Labour Movement might actually be able to implement a reformist program in the interests of its constituency: the working population.

The chief obstacle to the development of a Labor government in the second half of the nineteenth century—or even to securing positions for real labouring men in the colonial parliaments—was that members of parliament did not receive a salary. It was not until 1889 that members of the colonial legislatures—first in New South Wales, and soon after in the other colonies—received a salary on which to live. Prior to this, the fact that members of parliament were unpaid made it virtually impossible for men without means to stand for parliament. How would they and their families survive without a regular wage coming in? Occasionally, the trade-union movement agreed to pay an allowance to a member of parliament who had been elected as a friend of labour, but the unions could not afford to pay the salaries of all Labour Movement members who won elections.

Payment for members of parliament opened up the possibility that a majority of members could be elected in the labour interest, perhaps sufficient to form a government in their own right. Hitherto, it had been Labor policy for their representatives to support colonial liberal politicians against their more extreme opponents—the conservatives—in return for concessions in favour of the Labor platform. In its first election in 1893, sixteen members of the Queensland Labor Party won seats in the colony's Lower House. This made the Labor Party the second-largest grouping in the House, and therefore the party became, effectively, the Opposition. By 1896, the parliamentary organisation of the party continued to evolve, and a former miner from Charters Towers named Anderson Dawson emerged as the leader of the Labour Movement in the Queensland legislature.

Dawson had had a hard life. Brought up in a Brisbane orphanage, he had become a miner and the first editor of the *Charters Towers' Eagle*—a radical newspaper in the labour interest. For the rest of his life, Anderson Dawson would suffer from the miners' disease, emphysema, and from chronic alcoholism—also a product of the rough and ready mining environment. His final breakdown in health had much to do with both conditions, but they were under control in the late 1890s when Anderson Dawson was in his prime.

Under Dawson's leadership, the Labor Party staked out a number of policy positions, and demonstrated that it intended to take its stand on principle rather than on electoral popularity. Dawson demonstrated this in his outspoken stance in opposition to Australian involvement in the Boer War—then a very popular cause. The Labour Movement, said Dawson, was opposed to 'sending a mob of swashbucklers to South Africa to show off their uniforms'. This was an unpopular view, and, for his troubles, Dawson had his house pelted with rocks, and his family insulted.

In the Queensland Parliament itself, the balance of power began to tilt towards the Labor Party. At the 1899 election, the conservative government won 43 seats, the Labor Party 21 seats, and independent Liberals 8 seats. On the surface, the government should have had no trouble in hanging onto power, but there were splits within the government ranks, and these boiled over in a dispute over the leadership. The government began to fragment. Dawson was now the Leader of the Opposition and the alternative Premier. The tactical problem that emerged was what concessions was the Labor Party prepared to make to obtain the support of the independents and enough breakaways from the government ranks to produce a workable majority? Should the party embrace pragmatism, or stick to its principles? This situation provoked major soul-searching within the party, for nothing was surer than that a coalition with the Liberals would produce a raft of electoral and industrial reforms that were long overdue. On the other hand, too much dilution of the party's principles would make it virtually indistinguishable from the Liberals. The Labor newspaper, the *Worker*, editorialised:

> The pioneer mission of Labour in politics is to clear away all obstructions until it obtains first a monopoly of the opposition and secondly a monopoly of power. Until it can claim at least a monopoly of seats in any ministry it had better remain in opposition or be a cabinet maker or breaker. If it participates in a policy which it cannot control, it is sooner or later certain to have to commit itself to measures entirely antagonistic to its principles.[29]

Nevertheless, as the government became increasingly unstable, Dawson began to negotiate with the independents and the breakaways. In the meantime, the government's legislation was getting through the legislature on the single vote of a maverick Labor member, and the Premier took the view that his majority was too uncertain to continue. He resigned and recommended to the Governor that he send for Anderson Dawson, as the alternative Premier, and request him to form a government.

At this stage, Dawson's erstwhile non-Labor allies began to suffer from 'cold feet'. While the overthrow of the existing unpopular Premier had been their avowed aim, they had never intended to pass power to the Labor Party. The breakaways withdrew from all negotiations with the Leader of the Opposition. Similarly, the independent Liberals demanded a role, in any coalition with Labor, out of all proportion to their numerical strength in the Parliament. When they did their sums after the withdrawal of the breakaways, the Liberals realised that they alone with Labor still did not possess a working majority in the legislature. Consequently, they also withdrew from all negotiations with Dawson. In the interim, because he had had good reason to believe that he could rely upon wider support, Dawson had advised the Lieutenant-Governor that he could command a working majority in the Parliament, and he had received a commission to form a government. The new government was to have a wholly Labor cabinet, the first of its kind in the world.

Anderson Dawson put together an impressive ministry. He himself took the offices of Premier and Chief Secretary; the Attorney-General was a lawyer named Fitzgerald from western Queensland; Harry Turley, a former wharf labourer became Home Secretary; William Kidstone held the portfolios of Postmaster-General and Treasurer; Billy Browne, a former seaman and miner took the Mines and the Public Instruction positions; Herbert Hardacre, a butcher elected to represent the seat of Leichhardt received Lands and Agriculture; while Andrew Fisher, later a Labor Prime Minister of Australia, held the portfolios of Railways and Public Works.

The new government was sworn in on 1 December 1899, and went into the Parliament to take up office. There, Dawson's request for an adjournment of the House to permit the Government to formulate its program was defeated by a margin of ten votes. The following day, Dawson submitted his resignation to the Lieutenant-Governor, and, when the House met again on 5 December, he announced the resignation of the Government to the legislature. When a new conservative administration took office on 7 December, the first Labor government in the world had come to an end—without having introduced a single piece of legislation.

To be sure, Anderson Dawson had hoped to receive wider support on the floor than he was actually able to obtain, but that was not the only reason for Labor to take on such a hopeless task. As much as anything, it had to do with symbolism. The leadership of the Queensland Labor Party was anxious that Labor be taken seriously as a potential alternative government, and to establish with the

Premier Anderson Dawson (centre) and Cabinet members, 1899. (Australian History Museum, Macquarie University)

electorate and its own supporters that it was not just a lobbying group that would support whatever party gave it the most concessions. When he made his dignified speech after his defeat in the Parliament on 1 December, Dawson spelled this out: 'The action I have taken, is to a very large extent, if not wholly, to show members of this House and the country that we do not regard politics as a joke.'[30]

It was good advertising for Labor to be seen to be running the State, even if only for a short while, and to be demonstrating that it could—potentially— produce sound competent government with a heart and with the human touch.

Ironically, both Anderson Dawson and William Kidstone went on to future parliamentary careers that led both men into the ranks of anti-Labor. Dawson, when denied preselection for the 1906 Senate election, stood as an independent— and split the Labor vote. He never won a seat, and the three endorsed Labor candidates also failed to gain election. In the case of William Kidstone, he became the Labor Premier of Queensland in 1906, and in the election of the following year, he suddenly demanded that all Labor candidates take a pledge of loyalty to him personally. This split the party, and Kidstone ruled with a minority government—supported, reluctantly, from the crossbenches by the elected representatives of the official Labor Party. He retired in 1911, still Premier, but no longer a member of the Party.

Anderson Dawson, the first Labor Premier, died of chronic alcoholism in 1910. He was, for a short time, a Labor hero, but he died a Labor renegade.

33

Captain Bully Hayes

How did William 'Bully' Hayes come by his nick-name? Among a plethora of vices, for what was he especially notorious? Why did Hayes' ships often mysteriously change their colours and their names? How did he personally build upon the sailor's dream of 'a girl in every port'? And how did he finally meet his deserved fate?

William Henry Hayes, citizen of the United States of America, was one of the most colourful characters ever to set foot in the Australian colonies. In a population of eccentric and swaggering roughnecks, the aptly nick-named 'Bully' Hayes still stood out from the crowd—and his reputation in the annals of Australian history is that of a slave-trader and consummate villain.

William Hayes was born in Cleveland, Ohio, a thriving port on Lake Erie. His father worked as a bargee, and, when he was old enough, young William learned fresh-water sailing from working with his father. His formal education was of a rudimentary kind, although he could read and write, and, later in life, he proved to be quite good at figures. By the time he was eighteen, William shifted to salt-water sailing, where he found his life's vocation. He began in 1847, as an able seaman on a passenger vessel carrying would-be miners from the east-coast port of New York to the west-coast city of San Francisco—and thence to the Californian goldrushes. For the next six years he learned the fine art of seamanship—and the rudiments of navigation and the handling of men—as he worked his way up from able seaman to bosun on the California run.

By 1853, William Hayes—shipped out of New York as uncertified third-mate and part-owner of the barque *Canton*—headed for Melbourne and the Australian goldrushes with cargo and 85 passengers. Bully Hayes had arrived at the scene he was destined to dominate for the next two-and-a-half decades. William had, by this time, gained the nick-name by which he is generally known. It stemmed from the methods which he used to persuade his crewmen to obey him with alacrity and without question. He had developed into a tall man of just under two metres (six feet) in height, and weighing 90–95 kg (about 200 pounds). He was thickset and burly, with blue eyes and red-brown hair and beard. He had one other important attribute—he could brawl with a ferocity that meant he rarely ever met his match. Even in the tough world of salt-water sailing ships, Bully Hayes soon became something of a legend. No crewman on Bully Hayes'

The only known photograph of Bully Hayes. (Taken from Frank Clune, *Captain Bully Hayes: Blackbirder and Bigamist*, Sydney, 1970)

ships ever disputed who ran the vessel—and there is no record of any other man challenging him twice!

In 1853, the waterfront in Melbourne (and later Sydney) was rife with stories of men finding their fortunes in a couple of hours of prospecting on the goldfields, but Hayes did not pursue this course. His love of the sea led him to look for payable cargoes in the coastal trade between Tasmania, Victoria, and New South Wales. He proved to be unsuccessful in this, and he eventually sailed the *Canton* to Singapore, where he sold the ship for a good price, and returned to America. As with almost every sale of a vessel with which Bully Hayes was connected, there were questions concerning the rightful ownership of the *Canton*, but Hayes unloaded the ship on to a buyer from Britain and rapidly decamped for San Francisco.

From this time onwards, Hayes frequented the waterfronts of most of the major ports in the Pacific Ocean, the South Seas, and the China Sea. He commanded a multitude of vessels, and engaged in the carrying trade. Everywhere he went, he left behind people to whom he owed money. It became his normal practice to carry out extensive repairs and refitting work on his ship, to have it supplied with the best of food and equipment, and then to slip out of harbour before his creditors got wind of his intentions, leaving angry and ruined ships' chandlers and tradesmen lamenting in his wake.

He would carry any cargo that paid, and was prepared to ship copra and trade goods around the South Sea islands—including human cargo such as Chinese coolies to the island of Hawaii (to work on the plantations there), black women (whom he traded to the island chiefs of Melanesia and Polynesia), or shiploads of kidnapped Melanesian and Polynesian men (to work as indentured labour on the sugar plantations of Queensland). This shipment of coloured labourers to the sugar plantations of Queensland became known as 'blackbirding', and the labourers were known as 'Kanakas'. Recruitment of islander men as indentured labourers began in earnest in the 1860s and continued right through to the 1890s. The coloured men signed indentures—for a specified period of work in Queensland—with traders and ships' captains who often acted as agents for planters in centres like Brisbane, Townsville, or Mackay. The main question involved in this procedure was—just how voluntary were these contracts? There is considerable evidence to suggest that some of the more unscrupulous agents would actually kidnap islanders and force them to append their marks to open-ended contracts, or to documents which they were unable to read and did not understand. The man with the worst reputation in this regard was Bully Hayes, who specialised in providing Kanakas to planters who did not enquire too closely about where their workers had come from, or whether they properly understood their contracts, or whether they even knew that they had signed away their freedom and had agreed to work as tropical labour in north Queensland. By 1891, there were over 9000 Kanakas working in Queensland, and, in the next ten years, a further 11 000 were shipped in.

There is no doubt that racial discrimination and abuse of human rights was rife in the entire trade in contract labour. Traditionally, attention has been concentrated on this ill-treatment, but a more rounded picture has also to take into account the fact that more than half of the Kanakas working on the Queensland sugar plantations voluntarily renewed their indentures at the completion of the contract period—rather than opting to return to their homes.

The system was designed to suit the employers, by regulating and fixing wages, thereby ensuring a reliable workforce. It worked reasonably well, but its most serious shortcomings lay in the South Seas—beyond the reach of the regulations—rather than in Queensland.

Part of the problem in coming to some understanding of the role played by a man like Bully Hayes in the blackbirding game, lies in the general lawlessness of the islands during this period. The islands lacked any form of colonial government that could superintend the recruitment process, and the agents and ships' captains played off local chiefs against one another, and took full advantage of the inadequacy of British naval protection for the local native people. In 1868, the Queensland Government enacted legislation—designed to provide facilities for the registration and control of the process—involving the introduction of coloured labourers into the colony. There was also an attempt to establish minimum standards of treatment for Kanakas working on the colony's plantations, and the law insisted that all coloured labourers arriving in Queensland under indenture had to be examined by the colony's Immigration Agent to ensure that they were there voluntarily. All of this was, in part, a reaction to the dreadful catalogue of bloodshed and brutality that the activities of Bully Hayes and his fellow agents had produced. Stories were abroad which accused the unscrupulous sea captains (such as Hayes) of the cold-blooded slaughter of natives who resisted their forcible abduction by the blackbirders, and of the bringing of about 500 islander women to northern Australia, where many had been sold into prostitution. These stories reinforced the reputations of the sea captains as men who had become irredeemably coarsened by the savagery of their daily lives.

Hayes, himself, lived a life of defiance and contempt for the law and for the normal conventions of civilised society. In addition to leaving a train of unpaid debtors behind him, Bully Hayes was also a serial bigamist, with four 'marriages' to his credit, as well as numerous girls whom he loved and left in every port he visited. Moreover, Hayes also had innumerable native 'wives' throughout the islands of the South Pacific, with whom he had readily gone through native marriage ceremonies. Finally, he never sailed without a private harem of 6–8 women aboard his ship, and when he had tired of a girl he would often trade her to the chief of the next island at which he made landfall, and replace her with somebody new who took his fancy. In Australia, he was twice charged with rape, but was acquitted. He was gaoled only twice in a career outside the law which lasted almost 25 years—once in Sydney for debt; and once in Manila for helping prisoners escape from custody. A short-lived conversion to Roman Catholicism secured easier conditions in the Philippines, from which Hayes soon escaped, but his ability to avoid the authorities when he was sailing close to the law and carrying contraband cargo became a legend. On occasion, Hayes was boarded by

American and British warships, but, although they knew he was up to no good, they could never catch Bully Hayes in the act.

In part, this was due to Hayes' skill in altering his vessel's appearance. It became his practice to change the colour and the rig of his ships once he had left civilisation. He would repaint and rename the vessel in some small island port before sailing off to engage in his criminal activities. By the time the ships of the British and American navies had received a description of a vessel that was engaged in criminal activities in their area, together with its name and registration details, Hayes would have altered everything about his ship and reverted to his earlier legal identity and appearance. He infuriated the authorities, who could do nothing about his activities unless they caught him in the act of breaking the law—and Bully Hayes was always much too clever to allow this to happen. He had built up a network of informants at ports throughout the South Pacific, and was always well informed about movements of the naval vessels and the intentions of their commanders.

The period in which men like Bully Hayes flourished ended with the arrival of the undersea telegraph cable in Australia in 1872. From this time onwards, faster official communications began to make it increasingly difficult for blackbirders like Hayes to be protected by the erstwhile slowness of communications with naval headquarters—a slowness which had allowed them to disguise their ships, and to be protected from official reactions to their activities. Now, the Admiralty could receive a cable from a British representative on one of the South Sea islands reporting the illegal activities of a ship in the area, and the orders could be telegraphed to the local naval squadron to investigate immediately. Bully Hayes was therefore living on borrowed time, and the age of the freebooting maritime brigands—who had hitherto infested the South Seas—was drawing to a close.

In 1877, Hayes was battered unconscious by a crewman he had bullied. He had been taken unawares from behind, by a ship's cook who had become a rival for the affections of one of Hayes' harem. Bully Hayes was thrown overboard to the sharks—a fitting end for a man who had been a predator all his life.

34

Mary Penfold—the Mother of the Australian Wine Industry

Why should Mary Penfold be described as the 'mother' of the Australian wine industry? When did she begin cultivating wine grapes? How is this seminal date commemorated for all to know—even today? How was she under-estimated by her own son-in-law? And did she finally receive the recognition she deserved?

Mary Penfold (1820–96) founded and managed what is now an internationally recognised symbol of excellence—the Penfolds Wine company. Because it was not acceptable in nineteenth-century Australia for middle-class women to run a commercial business, Mary's role in the development of the South Australian wine industry has always been disregarded, and the credit has been incorrectly given to her husband, Dr Christopher Penfold. But, in a more enlightened age, Mary Penfold's accomplishment can now be celebrated as it deserves. In establishing a winery producing wines which became the recognised benchmark for quality, she has placed all Australian wine drinkers in her debt.

Christopher and Mary Penfold arrived in South Australia in 1844 as immigrants seeking new and better opportunities in a new land. Mary was an only child, and her parents were distraught at the prospect that their much-loved daughter would have to rough it in a primitive and pioneering environment. In many ways, Mary personifies the ambiguity in the middle-class emigration process—especially where it relates to the role of women. It has always been understood that convict women had no choice in the decision to depart from England, but it has also been assumed that free female migrants took ship as part of a conscious resolution to embrace the opportunities which emigration offered. Such a view ignores all the married women in Mary's situation, who, by their marriage vows, had placed themselves under the control of their husbands, and who therefore had no choice but to accompany their partners if the men decided to settle permanently in the new world. Mary's mother complained that Christopher Penfold 'would listen to no-one but the emigration agents'.

When the Penfolds arrived in Adelaide, they had their four-year-old daughter, Georgina, with them, and the family was attended by a servant and mother's help named Ellen Timbrell. They also brought with them a collection of fine

British and European porcelain, some handsome mahogany furniture (including a piano), and a collection of vine cuttings from the Rhône region in France. Clearly, the Penfolds were intent on pioneering in comfort!

For twelve hundred pounds, Christopher purchased a property of 500 acres (220 ha) in the foothills of the Mount Lofty Ranges. The acreage included a residence that the local Adelaide newspaper described as a 'mansion', and which the Penfolds named *Grange Cottage*. This house, a single-storey stone cottage like so many of Adelaide's houses in the colonial period—with a long verandah to keep the direct sun off the walls and to provide a cool place on hot summer evenings—became Mary's home and business office for the next four-and-a-half decades.

The full burden of farm management passed to Mary, as her husband had to work desperately hard to establish his medical practice. This involved prolonged absences as he rode on his rounds visiting his patients, and, when he was at home, he conducted his surgery in their dining room. By default, the supervision of the farm, its crops and workers, became Mary's responsibility—together with the education of their daughter. She was a methodical person, and her daybook shows her making payments for ploughing, receiving the payments from Dr Penfold's patients, purchasing agricultural equipment from Adelaide, as well as the brief statement: 'Began making wine'. Hereafter, wine-making became Mary's personal speciality, and it was she who tended and harvested the grapes from the cuttings they had brought with them from France.

Christopher prescribed the wine as a tonic for his patients, but the wine business under Mary's superintendence soon outgrew its role as an adjunct to the medical practice, and blossomed into a separate and prosperous business. The wine was sold in Adelaide and won prizes at local agricultural shows, and a taste for the Rieslings and clarets produced by the Penfolds winery began to spread. Mary expanded her range, and found a retail outlet for her wine in Melbourne, the capital city of the adjoining colony of Victoria. Penfolds wines sold well in Melbourne, despite the fact that they were subject to customs duties when they crossed the Victorian border. The agent for Penfold's wine in Victoria was a man by the name of Thomas Hyland, and he joined the family business when he and Georgina Penfold married.

The business grew from strength to strength, but Mary's role was always behind the screen of her husband's name, and most observers credited him with the success of the venture. It was just not acceptable for a woman of genteel background to be engaged in commercial activities. The true state of affairs emerged in 1870, when Christopher Penfold passed away after a long illness. Even her son-in-law, Thomas Hyland, had not realised the centrality of Mary Penfold to the wine business in which he was now involved, and he wrote to her

Mary Penfold in the late 1860s. (Read McCarthy Group)

advising that he had been able to build up a lucrative market for Penfold's Grange and other Penfold's wines in Melbourne, and that she should sell the property to some-one who would continue the business.

Mary had no intention of selling up, and replied with a terse letter to Hyland in which she informed him of her intention to continue the business of making wine, and sent him a balance sheet setting out the soundness and the prospects for the future of the enterprise. Two months later, Thomas Hyland replied with an offer to form a partnership. Under the proposed arrangement, Mary would continue to manage the manufacture of the wines, whereas Thomas and Georgina would control their retail distribution in Melbourne. Mary accepted the offer, and her position changed from being that of a doctor's wife who made wine as a hobby, to one much closer to the reality, in which her skills as a vigneron and entrepreneur were recognised at last.

In 1874, a journalist from the *Adelaide Register* cited the Penfold vineyards as an example of good management techniques, and he paid particular attention to the presiding role over wine production maintained by Mary herself—especially to the art of blending:

> Mrs Penfold makes four varieties of wine, sweet and dry red and sweet and dry white. Grapes of all kinds are used and the uniformity which is so great a consideration is secured by blending the wines when they are two or three years old. This is done under Mrs Penfold's personal supervision, not in conformity with any fixed and definite rule, but entirely according to her judgment and taste.[31]

In her cellars, Mary had stored over 90 000 gallons (about 400 000 litres) of wine which she was ageing in gigantic oak casks that contained 5000 gallons (about 22 700 litres) apiece.

In 1869, a further partnership agreement was signed between Mary Penfold and Thomas Hyland—together with Joseph Gillard, her cellar-manager. One of the stipulations of this compact was that Mary had to stay on as wine-maker for seven years, an unambiguous recognition of her position as the maker of what were already recognised as the finest wines in the country. The company also retained her name, and was registered as Penfold and Company. By 1881, the company had stored more than a third of all the wine produced in South Australia, and their product was sold in every Australian colony.

Mary finally retired in 1884, at the age of sixty-eight, and handed over control of the thriving viticulture enterprise to her cellar-master, Joseph Gillard. When he retired in 1905, Mary's grandson, Herbert Leslie Hyland-Penfold, took control, and another generation of the Penfold family continued the family business begun so modestly all those years ago by the young wife of a country doctor.

The motto of the Penfold Wine Company today echoes that most seminal event in 1844, when Mary first began the cultivation of the grape cuttings on the new farm that her husband had purchased. It reads: '1844 to evermore'.

Mary left South Australia in 1892, and lived out the last four years of her life with her daughter and son-in-law in Melbourne. She died in 1896, and her body was brought back to the estate for final interment. None of the death notices accorded her any credit for pioneering South Australian wine-growing, or for her establishment of one of the truly great wineries of Australia. Yet it is impossible to go past Mary Penfold as perhaps the single most important person in the history of the wine industry in Australia.

35

Alfred Deakin—Australia's Most Eccentric Prime Minister

Why is Alfred Deakin considered to be Australia's most eccentric Prime Minister? What was the unusual source of the most-valued political advice he sought? What was his connection with John Bunyan and *A Pilgrim's Progress*? And just who was the mysterious political correspondent of the London *Morning Post*?

Alfred Deakin was born in Melbourne in 1856, the year the Colony of Victoria began to exercise full responsible government. He was the son of an English migrant who had emigrated to South Australia, and who had then been drawn to Victoria by the goldrushes. His father did not make a fortune in the goldrushes, and found regular employment as a book-keeper with the coaching company Cobb & Co. Although Alfred's family was not wealthy, his father used carefully accumulated savings to ensure that Alfred attended Melbourne Grammar School before moving on to study law at Melbourne University. In 1878, he went to the bar, but he experienced difficulties in securing enough work to make a living.

In his politics at this early stage of his life, Deakin was a free trader with a conservative outlook, but in 1879 he met David Syme, the owner of the *Age* newspaper, and Syme converted Alfred from his previous beliefs into a liberal protectionist. This was a most important shift in Deakin's outlook, for David Syme was one of the most influential men in the colony—and a political career with Syme's support became a distinct possibility for the aspiring young lawyer. For the rest of his public life, Alfred Deakin never wavered in his commitment to the principles of liberal protectionism which he had imbibed under the tutelage of his mentor, Syme. He began writing for David Syme's newspapers, the *Age* and the *Leader*, and in 1879, with Syme's support, he stood unsuccessfully (as a Liberal Protectionist) for a seat in the Victorian lower house, the Legislative Assembly. The following year he stood again and lost, but in a further campaign later in the year, he exhibited the rhetorical skills for which he would later become famous, and easily won a seat. Within three years Alfred held the portfolios of Water Supply and Attorney-General in the Service–Berry coalition admin-istration, and had become Commissioner of Public Works. It was Deakin who, in the drought years of the early 1880s, brought out the Chaffey brothers from

California to plan the irrigation schemes on the Murray River in the Mildura district.

Altogether, Deakin's career in Victorian politics lasted from 1880 to 1890, when he lost office with the Gillies government. This change in his circumstances freed him to devote his time to the Federation movement, and he laboured unceasingly for the next decade to bring this about. Alfred Deakin probably became the single most influential person working to bring about the political union of the Australian colonies during the decade of the 1890s, and, because he could devote himself full-time to this work, he provided the driving force to turn the concept into a reality. He entered the first Federal Parliament of the new Commonwealth of Australia in 1901 under the Prime Ministership of Edmund Barton. In 1903, Alfred Deakin became the second Prime Minister of the new nation, following Barton's resignation to take up a judicial position on the new High Court. He held the office of Prime Minister for three terms, 1903–5, 1905–8, and 1913 until his resignation later that year. In his federal career, Deakin proved to be a progressive liberal, and—with the support of the Australian Labor Party—brought down a great deal of socially innovative legislation in which the government intervened in the economy to secure minimum standards of living, and enshrined these standards as part of a standard wage which employers were not permitted to undercut.

So far, we have looked at the main outlines of a fairly conventional political career. However, beneath the surface of conformity, there lurked in Alfred Deakin an unexpected and occasionally outlandish streak that he kept hidden from the public gaze. In his private world, Deakin was an eccentric with a bewildering and unusual set of beliefs and behaviours.

He first met his future wife, Pattie Browne, when she was a girl of fourteen, and he was her Sunday School teacher in the Spiritualist Progressive Lycaeum in Melbourne. When they married in 1882, she was still a teenager of nineteen and he was twenty-five years of age. It was clearly a love-match that lasted for life, and, for the next thirty years, Alfred commemorated each of her birthdays—and their wedding anniversaries—by writing her a sonnet to mark the occasions. These sonnets are not great poetry, but they are evidence of a warm nature and an affectionate heart.

In matters of religion, Alfred Deakin was distinctly not mainstream. He had—like many spiritual seekers of that time who wanted a direct personal experience of the transcendent—been drawn to spiritualism from the age of eighteen. He consorted with mediums and attended seances on a regular basis, and became very impressed when he received encouraging prophecies regarding his marriage and political career when both seemed impossible. Alfred received political advice from a variety of spectral sources, including Sophocles, John Knox, John Stuart

Mill, Lord Macaulay, and the great liberal statesman Edmund Burke, all of whom spoke to him via the agency of his enthusiastic amateur housewife mediums. Perhaps the most useful of his ghostly advisers was the spirit of Richard Heales, a former Premier of the colony of Victoria who had died in 1864.

Spiritualism proved to be the sort of eclectic and tolerant religion that suited the young Deakin, and, by 1878, he had become the President of the Spiritualist Association of Victoria, in addition to filling the role of the organisation's Sunday School teacher. To facilitate his work in the Sunday School, Deakin produced his first book in 1877 which bore the title *Lycaeum Leader*. This was a selection of extracts culled from the writings of a miscellany of poets, sages, and religious teachers from a variety of traditions and from all ages. Exhibiting the great moral earnestness of the Spiritualists, the publication also included a catechism of sorts,

Alfred Deakin

in which the precepts of conventional moral teaching stood alongside material extolling the virtues of communicating with the dead.

Nor did communications from 'the other side' come to Alfred Deakin only through his mediums. For a while, he believed that he, himself, possessed abilities as a medium—with a particular skill in the area of automatic writing. He found that if he emptied his mind of conscious thoughts, and sat ready to receive the messages from the spirit world, words flooded into his brain with such fluency that they could not possibly be his own. He believed that he was receiving the thoughts of the spirit of John Bunyan, who had chosen him as the conduit for the transmission of a sequel to Bunyan's famous book *A Pilgrim's Progress*. Alfred Deakin's effusion was entitled *A New Pilgrim's Progress*. It appeared later in 1877, although not to any great acclaim—even among the Spiritualists. It certainly was used to embarrass him during his political campaigns in 1880, when it was described by a Melbourne newspaper, the *Daily Telegraph*, in the most uncompromising terms:

> It is the record of the delirious dreams of an illiterate, ignorant and impure mind. But that it fell still-born from the press—failed to gain currency even amongst the small society in whose interests it was written—the book would have richly merited legal suppression, as a work outraging religion, morality, and public decency.[32]

In later years, Deakin rejected his book as being the work of the dead John Bunyan—and similarly rejected much of the teachings of the spiritualist organisations—but he always maintained an interest in the occult, and he moved on to an involvement in the Theosophical Society and an abiding interest in comparative religion, which he continued for the remainder of his life. He also found the area of prophecy fascinating, and remained convinced that the predictions made to him by the mediums he visited in 1876 and 1880— concerning his future marriage and political career—provided incontrovertible evidence that there was a great deal more than chance at work.

Inclined to see the hand of supernatural forces at work in the great movements of the age, Deakin felt quite happy in ascribing the success of the campaign for Australian federation to the workings of a greater destiny. Consequently, the man who had done more than anybody to bring federation about, stated that: 'its actual accomplishment must always appear to have been secured by a series of miracles'.[33]

Not all of Alfred Deakin's eccentricities were confined to the area of religion, and there are aspects of his behaviour that indicate youthful enthusiasm and idealism continuing well into his middle life. One good example of this emerges from the 1890s, when he lived a life of devotion to the cause of federation. In 1897, Deakin and other fathers of federation, including Edmund Barton and Charles Kingston—the Premier of South Australia—were in London negotiating the final shape of the draft constitution for the new Commonwealth of Australia. Negotiations had stalled on Clause 74 of the constitution—which related to appeals from Australian courts of law to the Privy Council in England—and the Australian deputation was split on the issue. Deakin, Barton and Kingston arranged an 'eleventh-hour' compromise with Joseph Chamberlain, the Secretary of State for the Colonies, and, on 17 May, the three had a private interview with Chamberlain at his room at Westminster, in which Chamberlain accepted, on behalf of the British Government, the suggestion proposed by the three Australians. Federation was now certain. When the British statesmen and officials finally left the room, Alfred Deakin described what happened next:

> When the door closed upon them and left them alone, they seized each others hands and danced hand in hand in a ring around the centre of the room to express their jubilation.[34]

Another unusual facet of Alfred Deakin's behaviour—which was also kept secret from the Australian public—was that the English newspaper, the *Morning Post*, employed him to write a regular column on Australian affairs from 1901 to 1911. The column was unsigned, and was attributed by the newspaper's editors to 'Our Australian Correspondent'. The money was a useful addition to the meagre parliamentary salary earned by Deakin, because, with a wife and three daughters to support, he needed to earn additional income to maintain the comfortable middle-class way of life to which they had all become accustomed. However, the fact was that the Australian correspondent of the *Morning Post* was writing on the political performance of himself and his own Party—even when he held the office of Prime Minister! The ethics of the arrangement—which has to be seen as a major conflict of interest—never seem to have bothered Deakin, and it was only pressure of work and failing powers that forced him to cease writing his regular assessments of Australian political affairs for his English readers.

One final endearing quality in this eccentric behaviour pattern is Alfred Deakin's continued refusal to accept a knighthood from the British Crown in recognition of his rank as Prime Minister, or his status as one of the Fathers of the Australian Nation. In this he has more in common with the Labor Prime Ministers—none of whom have accepted imperial honours—than with the non-Labor side of politics—the leaders of which have usually distinguished themselves by the unseemly scramble for titles, knighthoods, and the other bricabrac so beloved by conservative politicians in Australia until the 1970s.

Alfred Deakin retired from Federal Parliament in 1913. His memory was failing and his powers of oratory had deserted him. He died in 1917 following a massive stroke—one of the most loved, respected, and genuinely eccentric leaders Australia has ever had.

36

The Hornet Bank Massacre—Gender and Race Conflict on the Frontier

How did different cultural norms regarding sexuality lead on from misunderstanding ... to abuse ... to rape of Aboriginal women in colonial Australia? How did the blacks respond? How did the white settlers exact their revenge? And what was the practical effect of the official policy of 'dispersal'?

There has been a tendency by Australian historians to articulate frontier conflict between whites and Aborigines purely in terms of disputes over land and control of resources. Although there is a great deal of truth in such a framing of race relations on the pastoral frontiers, it is curiously one-sided, and little attention has been paid to the role of women as a focus for the convergence of outback racial hostility. The issue of relationships of station owners and their stockmen with black women has been overlooked, and white men on the colonial frontiers of Australia are often treated as though they lived lives of restraint and disciplined celibacy. But the fact is that white men did not live such saintly lives in the bush, and they often entered into relationships with Aboriginal women and produced mixed-race children—whom they usually refused to recognise. The Durack family's involvement in such situations, in the far north of Western Australia, has recently received considerable publicity, and the practice of white men taking a piece of 'black velvet'—whenever they felt like it—has been widely attested as the norm on the nineteenth-century frontier.

The situation was more complicated than a straight case of rape. The complication was the Aboriginal practice of sexual hospitality—whereby women were sometimes used by the tribes to establish a kinship relationship with the incoming whites. Under tribal customary law, the acceptance of a woman in these circumstances involved the white man in a reciprocal relationship with all the woman's relatives, and they had earned the right to a share of the white man's resources and his food supplies. Most white men had no idea of the obligations which they incurred when they took Aboriginal women as sexual partners, and assumed that the relationship was essentially one between a prostitute and a client. They despised Aboriginal men whom they accused of being willing to prostitute their women in return for a bit of flour, some tobacco, or a small amount of tea and sugar. Since the white men placed no value on the black women's consent to transactions of this sort, the practice grew up of many whites taking whatever black women they pleased—whenever they pleased. The Aboriginal girls were viewed as a sexual commodity, to be used by the pastoral workforce of both whites and black stockmen—as they deemed fit.

When whites failed to live up to expectations incurred under the reciprocity system of Aboriginal kinship, they broke the Aboriginal law. When they just helped themselves to black women, they broke the law. When they permitted their workmen and the male members of their families to take black women, they broke the law. Anger at white men's breaches of their law, and at their depredations against Aboriginal women, was the underlying element in much of the frontier conflict in the pastoral districts—and laid the groundwork for one of the most extreme reprisals that occurred in October 1857, at the *Hornet Bank* station on the banks of the Dawson River, in what is now north Queensland.

On the night of 26 October 1857, twelve Europeans went to sleep at the Hornet Bank homestead. Nine were members of the Fraser family who leased the station; the other three were employees of the family. Sleeping in the house, or on the verandah, were the members of the family—Mrs Martha Fraser, a widow, and her four daughters (aged 19, 11, 9 and 3 years of age), together with four of her sons (aged between 23 and 6 years). In a hut about 50 metres from the homestead were the other three Europeans—two of the station's workmen who had been paid off (and had therefore surrendered their guns), and a tutor responsible for the children's education.

Not long before daybreak, about 100 Aboriginal warriors crept up on the house. One of the white boys—a 14-year-old named Sylvester (West)—woke up to hear the warriors talking softly in his room. He reached over his head to pick up a loaded gun, but, before he could fire it, the weapon was knocked from his hand, and he received a blow to his head from a nulla nulla—which knocked him unconscious. When he came to in the darkness, he heard the deaths of his mother and sisters take place in the yard, and, when he later found the bodies of his brothers and the workmen, he realised that he was the sole survivor.

He reported that he heard his mother pleading for the lives of her daughters before she and the older two girls were raped, and all five females were killed. Young West also reported that the bodies of his two older brothers were both naked, and that their bodies had been mutilated. Mrs Fraser must have recognised some of the attackers as members of the local tribe, for West heard her talking to four of them—whose names she knew as Baulie, Jacky, Little Jacky, and Bobby.

The newspapers of the colony reported the massacre as another example of the wild sub-human savagery of the Aborigines, and called for rapid and

Contemporary nineteenth-century romanticised view of a settler and his family holding hostile Aborigines at bay. Images like this helped to legitimise the relentless reprisal killings of Aborigines following the massacre of the Fraser family.

widespread reprisals. The *Moreton Bay Courier* of 11 November commented:

> Last week intelligence was received of a fearful outrage committed by blacks under circumstances of peculiar atrocity. Of twelve persons residing on the station at Hornet Bank on the upper Dawson, eleven were barbarously murdered. One only escaped to tell the dreadful tale.[35]

By concentrating on the savagery of the attack—and especially on the rape and the mutilation of the bodies of the victims—the whites depicted the Hornet Bank massacre as evidence of the violent and malevolent nature of Aborigines. The fact that rape was a most unusual accompaniment of an Aboriginal attack did not apparently provide any incentive for further or closer investigation by the authorities, who seemed intent on casting the Fraser family as the innocent victims of bloodthirsty ferocity. Yet the data were there for an alternative explanation—had a search been made.

In fact, the Fraser males had a reputation for the frequency of their assaults on the women of the local Aboriginal tribe. Indeed, Martha Fraser herself had become so concerned by this that she had pleaded with Lieutenant Nicol—the European officer in charge of the local detachment of Native Police—and had asked him to intervene to prevent her sons 'forcibly taking young maidens'. Moreover, the white employees had recently whipped and raped two Aboriginal girls, and the tribe had first tried to use sorcery to punish the men concerned. When this had had no effect, they had sent an old Aboriginal woman to the homestead to explain what had happened and to seek redress, but again no action was taken. Finally (as was later reported to the Queensland Select Committee on the Native Police in 1861), a further contributing factor to the massacre was the Frasers' habit of allowing their black stockmen, 'to rush the gins' in neighbouring Aboriginal encampments.

When all the material is assembled, it emerges that the reasons for the attack on the white women at the Hornet Bank station—and for the mutilation of the naked bodies of the older Fraser sons and the hutkeepers—are to be found in the disregard of Aboriginal law, insofar as it related to access to women and the obligations thereby incurred. Martha Fraser had felt the greatest uneasiness about the consequences of her sons' activities with, and sexual attacks on, native girls. It was reported that she had told Lieutenant Nicol that she had: 'expected harm would come of it, that they were in the habit of doing so, notwithstanding her entreaties to the contrary'.[36]

The aftermath of the massacre amounted to a virtual declaration of 'open season' on the Aboriginal tribes in the area. Several parties of the Native Police were quickly on the scene, and a dramatic body-count followed. The eldest son, William Fraser, who had been away from the station at the time of the attack, claimed to have taken a vow at the graveside of his mother and sisters—with an uplifted tomahawk in his hand—never to rest until he had buried the tomahawk in the head of the Aborigine whom Fraser felt was personally most responsible for the attack. In later life, he claimed that he had carried out his vow. It must have been one of the four with whom young West had heard his mother pleading for the lives of her daughters.

Other settlers took the law into their own hands, and slaughtered Aborigines who had even the most tenuous connection with the tribe responsible for the killings. The full story of the retaliatory measures taken on surrounding stations will never be known. The Native Police detachments caught up with some of those involved in the massacre within a couple of days—and five Aborigines were killed and three wounded. The troopers recovered stock, clothing and firearms which had come from Hornet Bank station. Another party came up with Aborigines whom they thought to have been connected with the attack, and another four or five were shot. More were killed in other brushes, and some Aboriginal women were shot by the police for running away when they were called upon to stay still.

An official policy of 'dispersal' of any large gathering of Aborigines followed the Hornet Bank massacre—because the thinly spread white population felt vulnerable and afraid. Since many of the Aboriginal gatherings for ritual and ceremonial purposes numbered 400–500 Aborigines at a time, the dispersal practice that was followed by the Native Police impacted heavily upon Aboriginal traditional life, and helped in the overall process of detribalisation. The northern settlers regarded themselves as being at war with the blacks, and enthusiastically supported the policy of 'dispersal'. The phrase was a euphemism that received the following explanation in the Queensland Parliament by the Attorney-General in 1861, when he commented that the term meant 'nothing but firing at them'.

Under this policy—which was not rescinded until 1896—any large assembly of Aborigines would, as a matter of policy, be shot at by the troopers of the Native Police. In the long run, it was the blacks who paid, by far, the higher price for the white refusal to respect Aboriginal women and the law—despite occasional dramatic episodes of reprisal, like that at Hornet Bank.

37

The Parramatta Female Factory

When is a factory not a factory? How does one institution act simultaneously as a penitentiary, a sanctuary, a hospital, a labour exchange and a marriage bureau—as well as being a place of manufacture? Why did the Parramatta Female Factory attract such a storm of criticism from the 'respectable' areas of society in convict New South Wales? On balance, did this multi-functional institution do more harm than good?

The first establishment to carry the name was one begun in 1804—by Governor King—when he ordered the building of a factory above the gaol at Parramatta to house female convicts who were unable to provide adequate accommodation for themselves at the end of each day (when their work had been completed). Most of the women made their own arrangements, and many cohabited with male convicts in relationships which scandalised the colonial chaplain, the Reverend Samuel Marsden. An additional motive for King's factory was the need for some form of penitentiary in which to confine women who had committed further crimes in the colony, or who offended too greatly against the moral standards of the administrators of the colony.

Thus, from the very beginning, the female factory had an element of ambiguity about its functions—that is, whether it was an asylum or a penitentiary, and the priority of asylum or penitentiary was never clearly established. When the old factory was replaced by a new and purpose-built establishment—designed by the architect Francis Greenway for Governor Lachlan Macquarie in 1821—the same ambiguity also affected the new factory. Throughout its history, until it closed in 1848, the Parramatta Female Factory combined a variety of roles that were contrary to one another. It acted as:

- a place of confinement for criminal women;
- a work-house for poor women unable to support themselves;
- an asylum for aged and infirm women;
- a place of protection for vulnerable single women;
- a marriage bureau;
- a labour market; and
- a general hospital for women of the colony.

With expectations so diverse, the factory was almost bound to disappoint the colonial authorities, and, once again, there was no clear ranking among these mutually contradictory aims to guide those charged with administering it. Indeed, there were times when the stress shifted from one function to another according to local circumstances, and a complete lack of consistency became characteristic of the way in which the factory was run.

In order to satisfy such a range of functions, the factory operated a classification system through which it attempted to discriminate in the treatment meted out to a population that comprised non-convicted females at one end of the spectrum, and hard-bitten repeat offenders at the other. Although it varied over time, in general terms the factory operated three classes of inmates among a residential population that varied between 250 and 500 inmates. It became government policy that all communication between the women in the different classes be forbidden, and that they be kept rigorously separated to avoid the contamination of the blameless by proximity and contact with the vicious.

The *first class* of inmates was known as the 'merit class', and comprised women of good behaviour, sober, and respectable in deportment, who were allowed to receive visitors and make employment contacts on their own account. After twelve months in the merit class, a woman could marry or be employed on the internal domestic staff of the factory. One of the real advantages of being placed in the first class lay in the fact that the women received a payment for their work—which usually entailed the manufacture of clothing (for the convicts in government service); or duties as laundress, midwife, or schoolmistress. First-class women also received a privileged dietary allowance much superior to that allocated to the other two classes.

The *second class*, were women who had been disorderly or disrespectful to authority in the factory and accordingly had been demoted from the first class. It also included those who had been returned from assignment, and others who had been promoted from the bottom third class category. The women in second class had to serve three months before they became eligible for promotion to the merit class, and for this reason the second class was sometimes known as the probationary class. At this level of the classification system, the women were subject to a number of restrictions. they could not marry or be assigned. They were not permitted to receive visits, and after 1826, their diet was less generous in both quantity and quality than that enjoyed by the women of the first class. For example, second class women received no milk allowance, and were provided with maize cornmeal rather than the wheaten flour distributed to the first class. Second class women also received less payment for the work they performed in the factory, and half of what they earned was withheld from them until the time of their release.

The *third class* of women usually were the criminals convicted of further crimes in Australia, and under punishment of incarceration. These women had been found guilty of less serious offences, and the female factory's third class of prisoners included those committed for crimes that were not sufficiently serious to warrant confinement in the colonies of secondary punishment at Van Diemen's Land, Newcastle, Moreton Bay, or Norfolk Island (that is, in the first settlement of Norfolk Island—between 1788 and 1814—when men and women were both sent to the island). Drunkenness, petty theft, disrespectful behaviour towards authority, and other undesirable conduct, would normally suffice to secure their perpetrators a berth in the third class of prisoners in the Parramatta Female Factory. Conditions for women in this category were even tougher than those applying to the second-class prisoners—with further reductions in diet, clothing allowance, and living conditions.

One of the great injustices in the classification system—in a regime that included the free (but incapable) alongside the convicted criminals—was that women could find themselves punished for minor infractions of the factory regulations by wardens or matrons who were empowered to alter their classification without recourse to a magistrate or a court of law. So a free woman might find herself condemned to a penitential style of imprisonment as a third-class prisoner on the whim of one of the employees paid by the government to run the factory. A further injustice lay in the fact that first-class and second-class prisoners were, in fact, being punished twice—once by being transported to Australia for the crime they had committed in Britain, and again, this time in Australia, for being rejected by a labour system of domestic assignment that could not absorb them. As they were reported to have complained to Governor Gipps in 1843:

> they had been sentenced to be Transported, but not to be imprisoned after Transportation ... in a place where the discipline is as severe as in the Penitentiary, and the privations and discomforts greater.[37]

Women suffered further privations in the factory—in that they were forcibly separated from their children who were four years or older. The children were sent to the Orphan School, and were returned to their mothers when the latter left the factory. What contact they were permitted was a privilege conferred only as a reward for the women's good behaviour.

The Parramatta Female Factory also possessed a number of secondary functions connected with the regulation of female lives by the State. The working-class habit—of cohabitation in *de facto* relationships—a habit that the convicts had brought with them from Britain, appalled the colonial authorities (who came largely from the ranks of the more genteel classes). Cohabitation was considered by these people to be tantamount to prostitution, and that made New South

Wales a sink of iniquity in the eyes of middle-class observers. The women of the first class in the factory were therefore encouraged to marry—as a means of escaping from the confines of the factory and its discipline—and many of them took advantage of the opportunity. Serving male convicts were also encouraged into matrimony in Governor Darling's time by being permitted to have an additional day to work for themselves if they married. Most convicts received one day a week for their own work, but Darling ruled that married men should receive two. The combination of a drastic shortage of women, and official pressure to regularise common-law liaisons, caused many factory women to accept offers of marriage. Women still under sentence would then be assigned to their husbands.

Every Monday morning, the matron would parade the first-class women in their best regalia, for the purpose of meeting eligible bachelors looking for a helpmeet. Most of the men who attended the muster were emancipated convicts who owned their own small farms and were anxious to settle down with a woman who could be a companion, a lover, and a skilled assistant doing the dairy work on the property—dairy work being usually considered women's work at this time. Any couple who fancied each other could step aside for a more private conversation, and, if they both agreed—for the woman's agreement was just as necessary as the man's, and no woman was forced to marry unwillingly—then a special licence was issued and the couple were married, usually by the Reverend Samuel Marsden.

The factory also operated as a placement and employment agency for women of the first class, and requests for the assignment of women were regularly processed by the factory authorities. Similarly, the factory operated as a means of disciplining recalcitrant women who could be returned as unsatisfactory by their masters or mistresses, and they would be punished by being placed in the second class of probationers until good behaviour once again returned them to the first class, and eligibility for reassignment. This raises yet another function of the factory as a hospital for the women of the colony. It often occurred that a woman was returned to the factory because she had become pregnant to a man who could not, or would not, marry her. It might have been an already married master or servant, or it might have been that the woman genuinely did not want to marry the father. She may herself have been already married. In any event, a pregnant female convict was usually returned to the factory which then operated as a lying-in hospital for women waiting to give birth, and the women remained at the factory while nursing their infants.

The factory hospital had originally been intended for the exclusive use of the inmates, but, as early as 1826, Governor Darling was complaining that the hospital was being used by women other than those entitled to its services. Many of those using the hospital were paupers, and an enquiry found that the wives of free men and ticket-of-leave convicts were using the factory as a lying-in hospital, and were obtaining the services free. By the beginning of 1829, the Parramatta Female Factory accepted all colonial females who needed medical treatment—regardless of their civil status. At the beginning of that year, the Factory Board of Management requested an extension to increase the hospital's capacity to accommodate the increased number of women in need of its services. However, the hospital saw more than childbirth cases, and the factory records show that women received treatment for a wide range of conditions ranging from venereal disease through to dropsy and tuberculosis, as well as the treatment of accidents involving wounds or burns to the limbs, body or head.

The Parramatta Female Factory performed a wide variety of functions in colonial Sydney, but its primary and over-riding province was to act as a place of incarceration. That this was in opposition to its ancillary roles provided an ambiguity to its activities that was never resolved by government at the time, and has clouded its subsequent reputation with historians.

In balance, it would be fair to say that the factory did more good than harm, and that it afforded a sanctuary—no matter how limited in scope—for those women in colonial society who were too frail, old, infirm, or disabled to look after themselves. It also acted as a hospital, a labour exchange, and a marriage bureau—in addition to its function as a place of manufacture and prison discipline. Over the years it has suffered from an unnecessarily bad press—a reputation that originated in attacks by conservative clergymen and gentry on the morals and ability of its administrators and its inhabitants.

38

The Prison Boys of Point Puer

Where and what was Point Puer? How did it get its unusual name? Why was it considered both notorious and successful? And what unpleasant fate befell those overseers who were chosen for the honour of being 'crowned' by the inmates?

In 1834, the Lieutenant-Governor of Van Diemen's Land wrote to the Colonial Under-Secretary in Britain and drew that gentleman's attention to a problem in the practice of transporting male convicts to Australia without paying sufficient regard to the age of the felons. From 1788 onwards, about ten per cent of the male convicts had been mere children aged between nine and fifteen years, and these boys were placed in a particularly hazardous position when incarcerated aboard ship for the voyage out—and when barracked in Australia—as part of the main body of adult convicts. A number of enquiries into various aspects of the convict system had drawn attention to the moral and physical danger which young boys faced in such hard-bitten company, and George Arthur's despatch addressed this problem directly, although without any mawkish sentimentality concerning the youthful offenders:

> ... it is utterly impossible to imagine a more corrupt fraternity of little depraved felons—on their landing I examined them personally and collected much of their history from themselves—some, it appeared, had been trained in a vicious course from having been thrown upon the world totally destitute, others, have become so, from the tutorage of dissolute Parents ... and others, have been the agents of dexterous old thieves about London—but all are the objects of compassion ... To assign them is impossible, and I, therefore, caused about one hundred to be removed to Tasman's Peninsula, but to be there kept apart and quite distinct from the Convicts under sentence.[38]

The establishment was called Point Puer—the name being derived from the Latin word *puer* meaning 'boy'. It was adjacent to the adult settlement of Port Arthur for recalcitrant and recidivist convicts, and about a mile (1.6 km) across the bay from that hell hole. The boys were to be kept apart from the adult convicts at Port Arthur, and reformed into useful citizens of their new country. The Commandant of the Port Arthur settlement was in overall control of Point Puer, but a local superintendent of the boys' prison was appointed to run the place and to implement the policies laid down by the Commandant and the Lieutenant-Governor of the colony. Sixty-six boys were the first inhabitants of the new settlement in 1834, and they were put to work making the buildings, the walled exercise yards and cells, and the houses for the Superintendent and his overseers. The buildings were of brick with a very inferior mortar that contained no lime (which caused them to deteriorate very quickly), or they were of weatherboard (which lasted rather better).

From 1834 until 1849, when the establishment was disbanded, Point Puer became the home of over 2000 boys—most of whom passed through the institution and came out the other end with a smattering of education and a trade at which they could work and earn an honest living. They were not there under sentence for a fixed period of years, but until such time as they were considered able to maintain themselves by working with their skills in the wider colonial community.

While at Point Puer, they were subject to severe discipline. For example, in 1840, out of a total population of 494 boys, 351 were punished for committing 1011 infractions of the rules. These varied from cases of serious assault on overseers or other boys, to boisterous horseplay. Theft from boys and staff was a common occurrence—as was absconding, which usually consisted of boys running away to the caves on the cliff-face above which Point Puer was situated, and living wild there in the caves for a period of time before they surrendered to the authorities. Because the settlement was located on a peninsula that was open to the sea and lashed by fierce winds and dangerous currents, few boys ever succeeded in escaping permanently. They could not escape by sea, and the land connection led straight to a line of sentry boxes where soldiers and ferocious guard-dogs patrolled constantly.

Boys were punished in various ways:

- by flogging on the backside up to thirty strokes for serious crime;
- by confinement in a detention area with loss of recreation privileges;
- by attachment to work details that cleaned up the establishment, emptied latrines, cut wood, and worked in the potato fields; and
- by transfer to the full rigours of the Port Arthur Settlement (this last punishment being for the occasional major crime—such as murder of an overseer—following trial by the Commandant in his capacity as a Magistrate).

From the outset, four different classes of prisoners existed at Point Puer, and the treatment of each group was quite distinct, with different grades of punishment according to the class in which a boy was placed.

First, there was the *general class* which comprised the majority of the boys who arrived direct from Britain and did not call undue attention to themselves

Remnants of the underground punishment cells at Point Puer. (Archives Office of Tasmania)

The Isle of the Dead, Port Arthur. Boys who died at Point Puer and convicts who died at the main Port Arthur penal settlement, were laid to rest on this small island that lay close to the Point Puer establishment. (Archives Office of Tasmania)

by flagrant breaches of the rules. They worked in the general clean-up gangs for a few months, and, if their behaviour had been good, they could then apply for the trade of their choice where they would receive a full training and apprenticeship in their chosen field. Trades taught at Point Puer included boat-building, carpentry, nail-making and metal work, blacksmithing, stone masonry, brick manufacturing, furniture making, tailoring, shoemaking and gardening. Most boys were desperate to enter one of the trades on offer, and this provided an incentive for their good behaviour. Once they were in a training scheme, most boys did not want to lose their place and the assured meal-ticket it represented in the outside world, and therefore discipline problems were not as overwhelming as a boys' reformatory might at first suggest. The standard of the trade-work was high, and many of the surviving ornamental stone buildings at the Port Arthur site are made of stones cut and shaped by the Point Puer stone-masons. Similarly, much of the furniture in Port Arthur—and in the government buildings in Hobart during these years—was manufactured by the Point Puer furniture-makers, and most of the clothing and footwear issued to the convicts was also the product of the boys' work.

The *second* group were the *incorrigibles*, and this consisted of boys who made a persistent habit of cheeking the overseers or the Superintendent, who were found guilty of theft from their companions, or who refused to co-operate with the disciplinary regime of the establishment. Others included in this class were the boys who had absconded, or those who had been involved in crimes of violence. The more serious of these violations were punished by a spell of solitary confinement in tiny cells that were under two metres in length, and less than one metre in width. These boys often received a flogging as well.

It would be a mistake to assume that these were poor waifs and helpless lambs, and the overseers soon found that constant vigilance was necessary if they were to avoid becoming the victims of violent assaults at the hands of some of these dangerous boys. In 1843, an overseer was murdered by two 14-year-old inmates. When the body was found in the exercise yard, the cause of death was established in the following terms:

> by blow or blows on the right side of the head which were inflicted by a stick or a stone hammer, such blows having been inflicted by Sparks and Campbell.[39]

The two boys named above were transferred to the main Port Arthur settlement after being found guilty of murder, and from there they disappear into the limbo of history.

Any overseer who relaxed his attention could find himself the object of a night-time prank the boys called 'crowning the overseer'. Throughout the dormitories, the boys were provided with large night-tubs to cater for the calls of nature after they had been locked in for the night. These tubs of urine would be very full of a morning, and, at a given signal, the lights would be extinguished, and the unpopular overseer who had been chosen as the subject would have the night-tub turned upside down over his head. Of course, nobody knew who had done the deed, and the authorities commented upon the solidarity of 'a desperate and unscrupulous element' among the boys who kept up a general hatred of authority, and who were protected by a strong corporate feeling against turning anyone in for such misdemeanours.

The *other two* classifications mentioned by Charles Joseph La Trobe, the visiting Superintendent of the Port Phillip District in 1846, were further sub-divisions within the two major divisions—incorrigibles and general—already noted. These further sub-divisions related to degrees of *punishment* in the incorrigible (that is, second-class) group; or degrees of *privilege* in the general (that is, first-class) group of boys—where the best behaved became monitors and assistant instructors, and enjoyed a special extra ration of tea and sugar.

By and large, the boys were treated reasonably well at Point Puer, although later in the nineteenth century it became the subject of a myth that maintained that the treatment was so extreme and brutal that an outbreak of suicide occurred when young boys—driven to despair—threw themselves off the cliff into the sea. There is no truth to that rumour. Indeed, the records show that there were only 38 deaths at Point Puer during the whole 15 years of its operation. One boy, however, did drown while engaging in recreational swimming in the ocean at Point Puer, and this is probably the source of the myth.

The boys who did die at Point Puer were buried on the Island of the Dead, which is a small island just off Point Puer headland, where more than 2000 dead convicts from Port Arthur are laid to rest. Neither the boys nor the convict men received headstones on their graves, and it is impossible to discern the precise locations of any of these graves. Only the graves of officers and other free people have headstones to commemorate them.

The Point Puer establishment never became self-sufficient—for a number of reasons. First, the soils were too infertile for effective cultivation, although that did not stop the authorities from using fieldwork in the unresponsive soils as a most galling punishment. Secondly, the place had no permanent water-supply of its own, and although some water was saved from rain run-off from the roofs of the buildings, water had to be regularly shipped across the bay from Port Arthur, and, in that duty, convict boatmen from the main settlement were necessarily employed to bring it ashore. Furthermore, from a very early time, the faulty building of the main structures led to rapid deterioration in the buildings at Point Puer, and an official visitor in 1842 described them as being in a state of semi-decay. And finally, conditions were made worse on occasion by severe overcrowding as the population reached 730 in 1845, before falling away again in 1849 to 162 boys, at which time they were transferred to the Cascades in Hobart and Point Puer was finally closed.

However, despite the obvious shortcomings, the Point Puer establishment can be rated one of the great success stories of the penal era. As a result of the training received at its trade schools, hundreds of young criminals were given a second chance at life, and were equipped to make a living as skilled mechanics in the general workforce. Once they had learned their trade—and had been judged capable of looking after themselves—the boys were moved to a type of half-way house at New Town Farm, where they worked at their trades until the government placed them with employers who knew that skilled tradesmen could be obtained at the boys' hiring depot. From here they submerged into the general community, and their very lack of later notoriety attests to the advantages they gained at one of Australia's earliest reform schools.

39

A Bunyip Aristocracy

What lay behind W.C. Wentworth's plans to establish an hereditary aristocracy in New South Wales? Why were his proposals unpopular and unsuccessful? How powerful is the weapon of ridicule? And who coined the immortal reference to 'a bunyip aristocracy'?

In 1854, the partly nominated and partly elected Legislative Council of New South Wales was engaged in debating the draft constitution—prepared by William Charles Wentworth—for the full transfer of responsible Government to the colony. This was a momentous moment in Australian political history because the former leader of the lower-class emancipists had thrown in his lot with the exclusives and their descendants, and had included clauses in the draft constitution that would lead to the establishment of an upper chamber in the foreshadowed two houses of the colonial Parliament—an upper chamber that would become a colonial 'House of Lords', to be occupied by baronets of a new Australian hereditary peerage.

During the first half of the nineteenth century, the politics of New South Wales had developed into a contest between two broad factions fighting for political supremacy. These two broad factions could be characterised as:

- the *exclusives* who were comprised of the wealthy free settlers, and the civil and military officers and their descendants; and
- the *emancipists* who included the former convicts (who had become free at the end of their sentences), their families, and, over time, the lower classes of free immigrant labourers, who found that the social and political pretensions of the exclusives would deny them a voice in the running of their new home.

After the introduction of an elective element to the Legislative Council in 1842, the exclusives came to dominate the legislature because they were the class who could afford the luxury of politics in a time when members of the Parliament did not receive a salary for their work; and because there was a property qualification before a voter became eligible to have his name placed on the electoral rolls. There were a few liberals elected from the Sydney constituencies, but the bulk of the Legislative Council's membership was drawn from the conservative rural squattocracy.

As William Charles Wentworth grew older, he found himself increasingly sympathetic and drawn to the conservatism of the exclusive ideology. Once the transportation of British convicts to New South Wales was halted in 1842, the term 'exclusive' all but disappeared, but the attitudes of the faction persisted, and it became more cohesive under the leadership of the liberal apostate Wentworth. The conservatives did not believe that former convicts and working men should be given a say in the selection of the people who ran the country. They felt that the right to express an opinion should be limited only to those men who had made something of themselves, and who had accumulated sufficient property to qualify for a vote or to stand as a member of the legislature. While liberals argued for the vote as the birthright of all freeborn Englishmen, colonial conservatives wished to preserve their privileged way of life by drastically limiting the franchise.

What better way to limit the influence of the groundswell towards democracy in Australia, than by establishing an hereditary aristocracy? The principle of heredity is the very opposite of democracy, and positions dependent on birth—rather than on ability or the popular will—lay at the heart of Wentworth's proposals. The pastoral interest—according to Wentworth and his followers—had brought New South Wales to its present state of civilisation and prosperity, and it was (they argued) the important interests in colonial society that should be represented in the law-making bodies. Wentworth stated his beliefs succinctly

Only portrait of William Charles Wentworth, the convict's child and would-be aristocrat, taken in Australia. (Taken from Jack Cato, *The Story of the Camera in Australia*, Melbourne, 1955)

on this question when he discussed the six seats that the draft constitution allocated to the City of Sydney. According to a newspaper report of the day, Wentworth's view was that the provision for six seats for the City of Sydney:

> is much too large ... [and I can] see no reason why the City of Sydney has any right to claim to be represented at all, except that there is a large mass of people congregated together in it.[40]

To protect the colony from falling under the control of radical democrats and common folk—who had flooded in during the goldrush period—Wentworth proposed to establish an electoral college that would be made up of the descendants of the new aristocracy, and this would choose the members of the upper chamber in the future. At the beginning, he envisaged, the newly created peers would become the members of the upper chamber, but over time they would produce numerous descendants, and all of these were to constitute the members of the electoral college. It was a long-term plan that was designed specifically to produce an Upper House that would become a bulwark for the important interests of the country against the reckless democrats of the Lower House. Wentworth declared that he favoured the British model and wanted: 'a constitution that will be a lasting one—a conservative one—a British, not a Yankee constitution'.[41]

Portrait of Dan Deniehy, who almost single-handedly ridiculed the proposal for an hereditary peerage out of consideration. (Taken from Cyril Pearl, *Brilliant Dan Deniehy: A Forgotten Genius*, Melbourne, 1972)

He went on to justify his position and stressed the gradual nature under which the new hereditary system would come into operation:

> The principle of electing a portion of the Upper House from those holding hereditary titles is one which cannot be carried into practice for the next forty or fifty years; it is to be seen therefore that the committee proposed to sow the seed of an institution which will have ample time allowed it to grow to maturity.[42]

The reaction in the wider community to the thought of a colonial system of hereditary grandees was one of astonishment—astonishment that the pastoralists' delusions of grandeur had become so extensive.

The *Empire* newspaper, under its editor Henry Parkes, wrote that the draft constitution proved that Wentworth was in his dotage, and accused the elder statesman of abandoning every high principle by which he had stood in his better years in order to embrace a wretched patchwork of political absurdities that he would have opposed strenuously had it been offered two decades earlier. The proposed peerage would perform the dual function of keeping the lower orders as slaves while making Australia the laughing stock of every civilised nation. The *Sydney Morning Herald*, the mouthpiece of the conservatives, reacted with caution and little enthusiasm for the proposal. It pointed out that any colonial baronetcy would become the object of ridicule—rather than respect—in the robust environment of Sydney politics, and the effect of this would be to weaken respect for the constitution and any claim it might have to political legitimacy.

Two native-born opponents of the scheme now came to the fore, and the concept of an aristocratic upper house was subjected to the forensic wit and condemnatory ridicule of the radical poet Charles Harpur and the youthful political commentator Daniel Deniehy.

Harpur reviewed the qualifications of the aristocratic Governor of New South Wales, Sir Charles Fitzroy—whose haughtiness and sexual promiscuity had made him despised by the liberals—and used these to mock both the British peers and their would-be colonial impersonators. Harpur suggested that the phrase, 'as drunk as a lord', would prove most popular in the colony, while the Governor's receding forehead and large nose led to the suggestion that characteristics like these—that displayed evidence of 'intense sensualism, selfishness extreme, and a brute obstinacy'—would provide the hallmarks for the selection of the members of the Upper House. But, the undoubted sign of real nobility Harpur concluded, was 'a thumping great nose! a round robustious, broad-backed, elephantine, Wellingtonian, dodo-like upper mandible'. Harpur concluded his review by advising Fitzroy to fill the upper chamber with 21 personages possessing large noses who could perform ceremonial salutes with their snouts to rival the traditional 21-gun salute.

Daniel Deniehy made his first public speech at a large meeting held in Sydney at the Victoria Theatre on 15 August, and it is generally held that it was at this gathering—at the hands of the brilliant 24-year old—that the Wentworth plan received its final coup-de-grâce. Deniehy's speech aroused gales of laughter from the audience, as he conjured up visions of: 'these harlequin aristocrats, these Botany Bay magnificos, these Australian mandarins'.[43]

Deniehy described James Macarthur—the head of the Macarthur family—as the 'Earl of Camden' with a coat of arms on which featured a rum keg. He spoke further of titled colonial pygmies who would render the colony so ridiculous that even the poor Irish peasant in the streets of Dublin would sneer, and he went on to connect the proposed Australian peerage with the well-established tradition of antipodean monstrosities and reversals of the natural order:

> Here they all know the common water mole was transformed into the duck-billed platypus, and in some distant emulation of this degeneration, he supposed that they were to be favoured with a bunyip aristocracy.[44]

As the *Sydney Morning Herald* had already recognised, ridicule was a powerful weapon in a debate such as this, and the notion that the descendants of the exclusives would somehow be raised up into legislators of superior quality by virtue of being made into baronets proved to be eminently ridiculous. The democratic tide in Australia had gone too far for such an old-fashioned notion—the implantation of the hereditary principle to colonial soil—to be sustainable.

William Charles Wentworth did serious damage to his reputation as a far-sighted and liberal colonial statesman by campaigning for such a development. In many ways, the fearful and reactionary attempt to create an Australian aristocracy has always overshadowed Wentworth's later reputation, and formed an artificial demarcation between his earlier leadership of the forces of colonial liberalism and his final departure from Australia to live in permanent exile from the country of his birth because it had become too democratic. The bitterness and disappointment in the soul of the exiled Wentworth had much to do with the ridicule he had provoked with his draft constitution and its clearly self-serving attempts to elevate himself and his male heirs into the Barons of Vaucluse.

40

Teddy and the Jewboy Gang

Who was the leader of the outlaw group known as Teddy and the Jewboy Gang, and how many members of the gang were Jewish? Why were the members of this gang subjected to a public mass execution? Why did one member of the gang not wish to 'die with his boots on'? And what do scarves and ribbons have to do with bushrangers anyway?

Few bushrangers in colonial Australia had a more dramatic reputation—or a more interesting story—than Edward Davis. Edward was the son of Michael Davies (sic) and his wife, and this Jewish couple produced eight children in all—two of whom were destined to make their mark in colonial Australia. The family had come to the attention of the English police on a number of occasions, and the father had been transported to New South Wales in 1830 on a charge of false pretences. In 1832, Edward, aged just sixteen, was convicted on a charge of stealing from a shop, and was sentenced to join his father and his elder brother John in Australia. Edward had not stolen goods from the shop, but had attempted to grab the till and run off with it and its contents. Tills were heavy items, and Edward had been pursued and captured. In the following year, he arrived in Sydney, and the convict indents list his religion as Jewish, and provide us with a physical description. The young lad was only five feet (1.5 m) in height, and worked as a stable-boy and apprentice jockey. His horsemanship was later judged to be excellent.

There was a wild streak in the young convict, and, by Christmas of his initial year in the colony, he had absconded for the first time. Over the next five years, Edward Davis was to abscond four times in all, and, after the last attempt—in 1838—he re-emerged in the following year as a bushranger who became known as Teddy the Jewboy. The gang of escaped felons which he gathered about him became known as the Jewboy Gang—despite the fact that Davis was the only Jew among them. For the following two years, Teddy and the Jewboys operated over a large expanse of territory covering a region that included the Gosford area, through the Hunter Valley and up to the New England Ranges.

The gang was always well mounted, and they also possessed pack horses on which to load supplies and booty from the raids that they carried out all along the Great Northern Road. Davis had insisted that the gang avoid bloodshed at all costs, and a romantic aura surrounded them as they consciously modelled themselves on the dashing highwaymen of legend in Britain—such as Dick Turpin. They affected a gaiety of dress and manner, and decked themselves out in colourful silk scarves and ribbons for their horses' bridles. The gang came to be much admired by the convict and emancipist population of New South Wales, and became the subject of ballads and gossip in the sly-grog shops which this class frequented. The Jewboy Gang engaged in a protracted reign of terror, when, in a series of daring raids, they stole horses and cattle, raided homesteads, and held up the mail and other travellers on the highway.

The bushrangers were able to avoid capture for such a long period of time because the lower levels of colonial society refused to hand them in, or to provide information to the police about the gang's whereabouts. Edward Davis played the role of the convicts' avenging angel when he administered a public flogging to a squatter at Wollombi who was notorious for the cruelty with which he treated the convicts working for him. The gang tied him up to the public triangles in the market-place, and flogged him with the cat-o'-nine-tails used by the government flogger in the district. Such activities endeared Davis to the victims of squatter arrogance—and created considerable fear and panic among the gentry and better-off members of the local communities.

Similarly, the Jewboy Gang aroused fear and loathing in the upper ranks of rural society—and great enjoyment among the lower classes—by the ease with which they avoided the police sent out to capture them, and by the humiliation which they inflicted on the forces of law and order when it suited them. Whenever large parties of mounted troopers combed the bush looking for them, Davis and his gang—in keeping with their rule of avoiding bloodshed—would withdraw deep into the ravines and forests, where they concealed themselves until the police had grown weary of the chase. Upon the withdrawal of the baffled troopers, the gang would emerge from hiding and resume their careers as knights of the road.

Teddy and the Jewboy Gang also employed ridicule to undermine the reputation of the police. On one occasion they rounded up the district's Chief Constable and his men—the members of a mounted party of police and volunteers that was out in pursuit of them—captured and yarded them like a mob of sheep, took their horses, arms and money, and rode away laughing. A policy of causing the maximum of discomfiture to the representatives of authority and wealth seemed to underlie much of the gang's activity.

The run of luck could not last indefinitely, however, and the gang's plundering finally ended in a confrontation with a shop assistant during a robbery, in which a member of the gang, John Shea, shot dead a storekeeper's clerk named John Graham. Edward Davis' golden rule had been broken, and the gang fled from the scene of the crime in an attempt to put as much distance as they could between themselves and the inevitable pursuit. A party of police and volunteers tracked the gang for a distance of fifty miles (80 km), and, at sunset the next day, they finally caught up with the gang in camp. A shootout between the gang and the pursuers followed—in which Edward Davis received a wound to the shoulder— and all members of the gang were eventually captured. The bushrangers were taken to Sydney and committed for trial at the Supreme Court. Shea was indicted for murder, and the other members of the Jewboy Gang were indicted as being accessories to murder—in that they had aided and abetted Shea.

Edward Davis' lawyer mounted a defence on the grounds that it was widely known that Davis, as the leader of the gang, had always tried to avoid bloodshed, and that at the time John Shea had shot the victim, Edward Davis had not been physically present. In these circumstances, it was argued, there could be no question of Davis' being an accessory to murder. Despite the best efforts of the defence, the jury found all members of the gang guilty, and the Chief Justice, Sir James Dowling, sentenced them all to death.

Davis, as the flamboyant leader of this colourful gang, and as a man who had never shed blood himself—discounting the flogging of the squatter at Wollombi— received a great deal of public sympathy. An appeal was made to the Executive Council for clemency in his case—but the appeal was turned down and the sentence of death was confirmed.

On 16 March 1841, Teddy and the Jewboys were all publicly hanged in Sydney before a crowd of over 1000 people. Witnesses in the crowd reported that the only member of the gang who seemed at all repentant for his deeds had been Davis himself. Indeed, the hanging was the scene of one of the most bizarre events in the history of public executions in Australia, when James Everett, one of the gang members, took off his boots and flung them into the crowd from the hanging platform. He claimed that he had done it to spite his mother, who had long predicted that he would die with his boots on—that is, that he would be hanged—and that he had no intention of giving her that satisfaction!

Public admiration for the gang was already strong, but they had subjected the minions of the law to serious humiliation, and had held them up to the contempt and ridicule of the lower orders. In such circumstances, there was no possibility that an executive intent on revenge would have allowed any appeal on behalf of Edward Davis or of his companions. An example had to be made, and respect for law and order reinforced, so Teddy and the Jewboy Gang expiated their crimes on the Sydney gallows.

One great irony in this case lies in the colonial career followed by Edward Davis' eldest brother John—who had also arrived in the colony as a convict. Unlike his little brother, John Davis joined the forces of law and order, and became a policeman. By 1840, while his brother's gang was terrorising the

Maitland district, John was appointed as Chief Constable at Penrith. John resigned in March of the following year—after his brother's execution—when the family connection made his life intolerable. He moved to Melbourne where he was unknown, and his father joined him and ran a series of hotels and public houses in that thirsty city. John became a reporter for a local newspaper and a stand-up comedian on the Melbourne stage. After five years, when the notoriety of the Jewboy Gang had subsided, John returned to New South Wales where he became Chief Constable at Wellington. Thereafter, he secured a series of government positions which included: Inspector of Slaughter Houses, Inspector of Weights and Measures, Inspector of Distilleries, Bailiff of the Court of Petty Sessions and finally Chief Constable at Bathurst.

Following this glittering career, John Davis moved to Tasmania, where he became the founder of the newspaper the *Hobart Mercury*, and later became a member of the Tasmanian Legislative Assembly. John Davis died in 1872 in Hobart—a valued and respected pillar of that colony's society—none of the members of which had any inkling of his connection with that notorious and flamboyant bushranger, Teddy the Jewboy.

A multiple hanging of the type that was common in convict Australia. The Jewboy Gang suffered such a public execution.

41

Ben Boyd—Merchant Adventurer and the First Blackbirder

Why is Benjamin Boyd remembered as the man responsible for beginning the notorious 'blackbirding' trade in Pacific Islanders? Why did Benjamin Boyd and others like him endorse the use of indentured coloured labour with such enthusiasm? What was the ironic conclusion to his entrepreneurial career?

Benjamin Boyd was born in Scotland in 1796. He entered the stockbroking business in London, and became interested in the pastoral industry in Australia because of the huge profits that were made by investors during the decade of the 1830s. It appeared to many investors in Britain that virtually unlimited returns were available on capital placed in the wool industry, and unreasonable expectations became the norm for investments of this type.

In 1839, Boyd and a number of fellow entrepreneurs founded the Royal Bank of Australia in London with a capitalisation of one million pounds. Their intention was to invest large sums of money in a variety of colonial industries—with whaling, shipping, and wool as the main focus for the bank's endeavours. A Sydney branch of the Royal Bank was established, and, in 1842, Boyd himself—accompanied by a small party of business acquaintances—arrived in Australia to superintend the activities of the bank, and to speculate in land and whatever other investment opportunities lay to hand.

Ben Boyd travelled in style aboard his own steam yacht the *Wanderer*, which he had fitted out in the utmost luxury. The vessel carried thirteen cannon for protection from pirates and natives, and it was also equipped with a generous supply of firearms, cutlasses, and pikes for defence and to repel boarders if necessary. Boyd also sent to Australia two steam ships which he intended to use in the colonial carrying trade between the Australian colonies on the eastern seaboard of the continent—perhaps including New Zealand if the trade possibilities seemed encouraging.

Boyd's timing was unfortunate, as he arrived in Australia at a time when supplies of cheap convict labour for the pastoral industry were no longer available. The British abolished convict transportation to New South Wales in 1840, and the existing population of assigned convicts was rapidly declining as those still under sentence served out their time and were not replaced by any new shipments. Free labour proved to be much more expensive, and far less easy to coerce than convicts, and Boyd and the other large squatters complained that labour costs were unacceptably high in Australia, and were cutting deeply into profit margins. He also arrived at a time of drought and severe economic depression—as the capacity of the British textile industry to absorb unlimited amounts of Australian wool seemed temporarily to have reached saturation point—and at a time when the costs of production and carriage of wool in Australia had begun to reach a level where the more remote sheep stations were only marginally viable. The financial crisis could not be quarantined to the wool industry, but spread to urban areas as well, for the dangerous position of the mercantile and banking sectors lay in the exposure caused by their joint extension of credit on a large scale to the pastoral industry and to individual pastoralists. Anything that threatened the ability of the squatters to hang on and work their way into profitability again, also threatened the survival of the banks and large merchant houses. Colonial wage rates became one such factor.

Ben Boyd's vision of a steam-powered carrying trade proved to be unrealisable in the Australia of the 1840s. The volume of trade was too small to be worth the costs of running a mechanised service with all the additional expense involved. Even the mail contracts were unable to produce profits, as the increased speed of communications—which was produced by Boyd's mechanised service—came at an additional cost that rendered the continuance of the service prohibitive.

Boyd turned his attention to two other areas of operation where he felt sure that large profits could still be maintained—the whaling industry and the pastoral industry. He was essentially a speculator, and believed that he could turn a profit in both areas of enterprise if he could control the labour costs. However, he was quite wrong in his diagnosis of the reasons behind the colonial depression—for the depression did not lie in the high cost of labour in the colony, but rather in a cut-back in credit from Britain and in an over-production of wool in Australia that resulted in falling prices.

In 1843, Boyd purchased a great deal of land in the area of Eden and Twofold Bay in New South Wales, together with the licences on squatting runs of almost 2 500 000 acres across New South Wales. He built a town at Twofold Bay to become the centre of his business operations in both whaling and wool industries, and modestly named it *Boydtown*—after himself. He quartered his whaling vessels at Boydtown, and engaged in coastal whaling from bases on shore, as well as deep-sea whaling with ships operating in competition with established American and English whaling interests in the South Seas. As part of his constant effort to cut his labour costs, Ben Boyd developed a policy of using native labour or coloured labour in both areas of whaling. He was the first person to make extensive use of Aboriginal labour in the coastal whaling industry, and he had several Aboriginal boat crews whom, he claimed, were as good as any in the business. He paid them a pittance for their efforts, and saved a great deal of money on his wages bills. In his deep-sea whaling ventures, Boyd soon found that natives from the Pacific islands worked just as hard—and for considerably less wages—than did white crews, and he began to include Islanders in the crews of all his vessels. Even the *Wanderer*—his own private yacht—was not exempt, and, by 1851, its entire crew came from the Pacific region.

In his pastoral activities, Ben Boyd revealed in its starkest form the extent to which he was prepared to go to turn a profit. The free immigrants—who had come on assisted passages to New South Wales since 1831—did not suit the requirements of the pastoralists. They wanted single men with no dependents who were prepared to work as shepherds on the lonely outstations in the interior of the country. But the development of the colony—and especially the deliberate alteration of the nature of its population mix from criminal to free—favoured

Painting of Ben Boyd from his ancestral home. (Taken from Tom Mead, *Empire of Straw: The Dynamic Rise and Disastrous Fall of Dashing Colonial Tycoon Benjamin Boyd*, Sydney, 1996)

the migration of families rather than single labourers. Married men with wives and children might have secured the future of the colony, but they required amenities that the squatters like Boyd were simply not prepared to provide. Moreover, most migrants came from urban backgrounds in Britain, and were afraid of the outback and of the dangers faced daily by men working as shepherds. The possibility of being speared by Aborigines was one of the main fears of such workers, but other concerns included the primitive living conditions and poor wages provided by a class of employers who had become accustomed to dealing with a workforce of convicts—and who treated the free labourers like men serving time who had no rights.

By 1843, a paradoxical situation had arisen in New South Wales, in which there was widespread unemployment in the cities and towns of colonial Australia, but, at the same time, a massive shortage of labour in the pastoral districts. Urban workers preferred to take their chances without work in the urban areas rather than take certain employment with the squatters. The problem was that the work of a shepherd in the pastoral districts was lonely, dirty, and completely nomadic. The sheep herds had grown in size to about 1000 sheep or more, and they were attended by a single shepherd who travelled with the flock and camped out by them every night. This was not the sort of life for a migrant with a wife and family. Besides, once a pastoralist like Boyd had reached an agreement with a worker on the rate of wages to be paid, other rival pastoralists would entice the labourer away by offering an extra pound or so a year in wages. So a man like Boyd would find himself in the situation of having provided his worker with the funds to travel into the interior to reach the stations—and then having to watch helplessly while his neighbours seduced the man into breaking his contract. The process of enforcing the labour contracts in the courts was too expensive to be worthwhile.

A Select Committee of the Legislative Council of New South Wales was established late in the same year (1843) to investigate the program of assisted immigration and the dislocation of the labour market. In evidence given before this committee, it emerged that Boyd was offering the lowest wages paid in the rural sector, and—far from his problems being caused by immigrants who were work-shy and preferred to luxuriate in the fleshpots of Sydney—the problems appeared to be connected with his attitude of paying as little as he could to his workforce. The men he did employ did not stay with him, but moved on to other employers who offered them a better wage and better conditions.

One of the major complaints by workers in the pastoral industry stemmed from the way that they were cheated out of their wages by unscrupulous squatters who increased the size of the flocks for which a single shepherd was responsible, and then deducted from his wages the costs of any sheep lost or injured while under his care. The normal size of flocks had grown from about 350 head to around 1000 head in this way, but Ben Boyd expected his shepherds to handle flocks of around 2000 sheep. Losses of animals were unavoidable in such circumstances, and to deduct such losses from the shepherds was an injustice. Wages paid by Boyd to white shepherds varied according to the remoteness of the station. In the most remote areas, he paid his workers about $50 a year (plus keep); in the intermediate districts this was reduced to $40 a year (plus keep), while in the close-in areas Boyd tried to force the annual wage down to $20 a year (plus keep). As the depression bit deeper, the pastoralists reduced the wage to $20 in all districts—thus further discouraging the labourers from accepting engagements with them.

In 1847, Benjamin Boyd sent one of his whaling ships on a voyage to the South Pacific expressly to collect a cargo of Islanders to work as labourers on his sheep stations. From Vanuatu he collected 65 labourers—whom he employed as rural workers. The wages he contracted to pay them amounted to $2.60 per year (plus keep), and this provided a significant economy over the costs of comparable white workers. This policy was a development of his established practice of employing Islanders aboard his ships—but the new workers clearly had no idea what they were getting into. The fact that the Boyd family had been involved in the infamous slave-trade only exemplifies the attitudes of this man—who was prepared to enter into labour contracts with workers who had no knowledge of the country or conditions to which they were committing themselves. When Boyd landed his cargo of Islanders at Twofold Bay, observers noticed that they were all naked, and seemed to have no knowledge whatsoever of English. Since their contracts with Boyd had been prepared in English, they could not possibly have known the import of what they had marked with their signs. But they had committed themselves to work for Boyd on ludicrously low wages for a period of five years. Boyd had introduced a modified form of slavery into colonial Australia.

The Islanders were taken inland to the sheep stations, and it immediately became clear that they had been seriously misled. Many of them returned to the coast within a few days, and demanded to be taken back to their homes. It was winter time, and Melanesians from tropical regions suffered cruelly from the cold in inland New South Wales. Some of them decamped to Sydney where they received a paternalistic—although sympathetic—reception as men who had been unwitting victims of Boyd's greed. Governor Fitzroy ruled that the indentures were illegal and unenforceable, and when Boyd's ship returned with a further 54 Islanders in October 1847 the indentures were no longer valid. This is where Boyd showed just what sort of a man he really was, for—rather than return the stranded Islanders to their homes—he abandoned them to their fate, and took no further interest in them. His labourers still remaining on his stations were also released from their contracts, and turned up in Sydney where they hung around Sydney Harbour begging for transport back to their islands. Most were eventually given passage to the general area from which they had come, but many had no idea of exactly what island they had been recruited from, and therefore there must have been a significant number of them who never made it back to their place of origin.

Ben Boyd incurred considerable negative publicity throughout Australia—and back in England—for his behaviour. Rumours were already afoot concerning his arrogance and his speculative methods of investing the money raised by the Royal Bank. His position as Executive Director of the bank was withdrawn from him, although he did remain on the Board of Directors. But all his expenditures in Australia had turned out badly, and even the profits earned in the whaling activities were swallowed up by the immense losses in his speculations in the pastoral industry. Under something of a cloud, Boyd sailed off to the

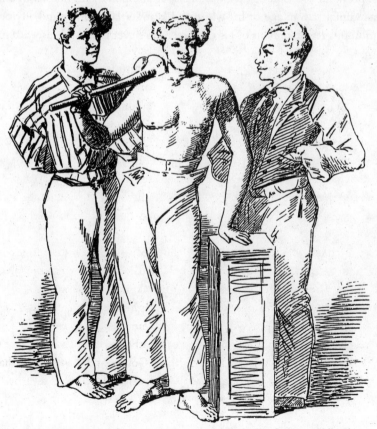

Three of Boyd's South Sea Island labourers, as shown in the Sydney publication *Heads of the People,* May, 1844.

Californian goldrushes in 1851 where he also failed. In 1853, he made landfall at Guadalcanal in the Solomon Islands aboard the *Wanderer*, and, heedless of his safety, he went ashore to hunt for meat for the ship. He never returned, the natives claiming that he had trespassed onto a site that was sacred to the women and *tabu* for men—so they killed and ate him. His shipmates turned the cannons on the native villages and exacted a ferocious revenge, but there does seem to be a certain symmetry to the fate of the first blackbirder. If anyone deserved to end up on the menu of a cannibal lunch, it was Benjamin Boyd!

Ironically, Ben Boyd's huge expanse of pastoral properties in Australia *did* represent a potential profit in the long term; and, in the period of the goldrushes— when the population grew rapidly and when unlucky miners swelled the workforce—his investments in the sheep industry would actually have produced a handsome financial windfall. But Boyd had been replaced as the Chief Executive of the Royal Bank by that time, and had already disappeared at Guadalcanal.

Ben Boyd's reputation as a feckless and arrogant financial buccaneer, who rated profit far above humanity, was firmly established by his notorious attempts to take unfair advantage of his white and Islander labourers—and any possible posthumous reinstatement of his character has never been seriously attempted.

42

Peter the Painter

Who was the mysterious terrorist known as 'Peter the Painter'? Did the Perth police get the right man? How did romantic jealousy cause an international incident? How could 'Peter the Painter' change Australian immigration policy—without even setting foot in the country? And what role did future Australian Prime Minister John Curtin play in the whole unlikely saga?

In a country such as Australia—where much of the population is made up of migrants from other parts of the world—the formative events and influences from the original homelands that helped to make the people what they are, have now become a part of Australia's social history. As human beings emigrate, they take with them whatever material objects that they can carry from their homes. But they also carry invisible luggage, in the form of attitudes and expectations that are the product of experience in their culture of origin, and these can impact in quite unexpected ways upon developments in their new countries. The story of 'Peter the Painter'—and the anti-tsarist terrorists from the Baltic regions of the Russian empire—is an intriguing example of this process.

By 1905, the Russian empire was in its final stages of pre-revolutionary turmoil. The very size of Russia was its major strength, and, at the same time, the cause of its greatest weakness. The power of the tsars stemmed from the huge reservoir of manpower that could be called up for military service if required. The Russians could produce literally millions of soldiers on demand, and this meant that Russia always had to be taken seriously by the great powers of Europe. Paradoxically, the weakness of the tsars was also derived from the same huge manpower reserves. The Russian empire was ethnically diverse, and included a whole range of vassal peoples who were subjected to vicious campaigns of Russification that were deliberately designed to expunge their separate racial identification—by outlawing the use of local languages and eradicating their cultures. The Jews suffered from this policy most grievously, but the Latvian, Estonian, and Lithuanian peoples also suffered serious interference.

Such attacks by the repressive regime of the tsars inevitably produced a violent and aggressive revolutionary reaction from the more militant members of the subject populations; and a spiral of ever-increasing bloodshed marked the progress towards the inevitable dissolution of the Russian empire. The more that official

Peter Piatkow *aka*
Peter the Painter.
(Corporation of London)

repression by police and army grew, the greater were the number of assassinations and attempted assassinations of Russian officials and imperial functionaries. Even the tsar himself was not safe from such attacks, and the Russian Premier Stolypin became a victim in 1911.

In 1905, an unsuccessful revolution against the tsar broke out in Russia's Baltic provinces. The revolution was a failure, and the tsar's forces re-established law and order with a series of bloody massacres of those suspected of being sympathetic to the revolutionary movement. The police became the agents of repression, and a state of undeclared war existed between the revolutionaries and the tsarist police, in which, when police were killed, their comrades responded with even greater persecution.

A flood of refugees abandoned their homelands, and fled abroad to escape the death squads. Many of these desperados found their way into the East End of London, where a ghetto of Jewish and Baltic emigrés took root. Part of the invisible luggage which such people took with them was an intense hatred of the police as the agents of a repressive capitalist system. They were also determined to carry on the revolutionary struggle from abroad, and to finance their activities by making capitalism pay for the revolution. This was to be achieved by robbing banks, post offices and businesses, and it made the host country very wary of accepting refugees from the tsar's territories. It is an unfortunate example of the power of invisible luggage, that the emigrés' hatred of the Russian police was transferred so uncritically to a hatred of the English police—who had nothing in common with Russian methods or practices. In London, after all, the police went unarmed, and relied on moral persuasion and the general consent of the community to carry out their policing functions.

When unarmed English police came up against revolutionaries who believed in the justice of their armed struggle against capitalism, the outcome could be both dramatic and tragic. In 1910, a London jeweller's store was selected for a robbery by a group of Latvian revolutionaries under the leadership of a shadowy figure known as Peter Piatkow—also nick-named 'Peter the Painter' because he had once worked as a painter of street signs in France. Peter appeared to be the 'brains' behind the group, but he was not present at the jewellery store when the burglars were interrupted by five members of the City of London Police Force, who had been alerted to the robbery attempt by neighbours in the houses adjoining the store. The police challenged the thieves, who responded by opening fire with automatic pistols—killing three police and wounding a fourth.

This was by no means the first violent crime in which the Russian refugees had been involved, but it was the first time unarmed English police had been gunned down in the street by them. The result was a massive explosion of anger and indignation by the general English population, who were furious that the sanctuary which their country had offered to the refugees should be repaid in such a brutal fashion.

Eventually, police investigations traced two of the gang to a hideout in Sidney Street in the East End of London, and armed police surrounded the building and evacuated the other residents in the early hours before dawn. The refugees opened fire on the police, and a siege ensued in which more than a thousand police and British soldiers became involved. The Home Secretary, Winston Churchill, personally directed the siege, and thousands of sightseers were attracted by the crackling gunfire. The shootout lasted for almost eight hours, and was ended only when the building caught fire. The refugees refused to be taken alive, and both men died in the flames.

As more information about the gang emerged, the police became increasingly interested in Peter the Painter. Warrants for his arrest went out throughout Britain, and the co-operation of European police forces was promised unconditionally in helping to secure the arrest and return to England of such a dangerous fugitive. News of the events reached Australia via the newspapers, and the hunt for the revolutionary with the picturesque nick-name aroused considerable interest in this country. Reports flooded in to London claiming sightings of the elusive terrorist from cities right across Europe, and he was also seen in Canada and the

August Maren.
(Archives Office of Western
Australia)

United States. Peter the Painter had become a veritable will-o'-the-wisp.

In 1911, however, a report reached London which claimed that the police in Perth, Western Australia, had arrested the fugitive and were holding him on a charge of conspiracy to give false evidence—until the British authorities decided how they wanted to proceed. It was a most dramatic story, and the local Perth police and newspapers revelled in the publicity. But there was a problem—the man whom they had under arrest was *not* Peter the Painter.

This is not to say that the man in custody was innocent of the London crime—it's just that he was not Peter the Painter. It is now quite clear that the Western Australian police had stumbled across one of the gang of terrorists under Peter's control. His name was August Maren, and photographs collected by the London police when they raided the gang's hideout show Maren posing with other known terrorists who had been involved in the murder of the police—and in the subsequent siege. Maren had fled from London just hours before the authorities pounced, and had taken ship as an immigrant to Western Australia. While in Western Australia's rural districts—where he had worked with other Latvian immigrants as a labourer—Maren had boasted of his revolutionary connections to impress a migrant girl in the same camp. The girl's boyfriend had objected to Maren's attentions, and Maren had responded by having him arrested on a trumped-up charge. In this way he had hoped to gain uninterrupted access to the girl, but his plans had backfired, when the infuriated rival had informed the police that Maren was, himself, Peter the Painter!

The story leaked to the newspapers, and Maren and his accuser were both kept in custody until instructions arrived from London concerning the extradition of the terrorist leader. This was to cause a great deal of embarrassment to the London police, because they were forced to confirm that—even if the man turned out to be Peter the Painter—they had insufficient evidence to justify his return to Britain, or to obtain a conviction against him. In the meantime, Maren embarked on a hunger strike to protest against his unlawful imprisonment, only consenting to resume eating when the prison authorities in Western Australia threatened to force-feed him. In fact, the Government of Western Australia had become caught up in the illegal imprisonment of August Maren, and the spurious nature of the charge on which they were holding him was revealed when the suit was dropped as soon as the reluctant confirmation arrived from London that the British Government was not interested in any extradition proceedings.

The aggrieved boyfriend had also to be compensated, and the records of the Western Australian police force show a series of small payments—in money, clothes, accommodation and food—that were paid to him for his services as an informer. The girl at the centre of the romantic tiff was handed over to the tender mercies of the Perth Salvation Army—presumably in the belief that they had ample experience in handling headstrong and wayward females. The legality of this action must also be open to grave doubt—as she had done nothing to deserve being deprived of her liberty.

August Maren was to spend the next two decades in a fruitless search for justice and an apology. He volunteered for service in World War I, and, after the war, wrote a series of letters to various ministers in Western Australian governments, in which he outlined his case and demanded recognition that he had been the victim of illegal treatment. In 1927, he received the written support of a rising power in the Australian Labor Party, the then-editor of the Labor newspaper the *Westralian Worker*—John Curtin. The future Prime Minister supported Maren's claim to have been shabbily treated, and described the imprisonment of Maren as 'a monstrous proceeding'. John Curtin's intervention brought a grudging admission that Maren—by then known as Peter Johnson—did have legitimate grounds for complaint, but suspect foreigners of dubious reputation and provenance had no right to expect either compensation or apology. Besides, as far as the Western Australian Government was concerned, Maren's (Johnson's) long fight for justice just proved that he was obsessed and not to be taken seriously. In the words of the Western Australian Minister of Police:

I have to state that the circumstances in connection with the case of Peter

Johnson occurred so long ago, viz. 1911, that it is very probable that few, if any, persons except Johnson himself remember the case. The only reason there was much publicity at the time was because it was alleged that Johnson was identical with the notorious Peter the Painter, who was connected with some crime in London. This aspect was communicated to the CID Scotland Yard, London, and a reply received that it could not be ascertained that he was in any way concerned in the crime in London, and no action was desired by that Department ... Not infrequently charges are made against individuals and they are kept in custody until the case is brought on. Even if they are brought to trial and found 'not guilty' no compensation is payable. The case did not even, in this instance, go as far as the charge being proceeded with, which would indicate that the Law Department at that time considered there was not sufficient evidence to sustain any charge.[45]

The personal injustice to August Maren pales into relative insignificance, however, compared with the wide-reaching administrative changes which were brought into being as a result of the authorities' recognising the possibility that Western Australia might be in danger of becoming a haven for international murderers and terrorists. Although immigration policy was one of the areas of administration taken over by the Commonwealth Government at the time of federation, the Commonwealth merely took over the existing immigration machinery that already existed in the separate colonies. In other words, although nominal authority now resided with the Commonwealth—and while any new enactments would be the responsibility of the Commonwealth Parliament—all the old colonial legislation remained on the books, and the separate states continued to tamper with immigration matters.

As a result of the fear that Peter the Painter had taken refuge in Western Australia, an inexperienced Australian Labor Party government—which had just taken office for the first time in Western Australia—panicked. Instructions were sent to the State's Agent-General in London to extend the policy of restricting the immigration of coloureds to Australia, and now also to exclude all Russians and Russian Jews—and any other foreigners of dubious European origins. The infamous White Australia colour bar had undergone metamorphosis into an Anglo-Celtic culture bar—and this sweeping change was rushed through on the basis of an unsubstantiated misapprehension that the arch-terrorist Peter the Painter had taken up residence.

This instruction was never contradicted by the Commonwealth.

43
The Sandakan Death Marches

What happened to Australian prisoners of war at the hands of the Japanese on the Sandakan marches? Why did it happen? What cultural differences played a significant role in the grisly events? And just what humanitarian values—if any—are universal?

Of all the many atrocities perpetrated by the Japanese forces during World War II, the cruelty of the treatment inflicted on the 2500 prisoners of war (POWs) held at Sandakan in Borneo has become deeply etched in Australian consciousness. More than 2000 Australian POWs were exterminated by the Japanese at Sandakan and Ranau—and another 500 British POWs suffered the same fate. In fact, of the full quota of 2500 men held by the Japanese in Sandakan Prison Camp, only six Australians survived the war—and they lived solely because they escaped into the jungle before the final executions took place.

At the Tokyo War Crimes Tribunal in 1946, it was shown that the POWs held by the Japanese suffered a 27 per cent death-rate while in captivity. By way of contrast, the death-rate among Allied POWs in the hands of the Germans and Italians was 4 per cent. Australian death-rates were higher than the average figure for all Allied forces' POWs, and out of 22 376 Australian POWs in Japanese hands, more than a third died. The death marches at Sandakan, therefore, are a case study of a much wider phenomenon.

Lying at the heart of the issue was a culture clash that could never be surmounted. According to Western codes of behaviour, a soldier was expected to fight the good fight, for as long as he was able to endure it. If he had fought with all his might—if he had done everything that could be expected of a warrior in battle and had still lost—then he had satisfied the code of behaviour of the Western warrior, and he forfeited no respect or status by making an honourable surrender. Becoming a prisoner in such circumstances did not involve losing the respect of the enemy or one's self-respect, and opposition soldiers knew that the shifting fortunes of war could make them POWs tomorrow. Both sides in a Western conflict, therefore, had a vested interest in treating prisoners humanely.

But the Japanese culture extolled the warrior code of *Bushido*, and the Japanese armed forces were inculcated with the belief that a soldier should *never* surrender. To be captured by an enemy was to suffer an irreparable loss of face, and involved the total forfeiture of honour. It was believed by the Japanese High Command, that to ratify the Geneva Convention which laid down the minimum standards for the treatment of POWs, would involve the Japanese in obligations, but would give nothing in return. They were sure that Japanese warriors would commit suicide rather than surrender, and the concept that there could be such a thing as an honourable surrender was so alien to this frame of mind as to be unthinkable.

When Allied soldiers surrendered to the Japanese in Singapore—and across Borneo and the rest of the Far East theatre-of-war—they had (in the Japanese view) lost all claim to be respected by their enemy. The Japanese considered that Allied soldiers had indulged in an abject surrender to preserve life at the expense of honour, and this belief led the Japanese to despise the Allied soldiers, and to dehumanise them. Once this psychological process of dehumanisation had taken place, then the POWs could be treated as a form of sub-human resource—to be mercilessly exploited and worked until they dropped.

In 1942 and 1943, approximately 2500 Australian and British POWs were shipped by the Japanese from Singapore to Borneo. They were marched to a prison camp about eight miles (12 km) from the town of Sandakan, and made to work on the construction of an airfield for the Japanese Air Force. This use of POWs as part of the war effort of their enemies was expressly forbidden under the protocols of the Geneva Convention, but since the Japanese had never ratified the Geneva Convention, they considered that they were not bound by its rules.

At the beginning, the treatment of the men was harsh, but bearable. However, as the war went on, and the Japanese began to suffer loss after loss in the extraordinarily savage battles fought in the Pacific, the treatment meted out to this dehumanised group deteriorated dramatically. Food rations for the POWs were continually reduced, although the Japanese forces ate a nourishing and well-balanced diet themselves for the whole of the war. Medical supplies for the treatment of the endemic tropical diseases—like malaria and beri beri, or the large skin ulcers on the men's legs and arms—were withheld from the prisoners, even though such medical supplies were in ample supply. (By the time of their rescue, the six Australian survivors weighed 84–78 lb (32–40 kg), and they were extremely sick men, all suffering the effects of malaria and beri beri.) The POWs began to die from the combined effects of brutal ill treatment—large-scale beatings of the POWs with rifle butts, boots, and bamboo staves became routine—and the reduction of the food ration until it would no longer sustain life.

The Japanese decided to use the remaining prisoners as pack animals to carry rice and food supplies to their forces which were preparing to withstand an Allied invasion at Ranau. The Commanding Officer at Sandakan organised two marches—of the men who could still walk—from Sandakan to Ranau, a small village about 160 miles (256 km) to the west. The marchers followed a track through some of the most inhospitable jungle they had ever encountered, and every morning those too sick to continue were gathered together by the Japanese and shot by the side of the track. Conditions were deplorable, with the mud knee-deep most of the way for the first part of the journey, and the hills so steep that the men had to crawl to get up them, and then slide to get down the other side. By the time the second group reached Ranau, the original party of 700 prisoners had been reduced to 203 men, and they joined the six men who had survived from the party of 407 POWs who had set out with the first group of marchers.

At Sandakan, nearly 300 men had been too ill to walk at all, but the Japanese had moved them all into the open, and then burned the entire camp, leaving all the stretcher cases without food or care of any sort. They all died, some quickly, and those who were not so lucky perished over a period of days.

The final 203 prisoners arrived at Ranau on 26 June 1945. No accommodation had been provided for them—although three long huts had been prepared for the Japanese. The POWs camped in the open air in constant rain. The only shelter available to them came from huddling beneath the surrounding shrubs. There were no medical supplies, water had to be carried by hand from a creek half a mile (0.8 km) away, and the food ration had been cut to one small cup of rice water with about an inch of rice in the bottom. On this meagre fare, the POWs were worked to death as pack-horses for the Japanese Army. By 18 July there were only 72 survivors left alive to move into the hut which they had built to protect themselves from the elements, and they continued to die from ill-treatment and diseases.

On 1 August, the Japanese rounded up all the POWs who could still walk, marched them into the nearby jungle, and murdered them. This left about 15 POWs who were too ill to move. The Japanese took this final group to a hill at the back of the camp, and shot them all. By this time, the original group of 2500 POWs had been reduced to six escapers in the jungle, and it was they—after their rescue and return to Australia—who alerted the Allies to what had gone on at Sandakan and Ranau.

The Japanese Government accepted the Allied demand for unconditional surrender on 10 August 1945, and the speed of the surrender—and the speed of the arrival of Allied recovery teams to look after the prisoners and superintend the repatriation of POWs from the Japanese prison camps in Singapore, Indonesia, Thailand, Burma, Vietnam, Borneo, Korea, Manchuria, and Japan itself—probably saved the lives of many more POWs. There is no doubt that, otherwise, the killing of prisoners would have been far more widespread.

To the defeated Japanese, the thought of surrendering to the very people whom they had treated so horrifically for the past four years—they were ordered to surrender their authority and weapons to the leaders of the POWs—amounted to a double loss of face. To be ordered to surrender was bad enough, but to be ordered to surrender to men whom they had become accustomed to thinking of as sub-human, added another entire level to their humiliation.

At the War Crimes Tribunal, the officers and men commanding Sandakan Camp and the two death marches to Ranau, were charged with crimes against humanity by ill-treating and killing POWs. Two senior officers received the death penalty and were hanged; others received 15-year terms of imprisonment with hard labour. On the scaffold, Captain Susumi Hoshijima, the Commandant of Sandakan Prison Camp expressed no remorse for what he had done. Rather, he had bitten the hand of the Provost-Marshall as he pinioned his arms for the execution, and had shouted *Banzai! Banzai!* before the drop. That such behaviour was incomprehensible to Australian observers at the scene is a further illustration of the depth of the cultural gulf between the two peoples. In fact, Hoshijima was attempting to live up to the code of *Bushido*, and—from a Japanese perspective— his death was admirable in the circumstances. To Australian witnesses, it was a terrible death because a human being was launched into eternity without seeking forgiveness for his crimes from God.

It may take a very long time to bridge such a gap in understanding.

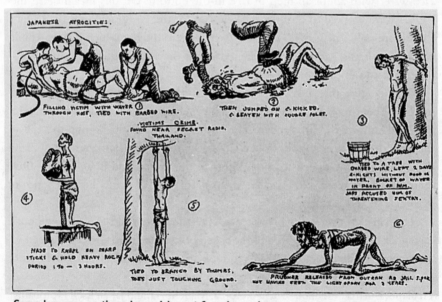

Some Japanese pastimes in punishment for minor crimes.
(Taken from Lord Russell of Liverpool, *The Knights of Bushido: A Short History of Japanese War Crimes*, London, 1958)

Acknowledgments

My thanks are due first to the ABC for allowing a history junkie to share his habit with fellow addicts. Special acknowledgment must be made of the support and enthusiasm of the premier compere Angela Catterns, who made the history component a permanent part of her national evening show. Thanks also to her producer, Steve Cannane, whose expertise and support has been much appreciated. Announcer Kevin Naughton and producers, Chris Norris and Doug Drew, were also part of the early days of the *Big History Question* before the baton passed to Angela Catterns.

At home, I have received considerable encouragement from my family, who know how much I enjoy talking about Australian history, and who have not begrudged the time it all takes.

At work, my friends and colleagues Portia Robinson, Linda Paoloni, Trevor McClaughlin, George Raudzens, John Walmsley, and Leighton Frappell have been extremely supportive; as has Valda Rigg, the Curator of Macquarie's Australian History Museum. To them I am most grateful.

Sources and Further Reading

1. Daisy Bates
Daisy Bates, *The Native Tribes of Western Australia*, Isobel White (ed.), Canberra, 1985
Daisy Bates, *The Passing of the Aborigines*, London, 1938
E. Salter, *Daisy Bates: The Great White Queen of the Never Never*, Sydney, 1971

2. Jack Howe—the Ringer or Gun-Shearer
Jim Gibney, 'Lest We Forget—Jack Howe', *Australian Tradition*, No. 36, December 1974
Hector Holthouse, *Up Rode the Squatter*, Sydney, 1970

3. The Battle of Brisbane
Richard Hall, 'The Battle of Brisbane', in *Good Weekend*, 25 November 1995
Dennis Phillips, *Ambivalent Allies: Myth and Reality in the Australian–American Relationship*, Melbourne, 1988
P.G. Edwards (ed.), *Australia Through American Eyes 1935–1945*, St. Lucia, 1979
L.G. Churchward, *Australia and America 1788–1972: An Alternative History*, Sydney, 1979

4. William Buckley—Australia's Wild White Man
Craig Robertson, *Buckley's Hope: Australia's Wild White Man*, Melbourne, 1980
Australian Dictionary of Biography

5. The Hungry Mile
Tom Nelson, *The Hungry Mile*, Sydney, 1957
C.M.H. Clark, *A History of Australia, Vol. VI*, Melbourne, 1987

6. The Rabbit Plague
William Lines, *Taming the Great South Land: A History of the Conquest of Nature in Australia*, Sydney, 1992
Eric Rolls, *They All Ran Wild: The Animals and Plants that Plague Australia*, Sydney, 1984

7. Black Mary—the First Female Aboriginal Bushranger
Julie Janson, *Black Mary*, Sydney, 1996
Jillian Oppenheimer, 'Thunderbolt's Mary Ann: An Aboriginal Bushranger', *Journal of the Royal Australian Historical Society*, Vol. 78, 1982

8. The New Italy Settlement
Anne-Gabrielle Thompson, *Turmoil—Tragedy to Triumph: The Story of New Italy*, Stanthorpe 1980

9. Frank Jardine—the Twice-Buried Pastoralist
Australian Dictionary of Biography
Glenville Pike, *Queensland Frontier*, Adelaide, 1982

10. Darwin and the Electric Telegraph

Michael Cannon, *Life in the Country,* Melbourne, 1973

K.S. Inglis, 'The Imperial Connection: Telegraphic Communication between England and Australia 1872–1902', A.F. Madden & W.H. Morris-Jones, (eds), *Australia and Britain: Studies in a Changing Relationship,* Sydney, 1980

11. Lachlan Macquarie—Slave Owner

John Ritchie, *Lachlan Macquarie: A Biography,* Melbourne, 1986

M.H. Ellis, *Lachlan Macquarie,* Sydney, 1978

Macquarie Journal No. 3, 29 December 1794 – 27 December 1799, Mitchell Library, Sydney

12. Sir George Arthur and the Black Books

A.G.L. Shaw, *Sir George Arthur, Bart 1774–1854,* Melbourne, 1980

W.D. Forsyth, *Governor Arthur's Convict System: Van Diemen's Land 1824–1836,* Sydney, 1970

13. James Stirling and the Pinjarra Massacre

C.T. Stannage (ed.), *A New History of Western Australia,* Perth, 1981

J.S. Battye, *Western Australia: A History from its Discovery to the Inauguration of the Commonwealth,* Perth, 1978

F.K. Crowley, *Australia's Western Third: A History of Western Australia from the First Settlements to Modern Times,* London, 1960

14. Brown Bess—Queen of the Frontier

David Denholm, *The Colonial Australians,* Melbourne, 1979

15. Samuel Marsden—Loathed in New South Wales; Loved in New Zealand

A.T. Yarwood, *Samuel Marsden: The Great Survivor,* Melbourne, 1977

C.M.H. Clark, *A History of Australia, Vol. 1: From First Times to the Age of Macquarie,* Melbourne, 1963

Bill Wannan, *Early Colonial Scandals: The Turbulent Times of the Reverend Samuel Marsden,* Melbourne, 1962

16. The Duke of Edinburgh's Braces

Keith Amos, *The Fenians in Australia,* Sydney, 1988

Robert Travers, *The Phantom Fenians of New South Wales,* Sydney, 1986

17. The Catalpa Rescue

Keith Amos, *The Fenians in Australia,* Sydney, 1988

J.S. Battye, *Western Australia: A History from its Discovery to the Inauguration of the Commonwealth,* Perth, 1978

18. The Spies Who Came to Sydney Cove

Alan Frost, *Arthur Phillip 1738–1814: His Voyaging,* Melbourne, 1987

Robert J. King, *The Secret History of the Convict Colony: Alexandro Malaspina's Report on the British Settlement of New South Wales,* Sydney, 1990

F.G. Clarke, *Australia: A Concise Political and Social History,* Sydney, 1992

Paul Fregosi, *Dreams of Empire: Napoleon and the First World War 1792–1815,* London, 1991

19. Mad Tom Davey
Coultman Smith, *Tales of Old Tasmania: The First Fifty Years,* Adelaide, 1978
John West, *The History of Tasmania,* A.G.L. Shaw (ed.), Melbourne, 1971
Lloyd Robson, *A History of Tasmania,* Melbourne, 1991

20. Walers and Gunners
A.T.Yarwood, *Walers: Australian Horses Abroad,* Melbourne, 1989

21. Michael Howe—Governor of the Ranges
Coultman Smith, *Tales of Old Tasmania: The First Fifty Years,* Adelaide, 1978
Russel Ward, *Finding Australia: A History of Australia to 1821,* Richmond, 1987
Charles White, *History of Australian Bushranging,* Hawthorn, 1970

22. Lola Montez versus Henry Seekamp
Australian Dictionary of Biography
Nancy Keesing (ed.), *History of the Australian Goldrushes: By Those Who Were There,*
  Sydney 1971

23. A 'Mill' on Sydney's North Shore
Pierce Egan, *Boxiana or Sketches of Ancient and Modern Pugilism,* London 1976
Peter Corris, *Lords of the Ring,* Sydney 1980
John O'Hara, *A Mug's Game: A History of Gaming and Betting in Australia,* Sydney 1988

24. Sydney and the Second Coming—the Star Amphitheatre at Balmoral
Mary Lutyens, *Krishnamurti: The Years of Awakening,* New York, 1975
Peter Washington, *Madame Blavatsky's Baboon: Theosophy and the Emergence of the
  Western Guru,* London, 1993
Jill Roe, *Beyond Belief: Theosophy in Australia,* Sydney, 1986

25. Ned Kelly and the Kelly Outbreak
Ian Jones, *Ned Kelly: A Short Life,* Melbourne, 1995
John McQuilton, *The Kelly Outbreak 1878–1880,* Melbourne, 1987
John H. Phillips, *The Trial of Ned Kelly,* Sydney, 1987

26. Aboriginal Sorcery—Singing a Man to Death in Northern Australia
John Cawte, *Healers of Arnhem Land,* Sydney, 1996
Tony Swain, *A Place for Strangers: Towards a History of Australian Aboriginal Being,*
  Melbourne, 1993
Douglas Lockwood, *I the Aboriginal,* Adelaide, 1971
Dick Roughsey, *Moon and Rainbow,* Sydney, 1971
David McKnight, *People, Countries, and the Rainbow Serpent,* Oxford, 1997
Harvey Arden, *Dream Keepers,* Sydney, 1997

27. Israel in the Kimberleys
Leon Gettler, *An Unpromised Land,* Fremantle, 1993

28. Sarah Wentworth—the Whore of Sydney
Penny Russel (ed.), *For Richer for Poorer: Early Colonial Marriages,* Melbourne, 1994
Helen Heney (ed.), *Dear Fanny: Women's Letters to and from New South Wales 1788–
  1857,* Canberra, 1985

Susanna DeVries, *Strength of Spirit: Pioneering Women of Achievement, from First Fleet to Federation,* Sydney, 1995

29. The Rebellion at the Eureka Stockade
John Molony, *Eureka,* Melbourne, 1984
Geoffrey Serle, *The Golden Age: A History of the Colony of Victoria 1851–1861,* Melbourne, 1963
Raffaello Carboni, *The Eureka Stockade,* Melbourne, 1963
Nancy Keesing (ed.), *History of the Australian Gold Rushes,* Sydney, 1967

30. Australians in the Boxer Rebellion
Bob Nicholls, *Bluejackets and Boxers: Australia's Naval Expedition to the Boxer Uprising,* Sydney, 1986
Raymond Evans, Clive Moore, Kay Saunders, Bryan Jamison (eds), *1901: Our Future's Past,* Sydney, 1997

31. Charles Joseph La Trobe—a Most Unlikely Governor
Geoffrey Serle, *The Golden Age: A History of the Colony of Victoria 1851–1861,* Melbourne, 1963
Penny Russell (ed.), *For Richer for Poorer: Early Colonial Marriages,* Melbourne, 1994
Australian Dictionary of Biography

32. The First Labor Government in the World
Ross McMullin, *The Light on the Hill: The Australian Labor Movement 1850–1907: Extracts from Contemporary Documents,* Melbourne, 1970

33. Captain Bully Hayes
Frank Clune, *Captain Bully Hayes: Blackbirder and Bigamist,* Melbourne, 1970
Hector Holthouse, *Cannibal Cargoes,* Adelaide, 1969
George Palmer, *Kidnapping in the South Seas,* London, 1871

34. Mary Penfold—The Mother of the Australian Wine Industry
Susanna DeVries, *Strength of Spirit: Pioneering Women of Achievement from First Fleet to Federation,* Sydney, 1995

35. Alfred Deakin—Australia's Most Eccentric Prime Minister
J. La Nause, *Alfred Deakin: A Biography,* Sydney, 1975
Alfred Deakin, *The Federal Story,* Melbourne, 1944
Don Whitington, *Twelfth Man,* Brisbane, 1972

36. The Hornet Bank Massacre—Gender and Race Conflict on the Frontier
L.E. Skinner, *Police of the Pastoral Frontier,* St. Lucia, 1975
Penny van Toorn, David English (eds), *Speaking Positions: Aboriginality, Gender, and Ethnicity in Australian Cultural Studies,* Melbourne, 1995
Henry Reynolds, *The Other Side of the Frontier,* Townsville, 1981
Henry Reynolds, *With the White People,* Melbourne, 1990

37. The Parramatta Female Factory
Annette Salt, *These Outcast Women: The Parramatta Female Factory,* Sydney, 1984
Portia Robinson, *The Women of Botany Bay,* Melbourne, 1993
A.T. Yarwood, *Samuel Marsden: The Great Survivor,* Melbourne, 1977

38. The Prison Boys of Point Puer
A.G.L. Shaw, *Convicts and the Colonies,* Melbourne 1977
Ian Brand, *The Convict Probation System: Van Diemen's Land 1835–1854,* Hobart 1990
F.C. Hooper, *The Prison Boys of Port Arthur,* Melbourne 1967

39. A Bunyip Aristocracy
Ged Martin, *Bunyip Aristocracy,* Sydney, 1986
J.B. Hirst, *The Strange Birth of Colonial Democracy,* Sydney, 1988
C. Pearl, *Brilliant Dan Deniehy,* Melbourne, 1972
A.W. Martin, *Henry Parkes: A Biography,* Melbourne, 1980

40. Teddy and the Jewboy Gang
Charles White, *History of Australian Bushranging,* Hawthorn, 1970
J.S. Levi, and G.F.J. Bergman, *Australian Genesis: Jewish Convicts and Settlers 1788–1850,* London, 1974

41. Ben Boyd—Merchant Adventurer and the First Blackbirder
Marion Diamond, *Sea Horse and the Wanderer: Ben Boyd of Boydtown,* Melbourne, 1995
Anne Bickford, *Ben Boyd National Park Bicentennial Project: Davison Whaling Station, Boyd's Tower, Bittangabee Ruins,* Sydney, 1988

42. Peter the Painter
F.G. Clarke, *Will-O'-The-Wisp: Peter the Painter and the anti-tsarist Baltic Terrorists in Britain and Australia,* Melbourne, 1983
Donald Rumbelow, *The Houndsditch Murders and the Siege of Sidney Street,* London, 1988

43. The Sandakan Death Marches
Lionel Wigmore, *The Japanese Thrust, Vol. iv of Australia in the War of 1939–1945,* series 1, Army, Adelaide, 1957
Lord Russell of Liverpool, *The Knights of Bushido: A Short History of Japanese War Crimes,* London, 1958
Yuri Tanaka, *Hidden Horrors: Japanese War Crimes in World War 2,* Colorado, 1996

Notes

1 *Sydney Morning Herald,* 27 December 1941.

2 Nelson Trusler Johnson *in* P.G. Edwards (Ed.), *Australia Through American Eyes 1935–45,* Brisbane, 1979.

3 K.S. Inglis, *The Australian Colonists: An Exploration of Social History 1788–1870,* Melbourne, 1974, p. 236.

4 Lachlan Macquarie, Private Journal, 24 January 1795.

5 Keith Amos, *The Fenians in Australia 1865–80,* Kensington, 1988, p. 73.

6 ibid., p. 240.

7 Phillip to Sydney, 15 May 1788 *Historical Records of Australia,* Series 1, Vol. 1, p. 18.

8 Paul Fregosi, *Dreams of Empire: Napoleon and the First World War 1792–1815,* London, 1988, p. 355.

9 Nancy Keesing (Ed.), *History of the Australian Gold Rushes by Those Who Were There,* Melbourne, 1971, p. 162.

10 *Melbourne Punch,* 6 March 1856.

11 Archives, Theosophical Society of Australia.

12 Mary Lutyens, *Krishnamurti: The Years of Awakening,* New York, 1975, p. 242.

13 Archives, Theosophical Society of Australia.

14 Charles Osborne, *Ned Kelly,* London, 1970, p. 126.

15 Ian Jones, *Ned Kelly: A Short Life,* Melbourne, 1996, p. 320.

16 ibid., p. 322.

17 Dick Roughsey (Goobalathaldin), *Moon and Rainbow: The Autobiography of an Aboriginal,* Sydney, 1995, p. 75.

18 Douglas Lockwood, *I, The Aboriginal,* Sydney, 1995, pp. 12–21.

19 Penny Russell (Ed.), *For Richer for Poorer: Early Colonial Marriages,* Melbourne, 1994, p. 121.

20 *Sydney Morning Herald,* 27 May 1847.

21 Russell, op. cit., p. 134.

22 Keesing, op. cit., p. 221.

23 *Adelaide Observer,* 11 August 1900.

24 *New South Wales Parliamentary Debates,* 1900 Vol. CIV, Legislative Assembly 205 July 1900, p. 1276.

25 *Australian Star,* 24 July 1900.

26 Douglas Pike (Ed.), *Australian Dictionary of Biography 1788–1850,* Vol. 2. Canberra, 1976, pp. 89–90.

27 Russell, op. cit., pp 83–4.

28 ibid., p. 91.

29 D.J. Murphy, *Labour History,* No. 20, May 1971, p. 4.

30 ibid., p. 7.

31 Suzanna De Vries, *Strength of Spirit,* Sydney, 1995, pp. 247–8.

32 J.A. La Nauze, *Alfred Deakin: A Biography,* Melbourne, 1965, Vol. 1, p. 59.

33 Alfred Deakin, *And Be One People: Alfred Deakin's Federal Story,* Melbourne, 1995, p. 173.

34 ibid., p. 162.

35 *Moreton Bay Courier,* 11 Nov. 1857.

36 L.E. Skinner, *Police of the Pastoral Frontier: Native Police 1849–59,* Brisbane, 1975, p. 331.

37 Annette Salt, *These Outcast Women: The Parramatta Female Factory 1821–48,* Sydney, 1984, p. 83.

38 F.C. Hooper, *Prison Boys of Port Arthur: A Study of the Point Puer Boys' Establishment Van Diemen's Land 1834–1850,* Melbourne, 1967, p. 1.

39 ibid., p. 15.

40 Ged Martin, *Bunyip Aristocracy,* Sydney, 1986, p. 119.

41 *Empire,* 16 August 1853.

42 Martin, op. cit., p. 120.

43 C.M.H. Clark, *A History of Australia,* Vol. IV, Melbourne, 1978, p. 38.

44 ibid.

45 F.G. Clarke, *Will-O'-the-Wisp,* Melbourne, 1983, p. 120.

Index